RESIL

RESILIENT

My Life Story

JANICE MCDERMOTT

Resilient: My Life Story
Published by Pomona Publishing Company
Arvada, CO

Library of Congress Control Number: 2019901470

ISBN: 978-0-692-15080-1

Personal Memoir

QUANTITY PURCHASES: Companies, professional groups, clubs, and other organizations may qualify for special terms when ordering quantities of this title. For information, email janicemmcdermott@gmail.com.

P
POMONA
PUBLISHING COMPANY

This book is dedicated to my loving husband, James Small, and to our two daughters, Sarah and Rachael, and their families. They have loved me unconditionally and helped me immeasurably on my great life-journey by holding me accountable as they share their immense wisdom. Words cannot express my gratitude for their gifts to me.

TABLE OF CONTENTS

"YOU are the hero of your own story. Stop making other people responsible for every twist and turn in your life. YOU made the decisions that got you from Point A to Point B. YOU worked hard. YOU navigated your way to where you are today. Your story is a heroine's journey. Tell it that way. Stop devaluing your story! Stop comparing it to others. Own it. Tell it in a way that makes you feel proud! You're a survivor, and you're not done yet!"

I've Been Thinking, by Maria Shriver

Viola Davis believes "Every story matters. . . We are all worthy of telling our stories and having them heard." She lives by a few simple rules:

- "I'm doing the best I can.
- "I will allow myself to be seen.
- "I apply the advice an acting coach gave me to all aspects of my life: Go further. Don't be afraid. Put it all out there. Don't leave anything on the floor.
- "I will not be a mystery to my daughter. She will know me and I will share my stories with her—the stories of failure, shame, and accomplishment. She will know she's not alone in that wilderness.

"This is who I am.
"This is where I am from.
"This is my mess.
"This is what it means to belong to myself."

Braving the Wilderness, pp. 86-87, by Brené Brown

INTRODUCTION

This is my story, the courageous story of our family and what happened after my father's death. My mother was in love with my father. She did reflect later in her life that it probably was not a good idea to marry a man who had had scarlet fever that resulted in a damaged heart. But she loved my father, so she married him. They were engaged for ten years before they were able to get married. It was the early 1940s, and even arranging time together was very difficult, though they lived only ten miles apart (that was a *very long way* in a horse and buggy). They were both from very poor families who were greatly impacted by the Great Depression.

They were married in a ceremony at the local Catholic parish in Farley, Iowa, followed by a small reception for twenty family members at my mother's parents' house. My Mom wore a knee-length white suit with a white hat covered with netting. They were married for nine years and had five children during their brief years together. In their tenth year of marriage, my father had a massive heart attack and died. His death so devastated my mother that she could never talk about him without crying, so we never talked about my father. She was completely dependent on him and became emotionally crippled after his death. Life as we knew it would never be the same. I was the second oldest (age seven) in our row of five children. My older sister was named Shirley. My "Irish Twin" brother, Paul, was born the same year I came into the world. My younger sister, Colleen, was born the next year, and my youngest brother, David, was only a year old when my father died. Five children in nine years!

To be clear, life was not great even before my father died. He was unable to work due to his heart being damaged from scarlet fever as a child. Then he lost his dream the night before I was born, when an electrical fire completely destroyed his newly acquired hatchery/gas station. His health issues, in addition to having only an eighth-grade education, made it impossible for him to find a good job. My parents, being strict Catholics, believed that they must accept all the children God was good enough to give them, so they would not, or could not, practice any form of birth control.

They also knew that they could not afford to have more children. They argued over how to feed and clothe five children with such a limited income—my mother working as a teacher in a one-room school house and my father always trying to find work. He ran a small gas station for a while. Then he borrowed money from his family to purchase the hatchery that later burned to the ground. He tried selling "Jewel-T" products. (Jewel-T was a company that hired workers to sell household goods door-to-door.) He eventually got too sick to do any kind of work. The doctors finally advised him to consider a risky and experimental type of open heart surgery. (My parents had a lot to consider because the doctors informed them that my father's heart wouldn't last much longer.) This was the early 1950s. They had no insurance—and no conceivable way to pay for the surgery. They were stressed and scared as they argued about what to do. The decision, however, was made for them: my father had the heart attack the doctors had said would kill him if he didn't have surgery.

Why my compulsion to tell this story? First and foremost, I must confess that I feel led by Spirit to tell this story. I would not and could not do this on my own. I believe my story will give hope to people who are suffering. My story is a study in courage and resilience. Resilience is the capacity to withstand stress and catastrophe. Psychologists have long recognized the ability of humans to adapt and overcome risk and adversity. They are able to rebuild their lives, even after devastating tragedies. Resilience/courage does not eliminate stress or erase life's difficulties. Instead, it gives people the strength to tackle problems head on, overcome adversity and move on with their lives. Even in the face of events that seem unimaginable, people are able to marshal the strength to not just survive, but to thrive and prosper. According to many experts, resilience is actually a common trait, and people are capable of learning the skills it takes to become more resilient. I believe that my life, and the life of both my mother and my siblings, is a great lesson in resiliency. I will make a case for this in my story. I will also describe the times that I wished that I had been resilient but came up short.

As this story was unfolding, I had the thought that someday I would tell this story. I don't pretend to understand this drive to write, but I do know that whenever anyone asks me about what I wanted to do in my life, I always end up telling them that I wanted to write my life story. I didn't have a voice as a child, but I now realize that I write to give myself the voice that I never had growing up.

At best, this story might be handed down to my children, grandchildren and great-grandchildren to help them understand their ancestors and the courage they exhibited as they lived their lives. At worst, I could write this story and place it in my file cabinet, to be discarded when my older daughter, who is efficient and a "thrower-outer" like me, cleans out our home after our death.

Actually, there are a couple of people who got me started on this book. Around 1989, I went to see a "palm reader". I am not the typical person to seek out a palm reader, but I had a neighbor who told me some incredible things about her life. I asked her how she knew these things. She said she had visited a palm reader in Boulder. I got her name, called her immediately and set an appointment to see her the very next week. At my reading, she looked at my hands and proclaimed, "You are a writer! You need to write your story." I immediately protested that it was not true. She was surely getting me confused with my older sister. She said: "No!" and assured me that I was the one who must write this story. I argued with her, but she insisted. She said my older sister had great writing ability, but she was still working on how to connect her head to her heart. I needed to tell the story because I realized that connection and could help my sister to do so as well. She would eventually be successful too, but I must lead the way. The palm reader suggested I "tell" the story to my father, who had missed so many things as we grew up. She got goose bumps as she said this, a sure sign that the universe was approving of what she told me to do.

When I came home after the palm reading, I started to think about how to write my story. Right away, I sketched out some chapters. It seemed easy and fun to me. I quickly wrote the first five chapters. They described my life in the convent, my time in the orphanage, my stay in a foster home, and all that I remembered around the time that my father died and about my painful teen years. I found it easy, and it actually turned out to be my first creative experience. I could sit at the computer for hours, with no idea of how much time had passed, while I was reaching into the deep recesses of my brain for things I remembered about my childhood.

But, because being a writer was so out of the realm of how I saw myself, I put the stories away after I wrote those first few chapters—and didn't think about them for years. I told myself I would get back to them when our children were older, when I had more time, or when they were out of high school. There were so many reasons to not dig these stories out of the file cabinet.

I was concerned about what my family would think about me writing and publishing these memories. A book about the trauma we experienced while growing up might reopen many old wounds. We had all done a good job of stifling our pain. We had developed coping mechanisms to deal with our lives, and I wondered if my family would resent me telling the world about our early experiences. I wondered how the residents of my very small town would react to hearing the truth about how we were treated when we were growing up. I still have family and friends who live there.

Another of my concerns was that it would force me to face so many of the painful experiences of my life. My life would no longer be "my life"—it would belong to anyone who chose to read about it. It might force me to deal with issues I have not wanted to face. I saw this, however, as an opportunity to heal, since it brought to the surface the emotions that had been buried for too long.

Yet another issue finally got me to take my writing seriously. I had been telling my close friends that I wanted to write, and had even asked a few people to read the chapters that I had written. They encouraged me on a regular basis, frequently asking me how my story was coming. I started to notice how badly I felt as I told them that I hadn't worked on it for a very long time. My children were now out of high school and college and married. How long would I wait? I needed to get this project underway, or stop telling my friends that I wanted to write. I felt like I was a phony. Really, the creative urge is so deep in our souls that we have to do the things we came here to do, no matter what they are.

Twenty-five years quickly passed. I started to wonder if I would ever publish my story. I believe our bodies are our best teacher, and they do have a very curious way of "waking us up" when we don't pay attention. It was around this time that I began to feel weak and in constant pain. I got scared. Maybe I was coming to the end of my life? Would I die with my story still in me? I decided I must finish my story. I was worried that writing about all those painful incidents might be making me sicker. I wanted to stop writing, but I realized that there was no turning back.

Nevertheless, I continued to get sicker. I could not lift my arms. My chest hurt if I moved it. I was in constant pain, not excruciating pain, but a dull pain that was always there. I couldn't ignore it. I went to an internist, and she ordered blood work, X-rays and CAT scans. Nothing was revealed except some pulled muscles near my sternum. I took muscle relaxants, but they didn't work. How did I pull my muscles? I had no real explanation. I was going to a chiropractor every month. He told me that I had a number of ribs "out"—sometimes up to eight ribs in the wrong place. Why? I went to an acupuncturist. He said I needed to take it easy; I was putting too much stress on my body. I had blockages between my liver and kidneys, between my lungs and my heart. I made an appointment to see a therapist who specialized in "inner-child" work. On and on it went. I started to believe that I must write this story in order to heal the painful memories stored in my body.

So I wrote my book, *What Would Your Father Say?* I self-published the book and sold all of the copies I had printed. I made a number of presentations to book clubs. Readers often said: "Why did you stop writing? How did you go from a fragile young girl leaving the convent to the strong, accomplished, self-confident woman you are today? We want to know the rest of the story!" I decided to finish the story; this book contains all the chapters from my first book—and the rest of my story.

I believe people love stories, especially stories that have a moral. It's said that people learn best by hearing stories, causing them to lodge deep in the heart. My own soul calls me forth to tell my story. Telling my stories gives me a chance to relive them and, eventually, to come to terms with the pain buried there and to accept and own it. Telling my stories carries me into the heart of where rebirth occurs. It puts me in an inner room with my suffering and allows me to see it in a new context, one where I find the courage to learn from it. Telling my stories helps me reorient myself to new truth and insight.

The gift of my first book was to hear countless people telling me that they had experienced many of the same things that I did as a child. I was surprised! I thought my suffering was mine alone. My readers said: "We could have had the same mother" or "I felt like I was reading my own story as I read yours" or "By reading about your life, I got to know my mom because she went to the convent." From my first book I got to see that, in the end, we are all one story. The human experience is the same, no matter the color, size or shape of our bodies, or the conditions in which we find ourselves as we live our lives.

To complete this book, I had no notes, only memories. I did have a copy of a journal that my friend, Sis, wrote during the summer that we hitch-hiked through Europe. I had saved the itinerary of my trip to China, and I checked that for accuracy. The affirmations in the appendices are taken from my journals throughout the years when I was passionate about writing affirmations. As I scanned my journals, I saw that I did not record the source of the affirmations, so I apologize to the Universe for neglecting to give proper credit. Around 1987 I read Louise Hay's *You Can Heal Your Life*; so many of my affirmations are from her book. Some of the affirmations are from Wayne Dyer. I attended a Church of Religious Science with workshops where we did affirmation work, and every Sunday the sermon suggested new ways to pray and to think about my life.

I do believe this above all else: There is One Mind and we all share that same mind, so we all share the same wisdom. No one has a monopoly on which insights they bring to the planet. We know all is in Divine right order, so neither I, nor anyone else, owns this wisdom. It is there for all of us to learn. I am grateful to all my teachers who have shared their wisdom. I will share what I know, and the readers of this book can take away what they can to make sense of their own lives.

In conclusion, my health has improved. I have learned to take better care of myself. I will speak of being resilient throughout this book. I believe my story alone is a story of resiliency, but I also write about the times in my life when I was NOT resilient. I do know that every thought we choose and every word we speak is creating our reality from moment to moment, so I affirm: "I am responsible for this"—both the times I am resilient and the times when I wish I would have been more resilient.

CHAPTER ONE

MY FATHER'S DEATH

His death on that gray, late October day in 1955 changed my life forever. It was the end of another beautiful fall season in eastern Iowa. The leaves had completed their glorious cycle of color and had drifted to the ground. The small Iowa town close to the Mississippi River was settling in for another hard winter, a winter that challenged everyone to simply survive. The moment my father had his heart attack, Mom told my sister, Shirley, and me to quickly take the three smallest children, Paul, Colleen and David, outside. None of us had noticed that there was anything wrong. Shirley and I quickly gathered everyone up. The hysteria in our Mom's voice told us we had better do exactly as we were told. We were used to doing exactly as we were told, so we didn't stop to question what was happening.

The five of us were sitting on an odd wooden structure, the one that our father was in the middle of building as an addition to the one-car garage. My older sister, Shirley, was holding David, who was close to turning two. I was sitting next to Paul, who was born only eleven months after me. I was seven and was holding Colleen's hand. I didn't want her to fall off the three-foot-high structure. We were all scared. We were concerned about what was happening in the house. From that spot we could watch everything unfold. We didn't have to wait long because momentarily our parish priest came rushing down the street in his car. He jumped out of the car and raced into the house. We knew it had to be bad if the priest had been called first; he would be there to save our father's soul, to administer the Last Sacrament so that, if he were to die, the blessings of the last rites would guide him straight to heaven where God would greet him with open arms. The second vehicle to arrive was an ambulance. It turned around in the driveway and parked in front of the house. We could not see them carry our father on a stretcher into the ambulance or our Mom climbing into the back of the ambulance with him. We certainly didn't realize that we were being left all alone.

It was only minutes before my Dad's sister, Aunt Delores, arrived. She told us that our Dad was sick and needed to go to the hospital and that we would go home with her. We all jumped into Aunt Delores' old dilapidated car. She had a good heart. She lived close to town and could get to us the quickest in such an emergency. She had eleven children of her own, so she didn't need five more. But her attitude was: WHAT DIFFERENCE WILL A FEW MORE MAKE? My siblings thought only about getting to play with our cousins out on the farm. I was not thinking that..... I was wondering what was happening to my father. I was the serious, emotional child in my family. Both Shirley and I knew something serious was unfolding.

After we arrived with Aunt Delores, she and a couple of the older children prepared lunch—a long line of bologna and cheese sandwiches.

We all squeezed together on wooden benches to enjoy our sandwiches. We knew it would be awhile before we learned how our father was doing, so we just had to wait. We didn't know Aunt Delores well, but we did know she had her own share of problems, with so many kids and an alcoholic husband. After lunch we played outside. As soon as we got outside, I asked Shirley when she thought we would hear about our father. She said: "Be patient." I sat and watched the long, dirt road, waiting for a car to come down the lane. That was the only way we would find out what was happening because Aunt Delores didn't have a phone. Nightfall came; there was no word about our father. We went to bed, four of us to a bed! I did not want to sleep so I tried to stay awake. I kept listening for anyone who might be coming into the house. No one came.

Finally, I fell into a restless, fitful sleep, but a couple of hours later I woke up needing to go to the bathroom, really bad. Aunt Delores did not have indoor plumbing, so I had to find my way through her unfamiliar house, in total darkness, outside to the outhouse. I got up and started to feel my way to the hallway. I thought I could make it down the back stairs and out the door where the sidewalk would lead me to the outhouse. I groped around, stepping on clothes, falling over shoes, running into walls, finally finding the creaky stairs that would lead me downstairs and outside. Sheer terror gripped me with each step. I had heard Aunt Delores say that her house had rats. With every move I imagined that I was going to step on a rat. I was paralyzed with fear. Finally, I made it outside. Even though I felt good to have made it without an accident, I was equally worried about finding my way back into the same room I was sharing with my cousins and siblings.

The next morning, wearing our cousins' clothes, we were dropped off at school. Aunt Delores said she hadn't heard anything, so she took us to school. We were only in school about two hours when a knock came at my first-grade classroom door. My teacher, Sister Anastasia, answered the door. Somehow I knew the person at the door would be for me. However, I could never have guessed who would be standing on the other side of that door. It was my Uncle Walter, my mother's brother, from Chicago. He whispered something to Sister Anastasia. Her face told me everything I feared! She came back to the center of the room, looking very ashen, and called my name. She told me to bring my coat and lunch box and instructed me to go with my uncle. He had Shirley and Paul with him in the hallway. He told us that our Mom was in the car waiting for us, with Colleen and David. When we got in she told us that our Dad had died. She announced this with little emotion. All five of us sat in the backseat, speechless. What did this mean? It was impossible for us to truly understand the implications of this astounding news.

From the school, my uncle drove us to the funeral home. We sat in front of the funeral home for the next hour while Mom and my uncle made all the arrangements. We were getting restless and we started to fight. At one point, mom came out and yelled at us: "Don't you know that your father has just died? Why aren't you crying? Don't you know that you just lost your Dad? What is wrong with you kids?" We had to quickly learn how to deal with this news. Our mother was not crying; she was angry with us for fighting. She was setting the tone for how we would deal with his death.

When we arrived back at our house, it felt so empty and quiet! There was something different about the house; something felt very strange. Very soon another one of my father's sisters came, Aunt Loretta. My father had thirteen brothers and sisters, a good Irish Catholic family. We were never very close to my father's family, but they did come quickly when they heard he was dead. Aunt Loretta took Shirley, Paul and me to her house in Epworth, a town about fifteen miles away. She volunteered to take us because she had money and two daughters about the same ages as Shirley and me. She was married to a man who owned a feed company. The plan was to loan us her children's clothes so we could look presentable at the wake and funeral. When we arrived at Aunt Loretta's house, we went straight to the girls' bedroom to try on some of her daughters' clothes. The girls did not want to share their clothes. They said to their Mom: "Mom, that is MY favorite dress. Don't give that one to them." They repeated that about everything we tried on. We finally got a cute dress that fit each of us. Aunt Loretta emphasized to her girls that we were only borrowing these clothes and that we would return them soon. I heard her admonish her girls: "You girls must learn to share and cooperate. These kids just lost their Dad!"

That night we were sitting at the kitchen table eating supper. The adults were not talking because the radio station, KDTH, was announcing the local obituaries. The radio announcer said: "Vincent McDermott of Cascade, Iowa, died last night of a massive heart attack. He will be waked at the Devaney Funeral Home for the next three days. Friends and family can call tomorrow evening at 7 pm for a rosary. Mass will be said at St. Martin's Catholic Church, and interment will be at the Cascade Cemetery." I did not want to look up or even take a breath. The silence was deafening. I wished someone would say something. Finally, Aunt Loretta announced that we should get ready for the wake. We had already laid out our clothes and taken baths and were ready to go to the funeral home.

We were getting dressed when one of my cousins decided to make a scene. She was NOT going to the wake. She did not want to see a dead person lying in a coffin. She refused to get dressed. She screamed and cried and kept repeating over and over that she would not go to look at a dead person. Her parents told her that she didn't have to look at a dead person. I stood there, wondering if she could understand that the dead person she was talking about was my Dad!

The wake lasted three days! It was decided that we were old enough and well behaved enough to handle sitting there for three nights, all in a row across from my father's casket. Only David was excused from this experience. He was almost two and wouldn't have to endure this ordeal. He would join us the last morning when they closed the casket and buried him. The four of us sat next to Mom for hours as people filed past the casket. They stopped and spoke to Mom, but few of them said anything to us. They mostly stared at us from a distance. We could hear people making comments: "Look at those poor kids. What is Helen ever going to do? How is she going to manage?" "How old are the kids, anyway? They all look so close in age."

In the eyes of my seven-year-old self, I liked seeing my father lying there in the casket. I thought he was sleeping, lying there so peacefully. He had a smile on his face; everyone commented on that! I wondered if that meant he was happy to be leaving us. People did say to Mom that he was smiling because that was his nature. He was a good, holy and happy man. To me he looked the way he did when he was sleeping on the couch in our living room. I had no idea about the meaning of death. I didn't realize that soon they would close his casket, and we would never see him again!

The next morning that is exactly what happened. We filed by his coffin for one last look. We all stared as my Mom said goodbye to him, and then the funeral home director closed the casket. It was at this moment that I realized that he was truly gone. I desperately wanted to cry, but everyone was being strong. I just walked out the back door with my siblings and into a waiting car that would take us to church and then to the cemetery. Shirley took care of David during the Mass. After the service, we followed my father's casket down the aisle and out to the hearse. All my aunts and uncles and cousins came to the cemetery. We watched as the pallbearers carried his casket to an open hole in the ground. The priest said some prayers, and then his casket was lowered into the ground. It was over for us. He was gone. Mom was stoic as my Uncle Walter guided her back to the car.

We all went back to our house. The children were all sent upstairs to play. It was time for the adults to grieve together. Grandpa (my Mom's Dad) came upstairs with us. Grandma had died two years earlier, and Mom was so glad her mother wasn't alive to see her suffer this way! Even though my Dad's parents were alive, they were not part of our lives, and they did not come back to the house that day. Grandpa brought us some food to eat; a lot of people had brought food to our house. We played some board games; our favorite one: "Sorry!" How sorry it was that we were not allowed to grieve or to stay with the adults. We could hear them talking downstairs.

When we were finally allowed to return downstairs, everyone was gone. Only Mom and the five of us remained. She told us to get on our pajamas and get into bed. The following days were filled with good food and company. My Mom's sister, Agnes, stayed for a few days to help Mom write thank you notes to everyone who donated food or gave money for Masses. We wandered around the house listening to the adults talking. We watched Mom's face, her every movement. We could tell she was overwhelmed and distressed. Gradually things returned to "normal". We did our chores, tried to be good and to cheer up Mom. She was in shock. How was she going to carry on? What strange twist of fate had landed her in this painful place? This was *not* how she had planned to have her life unfold.

CHAPTER TWO

THE ORPHANAGE

After my father's death, life changed dramatically for us. There were many problems before he died; he had been ill for a number of years and unable to work. He was facing risky major open heart surgery. Although these issues were there, we weren't so painfully aware of them.

Now, things were different. There was a new tension that was palpable. Mom had no one to talk to, and suddenly we were involved with every crisis. Serious problems seemed to arrive daily. We heard Mom crying at night after we went to bed; sometimes she talked out loud to herself. She wondered how she would pay the bills. How would she make enough money to buy shoes and school clothes for the five of us? How could she afford groceries on such a limited income? Could she do it by herself?

She was overwhelmed with the responsibility of raising five small children. Her job, teaching in a one-room school in the country, did not pay enough to support them. My father was painfully aware of the financial problems before he died. His eighth-grade education and his poor health made it difficult to support his family. He had no insurance and no pension. Most of my parents' fights were about money. At least, when she was working, my father was home to take care of the children. After my father's death our Great Uncle Charley, who lived up the street, became our life saver. He helped out with taking care of Colleen and David until Mom got home from work.

But Great Uncle Charley was old. He had lost his first wife early in his life, had no children and married Great Aunt Agnes later in life. They were to become very important in our lives after my father's death. Aunt Agnes was a wonderful cook. She was employed as a cook in a nursing home during the week, but on the weekends she cooked special treats for us. She helped us celebrate our birthdays and provided a sense of family when no one else was around. We could run up the street to her house when things got crazy around our house. We all did this, including Mom. Great Aunt Agnes's house was immaculate; everything had its place. When we visited we had to sit very still. Her beautiful things were to be looked at only from afar. We longed to play with her black and white ceramic dogs or the tall metal ashtray with the moveable top. That was not to be. The house was always quiet. We were expected to sit still and have a conversation with Aunt Agnes and Uncle Charley. Usually these conversations focused on the birds in the purple martin birdhouse outside the back door, the flowers growing in the yard, the vegetables sprouting in their garden or her angel food cake baking in the oven.

There was another reason we sat so still during these escapes from our stressful home life. Aunt Agnes sat very still. She was overweight from all her years of cooking (and eating). She needed to rest because her body had to work so hard carrying her weight. She did work hard when we weren't visiting her. She kept herself busy by cooking, cleaning, waxing floors, tending her flowers or canning. She always had fresh brownies, cookies, fudge or angel food cake, which she often offered us as a treat when we visited her and Uncle Charley. It was a wonderful escape from our stressful family life.

My father had died, but my brothers, Paul and David (they were two and six), were too young to be the father around the house, so Uncle Charley helped fill that role. He decided that our house needed painting, so he came on the weekends to work on the house. One Saturday he was painting right above the front porch, the ladder leaned against the steps and porch. Mom called him down for lunch, but as he started to climb down the ladder, he lost his balance. He fell onto the sidewalk and the bucket of white paint flew out of his arms. The whole bucket spilled onto the sidewalk right in front of the porch. Great Uncle Charley was bruised and sore, but the sidewalk took the most abuse. That spattered white paint remained frozen there all the days of our childhood.

Mom returned to teaching in a one-room schoolhouse after our Dad died. At that time, a teacher needed only a high school diploma and a few college courses to teach. She had taken a college class every summer to qualify. She not only had the responsibility of caring for her own five children, but also that of educating twenty other children ranging in age from six to thirteen.

She drove to school on graveled, country roads; in the winter it was still dark when she arrived at school. She had to shovel a path to the school if it had snowed, start the fire to heat the classroom, and have her lessons prepared for eight grade levels when the children arrived. If the roads were too dangerous to drive, some of the children arrived on horseback. At the end of the day, Mom made her way back home to cook dinner, help us with our homework and get us all into bed. When we were settled, she baked the bread for the next day. During these late hours she also prepared lessons for her students. She often told us: "Whatever you do, don't become teachers! It is a hard life. There is no end to the work."

In one respect, life didn't change that much for us after our Dad's death. A life of poverty and hard work was not new to us. We still planted a huge garden and worked in it most of the summer. We lived off the land, growing everything that we could to ensure a stock of food during the winter months. We canned everything that could be canned. We dug potatoes and onions and stored them in the basement. We raised chickens for their eggs. When the chickens got old and no longer laid eggs, we ate them. On late summer days we scoured the countryside for wild raspberries, gooseberries, blackberries, mulberries and strawberries. We canned these fruits to make jams and jellies. Canned fruit was a special treat at the end of a meal during the winter months.

Sometimes there wasn't enough money for shoes for all of us. Our maternal grandfather visited occasionally and helped out by buying shoes for the kids who needed them the most. Mom became an excellent seamstress; she sewed everything we wore, except for underwear and socks. She also taught us to darn our own socks using a light bulb and some darning cotton.

Even living so simply, we didn't have enough money to get by. Soon after my father's death, Mom was visited by a social worker who told her about two programs that could help us. One was called Aid to Families with Dependent Children (AFDC). The other was a food program called Commodities. She knew she had to take advantage of these programs, but she was embarrassed. She knew families that used (and abused) the system. They had a bad reputation in our small community. She was a proud woman who didn't want to take anything that wasn't rightfully hers. In her heart she did not want AFDC. There was a stigma attached to taking money from the government; people on welfare were generally considered lazy and unwilling to work. With great humility and sadness, she applied for both programs and finally got a letter of approval.

We were now part of the social welfare system. This meant that social workers regularly checked on us. My Mom could not make a cent of extra money without reporting it; if she ever got caught she would forfeit her monthly payments or have them reduced by the amount that she made. Mom was so honest that any dollar she made sewing a dress or hemming a pair of pants was reported, and that amount was deducted from our monthly check. The food program did enable us to enjoy some of the finer things in life. Every month we were recipients of a huge chunk of cheese, a large can of peanut butter, a couple of pounds of butter and some canned chunks of beef.

It was humiliating for Mom to drive into the city to pick up these food items. When we made these "welfare trips" we also stopped at a discount bakery store in town. Mom would buy a huge bag of crushed bread. The bags warned: "NOT FIT FOR HUMAN CONSUMPTION". These bags of bread were sold to local farmers who fed it to their pigs to fatten them up. It was always so much fun to split the bag open and see what goodies were stuffed inside. Sometimes, if we got a particularly good bag, there were donuts, cupcakes, and cinnamon bread, in addition to regular bread. We would straighten out the bread and re-bag it so we could make sandwiches; sometimes it was so smashed that we just had to throw it away.

Mom seemed more withdrawn and unhappy as the weeks and months passed. The stress was getting the best of her. She lost a lot of weight. At 5' 10" she weighed only 115 pounds. Anyone close to our family surely could have predicted what was about to happen. Mom simply withdrew after my father died. Secretly, she could not believe how her life had unfolded. Part of the problem was that there wasn't anyone close to us. After her husband's death, his family simply disappeared. He had thirteen siblings, but only one of his brothers remained close. He and his wife stopped in to check on how we were doing. My Dad's brother had a farm and a big family of his own, but they were kind to Mom. She really liked his wife. She could always cheer Mom up better than anyone else. She was a lighthearted, happy woman. She told lots of stories that made Mom laugh. They always brought little things to Mom. We loved it when they stopped by because she always felt better after they came to visit.

My mother's sister, Agnes, was very busy with her own life. She came to visit when she could but she lived ninety miles away. She had had difficulty getting pregnant, so she and her husband adopted a baby. She got pregnant immediately after the adoption, so she had two small children of her own. She worked part time as a nurse in a doctor's office; her husband worked in a factory. They were tired on the weekends, but they did join us for the holidays. These were fun times because Mom relaxed with her sister around. They would talk together in the bedroom. Mom told her sister all her troubles.

Mom kept saying she didn't feel well. We started to notice she was coughing a lot. She would cough up phlegm into a hankie, then walk away to look at it. She finally told us about the doctor's appointment. It was very unusual for Mom to go to the doctor; she really did not believe in doctors. We had been raised to believe that if you were sick, you should rest and wait for the body to heal itself. We did not take medicine and neither did she. But she was not able to rest and she continued to cough up blood and lose weight. It scared her enough to make an appointment. It was her sister, Agnes, who was a nurse, who convinced her that she MUST see a doctor.

Although aware of this appointment, we could never have guessed how this one doctor visit would change our lives. We were walking home from school on that fine, fall day. The leaves on the trees had turned their most beautiful shades of yellows, reds and oranges. We were walking along, kicking the falling leaves. We had just turned the corner to go down our street when we saw an unfamiliar car sitting in front of our house. We didn't recognize the car, so we picked up our speed to get to the house quickly. We were greeted by a social worker with an official name badge on her dress. She said that Mom was very ill. She was diagnosed with tuberculosis. She said most people call it TB. She would have to be treated at a sanitarium for TB patients. We could not stay alone, so she had arranged to have us stay at an orphanage until Mom was well enough to take care of us again. David was too small to go to the orphanage because it did not accept babies. He would go to Chicago to live with Uncle Walter, who had come to get us from school when our father died. Mom would be taken immediately to a sanitarium one hundred miles away. We would go to an orphanage thirty miles in the opposite direction. The house would be locked until we could return. Our family would be going to three different places.

There was no need to worry about packing our clothes. We weren't allowed to take anything with us. All of our things had been exposed to TB germs. We all said goodbye to Mom and then climbed into the social worker's car—to leave with a total stranger. Not a single tear was shed. Shirley, who was now ten years old, sat in the front seat and carried on a conversation with the social worker. She was "in charge". As we sat silently in the backseat she asked all the questions we were wondering about: When was Mom going to the hospital? Where was the orphanage? When would we get to see Mom again? Would we all stay together? Where was our baby brother, David, going? What about our clothes......

why weren't we allowed to take anything with us? We all had our school uniforms, but the school we would attend did not require a uniform.

Mom was still at the house when we got into the car, but she would be taken to the hospital by ambulance as soon as my Uncle Walter came for David. He had to drive out from Chicago. We were told that our first stop would be a clinic where we would all be tested to see if we were active carriers of TB. We could not enter the orphanage if we tested positive for TB. We waited at the clinic a very long time for the results of the chest x-rays and the skin test. We sat in silence the entire time, too scared to even imagine what might happen next. The social worker told us that as soon as the results came back, she would be free to take us to the orphanage. She explained that we would stay there only long enough for Mom to get well. No, she couldn't really tell us how long that would be. Yes, she would bring us back home as soon as Mom was well enough to take care of us.

Finally, we received word that, even though we had been exposed to the TB bacteria, we were all healthy enough to go to the orphanage. The social worker drove us up to the front drive of the orphanage which was a huge institution. We looked at each other with surprise upon seeing how big the building was. We wondered what was happening to us. Right away we were greeted by two nuns who seemed to know a lot about us already. They were expecting us. We learned right away that boys and girls were separated, so Paul went to the boys' wing. Shirley and I were placed in the same wing, Colleen was sent to be with the youngest girls in another wing. We saw each other only at meal times. In the cafeteria it seemed strange that we did not have much to say to one another. We simply said: "Hi" and then were on our way. I followed my sister and the bigger girls back to our wing.

Life in the orphanage was filled with mystery. Every time I met my siblings, during our recreation time, we asked the same questions: Do you know how Mom is doing? When do you think we will be able to leave? Have you heard from Mom? Do you think our relatives know where we are? Will someone come to see us? What has happened to other kids who live here? We told ourselves that we weren't *really* orphans because we would be leaving as soon as Mom was well enough to come for us.

Every day we went to a small school located in the orphanage. Shirley attended a Catholic elementary school close to the orphanage. She had homework. I was in second grade. Even though I never missed a day of school in the orphanage, I was there in body only. My mind was somewhere else. I was not interested in reading or writing or spelling or math. I wanted to know where my Mom was and when I could go home. I don't remember having any homework or even working in class; we sat around and talked a lot during our class time. I had a sense that the teachers felt sorry for us and didn't want to burden us with too much work, either during class or afterward.

We had been in the orphanage for about three months when we had our first visitors. It was a Sunday afternoon. We were called to the front parlor, a room that was off limits unless you had visitors. Our Great Uncle Charley and Aunt Agnes were waiting for us. They brought some of Agnes's wonderful fudge. We sat silently; Shirley did most of the talking. She told them what it was like to live in the "Home". It was called St. Mary's Orphanage but we all referred to it as the "Home". (It didn't feel the least little bit like home.) We asked them how Mom was doing. They had been to visit her. They told us that she was very weak and not able to get out of bed. She was doing everything she could to get well so she could come get us. We asked them how long they thought we would be here. They left with these parting words: "It will take a long time for her to get well. She is very sick." They told us she was not allowed to get out of bed; she was too weak to even write us a letter. This was not good news, but it did help us settle into the routine of the orphanage and accept that we weren't going to be leaving anytime soon. Even though we were not truly orphans, we would have to live as orphans until Mom got better.

It was in the orphanage that Shirley first started getting into trouble with the nuns. The nuns did not know how to deal with her, so they sent her to another school outside the orphanage. She asked too many questions. She was too smart. She had her own ideas about how things should be done. She refused to do something simply because the nuns told her to do it. She was used to being in charge: she had moved into her adult role as soon as Dad died, even though she was only nine years old. She was, out of necessity, strong willed and in control.

It was also at this same time that I learned about the facts of life. I was eight years old. One day we were all standing around outside in back of the building. All of a sudden a girl by the name of Theola started shouting. She was standing as stiff as a board and refused to move. I kept asking the older kids what was wrong with her. They told me that I was too young to understand. I refused to take "no" for an answer! I followed them upstairs, asking them what had happened. Finally, in the bathroom, they told me that Theola "got her period." That didn't help me at all because I didn't know what that meant. So I kept bugging them until they explained. They said that Theola had never been told about getting her period so she was very scared. When I went back to where she had been standing, I saw blood on the cement.

After that I heard lots of conversation about "getting your period." The nuns in the orphanage yelled at the older girls when there was blood on sheets or clothes. I was so fearful about that happening to me, but someone told me that I had nothing to worry about because I was still much too young. All I knew was "it" wasn't a fun thing.

In my bed at the end of a large dorm room full of beds, I lay awake at night, watching a light come through the windows and play across the walls. The search light from a small airport nearby guided planes onto the runway. I pretended the light was held by someone looking for us, saying to myself: "Yes, we are here. Come and get us." The rescuers would climb the walls, and take us away and return us to our home where all my family awaited us. I knew this was just a game in my mind, but it was a dream I could not escape. Other nights I dreamt about where that light would lead me if I could follow it. I wondered about what my life would be in that big unknown world out there. The search light both frightened me and comforted me. I was not alone when I lay awake trying to figure out how to get to sleep when I didn't have anyone to comfort me. I had to figure it out on my own so I kept watching the lights.

In my dorm room, I also learned about the "evils" of make-up. The older girls who were going on an outing hid their make-up in their pockets. At the movie theater they went straight to the bathroom to apply it, and they might have gotten away with it had they not forgotten to take it off on returning home. The nuns were furious. They all got extra punishments and, from then on, were unofficially labeled the "bad girls." Shirley was not part of this crowd. I was thankful for that. She was not interested in makeup. She had much more important things on her mind.

I was always the "good girl"—very quiet, didn't want to cause any trouble, shy, easy to deal with and did not want to attract attention. I tried to follow all the rules. I didn't even ask questions. For my good behavior, I was rewarded by being chosen to carry the crown for the May crowning of the Blessed Virgin Mary, as part of a long processional into the chapel. One girl was chosen to crown the statue of Mary. That was the highest honor. Almost as honorable was the second to last person, the one who carried the crown. (That was my job!)

I wore a beautiful long white dress that was loaned to me by the orphanage. My younger sister, Colleen, made her First Communion that same day, so she was also dressed in white. I carried the crown on a small white pillow. The procession had lots of singing and spring flowers—bridal wreath and lilacs. These were the only flowers blooming in late May in the Midwest. Everyone from the orphanage was there, and photos were taken to record the event. As part of the ceremony, we all made little shrines of our own, although I do not recall doing anything other than painting them. Someone snapped a picture of the four of us standing with our little Blessed Virgin Mary shrines. We were surviving the orphanage, but there was such a far-away look on our faces in that picture. There were no smiles. We were all lost in our own thoughts: When would we get to go home? Why isn't anyone coming to get us? Where is Mom? Is she getting better? Where are Aunt Agnes and Uncle Al and their two children? Does anyone know we are in this orphanage?

Our second set of visitors arrived a couple of months later. It was Uncle Cyril and Aunt Viola, the brother to whom my father was the closest. They had become regular visitors in our home to support Mom after my father's death. They gave us the same dismal news: she is resting comfortably but is very weak and confined to bed. Her recovery will just take time. They promised that, when she was well enough to come home, they would come and get us. It was comforting to know there was a plan once Mom was strong enough to return home.

During that year I do remember one other set of visitors, our Aunt Agnes (mom's sister) and Uncle Al. I was so happy for their visit because they were our favorites. (We also believed they would know best what was happening with Mom.) I wondered why they didn't bring their children. They were our closest cousins. Were they embarrassed about us living in an orphanage? Would it have scared them? I wondered if they felt guilty to have not taken us into their home. I kept telling myself that I wasn't a *real* orphan because I did have a mother. We were patiently waiting for her to get well enough to come and take us home!

Shirley was not so patient. She wanted to go home. She was getting into a lot of trouble. As good as I was, she was equally choosing to misbehave. I don't think she was really bad; she just became accustomed to being in charge since our father's death. She got into trouble for running in the hallways or saying something inappropriate to the nuns. She was regularly punished for her transgressions by having to kneel in front of the entryway to the chapel. She was too bad to even go into the chapel to ask for forgiveness! It was a lesson in public humiliation. She knelt there as we all filed into chapel. I was so sad to see her there and I just wanted to run away. Why did the nuns have to be so mean to her? Didn't they know she was sad and angry about her abandonment? Didn't they know she was just playing the role she had taken on as a result of having a mother who was incapable of being the adult in charge? Why couldn't they be kinder to her?

In fact, the nuns did try to help her. There was a psychiatrist who visited the "Home" once a week to help the nuns deal with the most difficult children in the orphanage. Shirley got to talk to him on a regular basis, but I am not sure he helped her because she continued to misbehave and get into even more trouble. I, too, had one visit with him. I liked going to see him. I must have passed all the "tests" he gave me because I never got to go back. I liked seeing him and wanted to return. I wanted someone to talk to me so I could understand all my thoughts and feelings, but I had learned to play the game; I was the good girl and didn't act out, so everyone assumed that I was adjusting perfectly to this situation. (This was so far from the truth. In reality, my heart was breaking.)

Yes, the whole school year passed. I finished my second grade at the orphanage. I had actually "missed" a whole year of school. Little did I know how much requiring so little work of us because we were "orphans" would affect my academic progress. Letting us play games and sit around talking, instead of doing our school work, did not serve us. We got away with "murder." We used our status as "orphans" to be very manipulative, employing every excuse in the book to get out of doing work. It worked; the adults in the orphanage fell for our tricks. They felt sorry for us and we used this for all it was worth.

We were approaching our first-year anniversary of living in the orphanage. We were all getting impatient with not hearing about Mom. I would constantly ask Shirley if she had heard anything. Finally, we got word that we could go home. The nuns had arranged for us to leave the next morning. Mom was going to be released from the hospital. Aunt Viola and Uncle Cyril would drive us home after Sunday Mass. We left as quickly as we came. We came with nothing and we left with just a few mementos of our year in the orphanage. The clothes we wore would find their way to the next children who came to the "Home." Again we waited in the front parlor. All four of us just sat there staring at each other. What would happen next? How would Mom look? We hadn't seen her in a year. What would happen once we got home? Would we be able to keep our family together? The nuns told us we would need to help Mom because she had been in the hospital so long and was very weak. Shirley and I assured them that we would be able to do that. We were determined not to have to return to the orphanage. Shirley was eleven and I was nine. Fear gripped our hearts; we were unsure if we could do what it would take to keep our family together and also make sure Mom got the rest she needed.

It seemed we waited for hours before our aunt and uncle showed up but I doubt it was that long. We were so eager to leave. When our aunt and uncle arrived, we were told that, instead of taking us straight to our home, we would spend the afternoon on their farm. We would eat dinner there, my uncle would do the chores and then they would be free to drive us home. It seemed too much to ask! We had waited so long to go home and now we had to wait for my uncle to finish his chores. I felt angry but I didn't say a word. I just waited. I tried to play with my cousins but I JUST WANTED TO GO HOME. Couldn't anyone understand that? This day seemed like an eternity as we went through the motions of waiting patiently to be taken home and see our mother.

Finally we were in the car driving into town. Our home town looked strange. It seemed like we had been away for so long. The biggest surprise was about to come into view as we drove down our street and caught a glimpse of our house. The house looked the same but the grass had not been cut in a year. It looked like an abandoned home. Someone had trampled down the weeds to make a path to the front door. We walked through the weeds to the front door. We saw Mom, attended by a nurse. We gave her a group hug. She looked different; she had gained so much weight because she had been in bed for so long. She seemed weak and helpless. The nurse gave us her little speech about needing to be "big girls" and help Mom. It was up to us to keep the family together. If Mom did too much, she would get sick again and have to return to the hospital. (The message was that it would be our fault if Mom got sick again.) We assured her we would do everything to help Mom rest and "continue her recovery." We were determined to NOT return to the orphanage. We told Mom we didn't ever want to live there again. She promised us we would NEVER have to go away again. We slept well that night. I took such comfort in knowing that I would never again have to follow the landing lights from the nearby airport when I couldn't sleep.

The research shows that resilient people do not let adversity define them. Resiliency is the ability to fall and get back up quickly. My siblings and I all got up quickly. We transcended the pain and grief we felt by believing that this orphanage experience was a temporary state and we would be back with our Mom soon. Now, it was coming true. We were back together, and we would do everything we could to stay together.

CHAPTER THREE

THE FOSTER HOME

Shirley and I both wanted to do whatever it took to keep our family together. This was a big order to fill for a nine- and eleven-year-old. I was starting third grade and my older sister, fifth grade. We took charge of the cooking, cleaning and laundry. Mom was there telling us what to do—a frustrating situation for her. She said that it would be so much easier for her to just do it herself. We begged her to sit down and rest. She needed to sit and tell US what to do. However, as she got stronger, she didn't listen to us anymore, or perhaps she could not stand to see us working so hard. She felt compelled to help, so she ignored the warnings of the nurses and doctors.

David, my youngest sibling who was living with our Uncle Walter in Chicago, arrived a couple of days after we got home. He had grown up during the year he spent in Chicago. He seemed subdued and distant when we saw him after that year. He had lost his baby looks and become a cute little blond-headed boy who was nicknamed "Whitie". We all wanted to pick him up and carry him around, but he would have no part of that. He had grown so independent. Only if Mom wasn't around would he go to his big sister Shirley.

Our home was located in eastern Iowa close to the Mississippi River. Because of the climate and humidity, the grass there continues to grow green and lush well into September and October. Three seasons of the year, spring, summer and fall, the grass required mowing every week. We had left in late summer so the grass had grown for almost a year. Now we had returned in June to see our home surrounded by weeds and overgrown grass. It was an overwhelming task but was the first thing we had to do once we arrived home: get the grass cut. We all took turns with the scythe—chopping, slicing, and cutting down the weeds; our old push mower was useless in such high weeds and grass. Once the tall grass was cut, we went over it again and again with the push mower. We had over a half acre to mow by hand. This seemed like an endless, thankless task. We worked on it every day. After two hours of work, only a small area was cleared, but it was important to us to return our house to looking like someone lived there, like we had come home. Paul, always a wise one and acting as the "father of the house," suggested we buy a couple of sheep and have them eat the grass. That was a great idea. We could also shear their wool every year and then sell the wool for cash. Mom bought four sheep. Every spring the shearers came, and Mom sold the wool in the nearest large city. In return she received enough money to buy us some of the things she could not make herself for the coming school year.

Doing the laundry was yet another huge challenge that we faced weekly once we were all back together. We spent all day *every Saturday* doing laundry. First, we heated the water on the stove, and then we poured the hot water into the old wringer washer. As the machine washed the first load, we heated more water for the rinse tubs; the first rinse tub removed the soap from the clothes; the second tub was to whiten the clothes with bluing. (That never made sense to me—adding a blue liquid to the water to whiten the clothes—but it seemed to work because the white clothes were whiter after that tub.) Then we scrubbed all the socks by hand with a bar of special soap for really dirty items. Our hands turned red and raw from the scrubbing. As I stood at the sink scrubbing the socks, I often wished that somehow, white socks would go out of style; any dark color of socks would have been so much better, but the fashion at the time was white and we all had white socks.

We put every piece of laundry through the wringer one by one after each rinse. After the third wring they were ready to be hung. In the spring, summer and fall this was no problem. Winter was another story. Winter presented us with a whole new set of challenges. Winter in Iowa is brutal, with temperatures frequently falling to 20 below zero and a wind chill factor of 30 or 40 below. The wind swept across the fields, blowing and drifting the snow. We didn't have extra clothes, so we could not skip a wash day. No matter what was happening outside, we washed. The first step in doing winter laundry was to dig a path through the snow to the clothesline. That allowed us to run outside to the line with a basket of wet clothes. The clothes would often freeze before we could hang them on the lines, as did our hands. Our hands got so cold that we would run back through the snow into the house to warm our hands, then race back to finish. The clothes would hang there "stiff as a board," as my Mom would say. We argued with Mom: How could they dry if they were already frozen? Somehow they did. If it started to snow we put on our boots and heavy coats to run out and snatch the stiffened clothes off the line. We stood them up in the kitchen and after a few minutes they started to thaw and crumple onto the floor. We had only one drying rack, so we used every available spot in the kitchen and living room to drape the drying clothes. These were the only rooms with heat; the kitchen had a wood-burning stove, the living room, an oil-burning stove.

One of the biggest problems we faced on laundry day was disposing of all the dirty water. The washing machine had a hose to release the dirty water, so we were able to pour the water into buckets. Carrying all the buckets of dirty water outside, however, was too much work, and we spilled lots of water. At one point Paul and David got creative. (Getting rid of the water was their responsibility.) They found some old downspouts and gutters from the side of the garage, hooked them all together and attached the washing machine drain to the downspout/gutter system they had created. It was pretty ingenious, and we were all excited when it worked well. Usually, some water would spill, but it flowed pretty well through the downspout into the gutters that snaked their way through our kitchen and out the back door! Then there were times when, for no apparent reason, one of the gutters tipped over, causing a huge flood in the kitchen. We were all called into service to grab the rags from the rag box and start wiping up the water. It usually caused a ruckus, and we would all laugh at our failed attempts at "saving time."

The next stage of the laundry process was mine exclusively. I was in charge of the ironing. First, I filled the 7-Up pop bottle with water. This 7-Up bottle had a special cork top with lots of tiny holes on it, and I used it to sprinkle all the clothes. It was important to get the top on tight or the clothes would be drenched with water. On occasion the cork came loose, and I would get very upset at having to return the clothes to the line to dry enough to iron them. I sprinkled every item of clothing, rolled them up and placed them in a plastic-lined wicker basket to be ironed. I couldn't wait too long, or they would start to mold or dry out. It was crucial that I put enough water on them; if not, I would have big wrinkles that would not come out when I ironed them. We ironed everything—sheets, pillowcases, tablecloths and all our clothes. There were reasons that I did this job exclusively. One was that I hated to cook. If I was ironing, I didn't have to cook. Another reason was that I was always cold. The iron warmed me up. Ironing made me feel good. Besides, I was very good at ironing. Actually, there was yet another reason. If I was ironing, I was in the kitchen with Mother. I needed to be close to comfort her. We could talk. I was vigilant in my companionship with my Mom. I tried to say things that would help her cope with her life. I would encourage her, console her and reassure her that things would work out. Mom always felt bad that we were working so hard. My two brothers hung out together and my two sisters were good buddies, so I was the middle child. It was the role I played in my family.

After finishing the laundry, we scrubbed the large linoleum kitchen floor on our hands and knees—and waxed it with Johnson's Wax—a job that seemed to take forever. After my Mom's illness, Shirley and I tried to take over the task of making bread every couple of days. Setting the bread to rise in a sunny spot in the kitchen, we waited until it had risen past the top of the bowl, and then punched it down to rise again. From the dough we made loaves of bread, dinner rolls and cinnamon rolls. Cinnamon rolls were the best. After rolling out the dough with a rolling pin, we sprinkled the dough with butter, sugar and cinnamon, and then we rolled it into a long cylindrical roll to cut into slices. These slices were placed on a pan to rise and, when they were high enough, baked in the oven. We always wanted a fresh roll when they came out of the oven, but Mom gave us only the end pieces. The good rolls were to be consumed on Sunday morning after church, when we had a big breakfast of eggs, bacon and the rolls. It was so good! Sunday was a day of rest when, depending on the time of year, we would do different activities. In the summer and fall, we went on picnics to gather berries or nuts. In the winter, we went ice skating on a rink next to the park across from our house.

During this time I got reacquainted with my best friend, Donna. She was a wonderful friend. She was lively and cute and never lacked for great ideas for fun things to do. I had been gone for a whole year, so she was very excited when she learned I was home. The first time she came by the house, she asked me to come out and play. I sadly told her that I couldn't because I had work to do. Mom overheard me saying this, and she told me that I could go play with her. I felt weird, being home and seeing my friend for the first time after my absence. I had been through so much. How could I tell her all the things I had experienced? I quickly learned that she really didn't seem to want to know. She just wanted to take up where we left off. I wasn't the same kid, but she didn't know that. I complained about how much work we had to do. She told me to stop feeling sorry for myself and just get playing. She said I acted like I was the only one with problems, which angered me because I truly thought that she had no idea what my life was like or how I was feeling. After all, she did have the perfect family (or so I thought at the time). Even then, I knew that Donna was the best thing that happened to me because she did not let me stay focused on my painful life. She was there to show me that, even though you have challenges, you must move on, and the best way to do that is to forget about what is happening and just go outside and PLAY.

Her father worked as a delivery man for the Texaco Oil Company, delivering oil to all the homes in the area with oil-burning stoves. He often drove past us in his big red delivery truck with the Texaco sign on it. Sometimes he would stop to say: "Hi." If he could, he would give us a ride home from school. The best part was that the truck had a small box of red suckers sitting on the passenger-side floor board. He gave us a sucker when he stopped. We felt so special, walking down the street with those red cherry suckers in our mouths!

My older sister Shirley was working doubly hard. She had the most responsibility for making sure things did not fall apart. She was our mother when Mom was not able to be present, either physically or mentally. She fought the battles Mom was too weak to fight, such as taking on the nuns at school, the electric company and the traveling salesmen who often preyed on my Mother. That job fell to my sister.

At one point Mom was notified that Paul would be placed in special education classes. He didn't get a good foundation during his first-grade year in the orphanage. He was in kindergarten when he lost his father so he really "missed" his first two years of school, there physically but not able to attend. The nuns decided that, because he was behind, he should be put in classes for "retarded" students. Well, Shirley would hear nothing of that! She marched up to school and told everyone that her brother was not "retarded," and that NO ONE was going to put him in a class that would damage him even more. She had watched him take over as the man of the house. He was able to fix everything mechanical: he had even taken apart the lawn mower and put it back together so it worked perfectly. He had fixed the car when it broke down. Shirley could see he was so gifted mechanically. No one to teach him, he taught himself. She knew he had no signs of being "retarded."

Gradually, Mom was up and around and working harder than she should have been. She proclaimed that we were not strong enough to do some of the chores, so she had to do them. Kneading the bread was one of them. She baked bread every other day. It took a lot of strength to knead the bread, and she would have coughing spells when she was working. We all begged her to stop, to buy the huge bags of bread at the discount bakery marked: "NOT MEANT FOR HUMAN CONSUMPTION."

We now had another reason to buy the bread. Uncle Cyril had given my brothers a couple of runt pigs. If my brothers could keep them alive we would take them to market with Uncle Cyril's pigs. So we really did want some of the bread for the pigs—the parts that were too crushed for us to eat. But mostly we had the great pleasure of eating the soft white bread that was store bought!

It was tense at our house. There were just too many obstacles to overcome. We were struggling to keep everything from collapsing, but we were so glad to have a roof over our heads and to be all under the same roof. In one of the few instances that Mom mentioned Dad, she said that one of the best decisions he ever made was to purchase the house right after their marriage. He had great plans for that property. There was the hatchery with a gas station attached, potentially a great source of income to support the family. This dream was short lived, however, since the hatchery burned to the ground just days before I was born. Both Mom and Dad were thankful that everyone in the family was safe and that no one died in the fire. Even though the property was only one block from the main street of our small town, the hatchery burned to the ground because there was no fire hydrant on that street, and the volunteer fire department could not respond quickly enough. The water tower sat at the top of our street, but that didn't help. After the hatchery burned, plans were made to transform the other side of the property into a roller skating rink, another potential money-making venture. The trenches were dug to build the rink but my father's lack of funds and his poor health put these plans on hold. The grass eventually grew, providing lovely sloping hills for the sheep to graze. These trenches always represented for us our Dad's unfulfilled dream.

It was around this time that I realized Mom had never wanted any kids, and here she was, "stuck" with *five* kids. Mom felt she wouldn't be a good mother for even one child. She said that it was my Dad who wanted a big family. She was angry for the situation she found herself in: this was not how she thought her life would unfold. She was getting more and more depressed, but she couldn't give up. She had five children, all totally dependent on her. When her sister, the nurse, came to visit, she cried. She listened but honestly didn't know what to say to her. She told her to rest more, to relax. This advice fell on deaf ears. There were clothes to make, mouths to feed, money to be made.

After my father's death we embarked on clearing the plot of land to plant a garden at our home (when my father was alive he had a very large garden, on the land owned by his parents). Clearing the land required hard work by all of us. First, we used a shovel to dig up the whole plot which had to be big enough to grow sufficient food for a family of six to make it through the winter. Mom set up the rows with strings so they would be straight. We planted tomatoes, potatoes, onions, carrots, squash, peas and green beans—row after row of vegetables. Through the summer we weeded nonstop; we were well aware of how critical it was to take good care of the garden. Mom knew how to can every vegetable. We helped with the whole process. Those canned vegetables got us through the winter months.

Sunday was the one day of the week we did not work. Our preparations for Sunday started on Saturday night. The cinnamon rolls were made. Now we all needed to take a bath. First, we heated the water for the large tub that was set on the kitchen floor. The kitchen then became off limits to everyone except the person taking a bath. The kitchen was the warmest room in the house because of the wood-burning stove, so it was the best place to bathe. We all used the same water, so it was very good to get to go first! The oldest was first and I was second. (There were some benefits to being almost the oldest!) We did have a tub upstairs, but since it had only cold water, we didn't really use it. With no heat upstairs, we also dressed for bed in the warm kitchen.

We each had one good Sunday church outfit, made by Mom. These outfits were worn only on Sunday morning when we went to Mass. As soon as we got home from church, we went immediately upstairs to change so they would stay clean and in good shape for the next church service. She sewed our outfits in the evenings, attempting to keep up with us as we grew. Sewing was luckily one thing that Mom could do without a lot of exertion. It was important for her that we look good for Sunday Mass.

As a child I was fascinated by the rituals of the Catholic Church. We NEVER missed Mass. That service seemed to be an island of calm in our stressful lives. We prayed that God would help us, would look favorably on us, and would be there for us. It seemed however, that God was moody and silent. I wondered how we could convince God that He needed to help us. Couldn't He see we were in trouble? Why was He so silent? Why did other people seem so lucky? I believed there must be a magic formula that we needed to learn. Mom believed that we must strive to be the best Catholics possible; if we did our part, God would be good to us. That included attending every single service offered by the church...... daily Mass, Stations of the Cross, Novenas, Confessions every Saturday, etc. We had our pew and nobody else sat in that pew. We were all expected to behave in Church and we did.

Although we were "making it," there was clear evidence to anyone close to our family that Mom was barely hanging in there. The problem was that there *was* no one close to our family except Mom's sister, who had her own problems. She lived ninety miles away and worked part time so they were not able to visit often. Mom went every month to get a checkup at the TB Sanitarium. We dreaded these monthly checkups because we knew that if her chest X-rays showed evidence of TB, we would be in big trouble. We had seen Mom coughing and spitting up blood. Our fears were well founded.

We feared the worst, and that was exactly what happened. She returned from a doctor's visit to tell us that her TB had come back. She would be forced to return to the sanitarium, one not too far from our home town. We realized that the thing we dreaded the most was about to happen to us again. We were still too young to stay alone without a parent. God only knows how they figured out where to send us this time, but it was decided that we would go to foster homes, rather than the orphanage. How would they find foster homes for all of us? Would we be close together? The social worker came the very next day to tell us that they had made arrangements for us. We would each be in a different home, except for my youngest brother, David. He would stay with my older sister, Shirley. He had already been traumatized by his stay in Chicago with his uncle that he didn't know very well. This time he would be with Shirley, who really was his main caretaker since our Dad had died.

The same procedure was followed as when we went to the orphanage. Mom was taken to the sanitarium in a city only twenty-five miles away. We were all taken again to the clinic to be tested for TB. By this time we were deathly afraid of doctors. I had a problem with fainting: when I got scared I would faint. I could tell when this was going to happen. I prayed that I wouldn't faint. I didn't want these strangers to know how scared I was. We all had chest x-rays and the TB test in our arms. If we had a reaction, we would have further tests. After we were told the good news, the doctor asked to see me again; I thought he was going to tell me that I had TB. I could barely breathe. I hadn't noticed that I had red splotches all over my body. He told the nurse that he thought I had chicken pox. I tried to convince him that I was just nervous. He was sure I had the chicken pox, and that my foster parents should be told that I must stay home for a week to recover.

This seemed like more than I could endure. I was going to a foster home with a family I didn't know, and then immediately I had to be put to bed for a week. I didn't feel like God was hearing me, so I didn't even ask for God's help with this situation. I was despondent.

As we waited for our test results, we were told about our foster homes. I found out I would live with a family in a town twenty miles from home. The father was the mayor of the town. He already had three little girls. Surely, he didn't need another little girl. These girls didn't need any more competition! The house was small; I slept in the same room as the three daughters. There were two sets of bunk beds and I was assigned to the lower bunk of the beds closest to the door. I wondered if the mayor had taken me in for political reasons. (I might have invented this story because the truth is that no situation would have made me happy.) I was shy and distant and just wanted to go back home. I didn't give this family a chance.

I was miserable in my foster home. For the first time in my life, I started getting sick. After recovering from the chicken pox, I started complaining about many symptoms. First, my legs hurt and then my stomach hurt and then my head hurt. My foster Mom took me to their doctor, but he could never find anything wrong with me. My symptoms were real. I remember sitting on the examination table, the doctor trying to guess what might be making me sick. I thought to myself: "You just don't get it. I want my Mother. I will get well as soon as I can go home and be with my Mom." Nothing else would get me well. I was sure of it. I did not share this with my foster parents. They continued to try different medicines and continued to be frustrated with not being able to figure out why I was sick. I put them through a lot, but I didn't care because I was miserable.

My younger sister's foster home was not far from mine, but in the country. I think she was too young to go to school because I don't ever remember seeing her there. She seemed unaffected by the situation our family was facing. She liked her foster home. She was the only girl in a home with three boys, and she quickly turned into a real tomboy. She was so cute and had a great personality; they all doted on her. I heard how much she loved being with that family.

My younger brother, Paul, was placed in a foster home owned by a brother and sister who lived on a farm, in the country not too far from the town where I lived. Neither of them had children. I don't remember seeing my brother at all during that year. At some point, he got sick too. He was diagnosed with rheumatic fever and placed in a hospital several hours from our hometown. I don't remember being told that he was sick; I was so focused on my own situation. I only learned about his illness when he did not return home with us.

I did get to see Shirley and David. They had been placed with an elderly couple who were not able to have children of their own. They lived on a farm within driving distance of my foster home. They needed help with the farm work because they were getting older—a couple of kids to gather eggs, clean the barn and help with the chores sounded good to them. This couple shopped in the town where I was living and once a week came into town for groceries. The house where I was staying was a block from the grocery store, so I watched for their arrival each Saturday. Sometimes my brother and sister were with them, and other times just my sister was there. Whenever I got to spend time alone with my sister, I told her how miserable I was. She told me she was sorry that I felt so bad, but she was facing her own miser—and was plotting to run away. But she couldn't run away without taking our brother too. She knew that if she went down the country road, one of the neighbor farmers would come along on a tractor, pick her up and take her right back there. This childless couple did not know how to deal with a preteen and a small child. They had no understanding of the trauma we had faced and the failure we felt at not being able to keep our family together. We had tried so hard, and yet, we found ourselves scattered all over the countryside, in different situations.

After my week of recovering from the chicken pox, I dreaded going to a new school by myself. I was painfully shy. My classmates were friendly, but I felt so alone. I tried to play with a few children at recess. I would be having fun and then, all of a sudden, I would remember where I was and that I had no idea where my mother was, or when I would ever see her again. I lived in a world of my own, worried about what would happen next.

One of the best things about my situation was that my foster home was right across the street from my school; I could run home for lunch. My foster Mom was a stay-at-home mom so she had lunch ready for us every day. We had peanut butter sandwiches she made with fresh, soft white bread and a glass of cold milk, with a couple of cookies for dessert. I had always wanted such a lunch at home, but Mom made the homemade bread that you couldn't cut into nice, even slices. I wanted a mom who was at home to make our lunches and to talk to us when we came home from school. I had that now. That made me happy, even though it wasn't my real Mom. I always delayed leaving the house after lunch—so I wouldn't have to go to the playground. My foster Mom always reminded me that it was time to go back, but I waited until I heard the bell ring to run across the street.

In class, I become a master manipulator. I made sure my teacher didn't call on me or ask me to do any hard work. She knew I was shy and not capable of doing the same work as others. I simply had to sit quietly and not respond. The teacher would skip me; the kids would whisper to each other that I was a "foster child." That was my excuse for not doing what was required of other students.

Did we get to visit our Mom that year? The answer is YES; we got to see her once. We were picked up one spring day by a social worker who drove us to visit Mom in the TB sanitarium. It had been nine months since we had last seen her. In the lobby of the hospital, we sat there speechless, as a nurse wheeled Mom toward us. We didn't know what to do or say because she looked so different. Again, she had gained so much weight, lying flat on her back in bed all those months. What could we say? Where to start to tell our Mom what we had experienced the past nine months? There *was* nowhere to start to express how traumatic this second period of separation from her was, so none of us said much. Shirley took charge and asked her the question we all wanted to ask: When would she be well enough to go home? (None of us complained to her about our foster homes. In fact, we didn't say a word about them because Mom was telling us how wonderful it was for these families to take us in.) She told us she was getting better and thought she would be released some time in late spring or early summer. That was enough for us. We returned to our foster homes knowing that we would be together again soon. I told myself, again, that I wasn't really a foster kid because my Mom was coming to get me! (Just like I had convinced myself that I wasn't an orphan because I did have a real Mom.) Every day I waited to hear the news that I was going home.

As the end of the school year approached, I realized that I had managed to complete third grade without doing much of the work. On the last day of school, I was walking home with a young girl I had started making friends with, so I told her that I would not be returning to the school in the fall because my Mom was finally recovered enough for us to go home. My friend said she was sad that I would be leaving and would miss me a lot. I was surprised she said that because I didn't think I had any friends.

Again, Aunt Viola came for us. She picked up both my sisters and my youngest brother, but not Paul. We learned that he had spent the last month in traction in a state hospital because he was diagnosed with rheumatic fever. I was sad that he was not there and even more sad that we didn't even know that he was sick. When we arrived home, it felt terrible not having him there. My Mom told us that we would visit him as soon as we could.

The arrival home this time was not as traumatic as before. We had grown accustomed to returning home after being gone for a year. The grass didn't seem quite so long. Our friends came by the house, and everyone knew we were home again. No big deal this second time. Our Mom said: "Yes, you can go out to play until it is time to make dinner," or "No, you can't go out to play because today is our wash day." We picked up where we left off. There was, however, one difference now. Shirley and I vowed that we would NEVER again allow our family to be separated. We knew in our hearts that we would NEVER again tolerate a social worker taking us away. We felt we were now old enough to be in charge of running our home if our Mom got sick again. That is a lot of resiliency for two girls aged nine and eleven.

Two weeks after we got home, Aunt Viola picked us up to take us to visit Paul at the University of Iowa Hospital. All five of us climbed into the car with Aunt Viola and headed to Iowa City. We were not allowed to enter the hospital. Luckily, he was in a room on the first floor. We waited patiently for Mom to signal to us so we would know at which window we could see him. We had to stand on our tiptoes to see through the window. He shared a room with two other patients, but none of them looked like our brother. That young boy in the bed in the corner surely didn't look like him, but that was indeed where Mom was standing. He was way too chubby. He seemed weak. Where was the brother we knew? We were so excited to see him, but this young boy in the bed where mom was standing did not look or act like my Irish Twin brother. We wondered when he might come home. We were all silent on the ride home. We had all wanted to see him, but seeing him only made us feel worse!

Sometime during the summer, he was released from the hospital. He was not able to take on his role as "man of the house" at this point because he had to be very careful as his heart grew stronger. Mom said he needed to be outside to get sunshine and fresh air. He was not able to walk and too heavy to carry, so we pulled him in a wagon. He was eight, but we looked forward to the day he could resume his role as a main contributor to all the outside chores.

How could we make sure that we were never separated again? We worked hard to make sure that didn't happen. We were so cooperative when we first returned. "Sure, Mom, I can do that!" "Let me help with changing the sheets." "Just tell me what you need." We were used to working hard, and so we continued doing all we could to keep our family together. We knew nothing other than hard work, even though I do think we did our share of complaining.

CHAPTER FOUR

THE FIRE

After our return from the foster homes, we quickly settled into a routine, doing our chores and making sure that Mom didn't work too hard. Mom seemed better, rested and stronger. She knew she needed to take it easy in this second recovery period. This time, it didn't feel like there was a sense of impending doom around us all the time. The issue of not enough money was ever present—how to stretch it to pay our bills and have money for food. Mom often talked to us about money, saying she didn't see any way out of this life of poverty for her. She believed that, in this small town, your fate was determined by the family you were born into, or whether you lived on a farm where you could raise cows or pigs to sell. (Every time we drove by a farm that really stunk, she would say, "That is the smell of money.") Lacking one of these two advantages, your only option was to marry a man who had a lot of money. She always said, "It is just as easy to marry a rich man as a poor one." She also told us that it was very important for the girls in the family to get an education so we could support ourselves, that we should never rely on a man. She had learned herself that you should not depend on a man.

She kept us on the straight and narrow by using a yardstick and by reminding us that if we misbehaved, she would get sick again and be forced to return to the hospital. It was a very effective way to keep us in line. But we were kids, and we were frustrated. We were unable to deal with everything that had happened to us, unable to try to be adults when we were still kids. We acted out our frustrations by fighting with each other. Actually, we would beat on each other. We would scream and cry and scratch each other. We would chase each other through the house. It didn't seem normal. Mom didn't know what to do with us. She would get out the yardstick or the belt and come after us, but she wasn't strong enough. When she started coughing, we would freak out, knowing it was us, again making her sick. We truly believed her illness was our fault because she couldn't deal with five children. She had said she didn't want even one child, and now she had five children to contend with all by herself.

Other times she tried "psychological force" to control us. She would send the two siblings who were fighting outside in the dead of winter—to work it out. This process took forever because we were stubborn, and refused to admit to each other who was in the wrong. It was always the other person's fault for causing the fight. Paul and I might decide to get along, but the minute we stepped back into the house, we would start fighting again. Mom would send us right back outside.

Another effective method that Mom used to deal with all the sibling rivalry: She just walked out. She strode up the street to visit with Great Aunt Agnes and Uncle Charley. We fell into silence as soon as she left. We would watch their house as long as she was up there, to make sure she was going to come home. We definitely had a fear that one day she would walk out and never come back; after all, she had left us for two years in a row. I always experienced a tremendous sense of relief upon seeing her walking back down the street. In defense of Mom, we fought a lot. We didn't know how to deal, or have any help with dealing, with all that the fates threw our way—the discrimination of poverty and the insecurity of having no security.

Mom tried hard to create a life for us. But after lying on her back for two years in the hospital, she was not only physically weak but emotionally crippled. She believed herself to have been victimized by everyone and everything. She couldn't sort out how it was that life had dealt her such a cruel blow; this was not the way she had envisioned her life. She often lamented that there was no way out of this life of poverty. She was depressed, and she often cried with the most desperate of sobs. None of us knew what to do. I prayed that someone like Aunt Viola or Aunt Agnes (her sister) would visit and cheer her up. We all got very quiet when Mom was like this. I tried to stay nearby so I would be there just to talk to her, to comfort her, if I could only figure out what to say.

That first Christmas, after our return from the foster homes, was marked by a visit from a Catholic priest from a country parish. He said that his parish had collected Christmas presents for us. This priest was not from our parish but from my grandparents' parish. He not only brought presents, but also a basket of food. We were all so happy! The biggest surprise that Christmas was that we all got a two-wheel bike to share. Santa had dropped it off at our next door neighbor's house by mistake! Our neighbor was an elderly man who was way past the bike-riding stage. We were all thrilled when we saw the bike. Even though we were experiencing a typical—below zero—snowy winter, we found a path through the snow on the pavement in front of the house to practice learning to ride. All four of us wanted to ride. We could not believe our luck to finally have a bike. We all stood in line waiting our turn. David was still too young for a two wheeler so we shared the bike among the four of us.

The spring after we got our bike, Shirley decided to give David a ride on the back. He sat on the bike seat as she pedaled down the blacktop just beyond our house. All of a sudden, my brother started screaming. Shirley jumped off the bike to see that his right leg was caught in the spokes of the wheel. He was still little enough to be carried, so she rushed him into the house. We all came running because he was screaming so loud. Mom knew immediately that he had a broken leg. David screamed the whole way to the clinic. Mom drove as fast as our old car would go, to the nearest large city where there was a clinic. (It was the same one that we had visited for our TB tests and chest x-rays the past two years.) We sat in the car while Mom carried him into the clinic. It seemed like we sat for hours while they put on his cast. When they returned we asked Mom if we could sign our names on his cast, she said we must wait until we arrived home to make sure the plaster was completely dry. David fell asleep, exhausted from all the crying. Shirley felt terrible about the accident; she had always taken special care of him. Now she carried him everywhere. He liked this. He wanted only her to carry him.

Somewhere around this time we got indoor plumbing. We continued to use the out-house in the summer because it was more convenient when we were outside playing. We also had problems with the pipes freezing in the winter, so we didn't really use the bathroom in the winter. Instead we would use a bucket that sat in the bathroom, taking turns each morning to empty it into the outhouse. That was NOT a fun chore. I did not like bringing the bucket to the outhouse. A particularly embarrassing episode happened to me at the outhouse, but it is too soon to tell that story.

We were "making ends meet" by planting a huge garden every spring, canning large amounts of produce during the summer, and raising chickens that generously gave us plenty of eggs every day. Every spring the local feed store gave away baby chicks. They did this so customers would then buy feed for the chickens. We kept ours in a make-shift pen on the floor of the kitchen. We enjoyed picking them up and petting them, so soft and fuzzy. Mom didn't like us to pet them too much because she thought handling them might make the chicks get sick and die. It was critical for us to keep them alive to produce the eggs we lived on each day.

At some point, the chicks got too big to stay in the kitchen and were moved out to the shed that sat on the front of our property. The shed was originally a gas station but it was never used that way. It stood in front of the hatchery but remained standing when the hatchery burned to the ground years before. We used it every spring to keep the baby chicks safe and warm. One night Mom heard that the temperature would fall below freezing, so she plugged in a light bulb close to the floor to keep the chicks warm. She had done that a number of times before. In the middle of the night we were awakened by Mom's screaming. We looked out the window. The whole side of the house was lit up. The shed, our chicken coop, was on fire. The winds were blowing the hot embers directly onto the house. Mom was screaming for us to stay in bed. Given the pitch and intensity of her screams, it sounded like she should be telling us to GET OUT of the house. She did, indeed, mean to tell us to GET OUT, but she was so frightened that she was confused and was saying STAY IN BED. Uncle Charley came to the rescue. As we watched the fire burn out of control, he ran up the stairs and yelled for us to come downstairs right away; he knew the house was in danger of catching on fire. We were downstairs and outside in a flash. We watched as the chicken coop burned to the ground. We all stood there, praying that God would spare our house. What would we do without a place to live? The fire department was at the scene, but the same tragedy was repeated as when the hatchery burned: we lived less than a block from the water tower, but with no fire hydrant near the house, there was nothing the volunteer fire fighters could do, except watch it burn to the ground. They used what little water they had in the truck to put out the embers that were falling on the house. We stood outside watching the firemen, but it was very cold. so finally the firemen said it was safe to go back inside our house. It took forever to fall back asleep that night.

The next morning came all too soon. We were exhausted, but Mom insisted that we go to school. None of us had recovered from the trauma, but we stumbled down the stairs and climbed into our school uniforms. We instinctively knew we were to act as if nothing had happened. I was still shaking. Everyone at school knew we had had a fire. News like that travels very fast in a small town. When the fire whistle blew, many, even in the middle of the night, would look to see where the fire truck was stopping. Even if they hadn't heard the news, everyone knew because all our clothes smelled like smoke (so did our whole house). None of the kids or adults said anything to me, but I desperately needed someone to tell me that things were going to be okay and that they knew what I was going through. Instead, I remember standing close enough to hear two of the nuns talking on the playground. They were talking about our family and all the tragedies we had experienced and "what a pity it was." These situations were helping me to form career decisions that I wasn't even aware of at the time.

This experience made me deathly, irrationally afraid of fires and would be the subject of scary dreams and nightmares for years to come. It was the combination of the hatchery burning a few days before I was born and the chicken coop burning in the middle of the night that made me fear fires so much.

When I was about ten years old, I remember being invited to a friend's birthday party. I was truly excited to be invited and knew I needed to buy a present. I asked my mom about what to get for my friend. She said, "Get her something you think she will like." She gave me a quarter to buy the present. I could stop at the dime store on the way to school, buy a present and then go to the party right after school; this friend lived close to school. It was a good plan. When I went to the dime store, I couldn't find anything that cost only a quarter. I kept walking around the store and finally the owner asked me, "Can I help you find what you are looking for?" I told him, "I'm not sure what I am looking for." He smiled at me and replied, "Then I guess I can't help you find it." I knew I was going to be late for school, so, in desperation, I grabbed a bottle of bubbles. I carried it in my lunch box to school and never thought about it again until I was at the party.

The party was in the basement; everyone carried down their presents and put them on a table in the middle of the room. I very carefully took the bubbles out of my lunch box and placed them on the table when no one was looking. (Not sure how I was able to accomplish that.) The party was fun. When it came time to open the presents, I held my breath. I was embarrassed that I had not wrapped my present and had no card to give my friend. After all the presents were opened, my friend held up the bottle of bubbles and said, "Where did these come from?" I was too scared to say that I had brought them. She looked at her mom, who gave her a curious look and motioned to set them down.

During those years following our stay in the orphanage and the foster homes, we were adjusting to not having two parents. I was becoming painfully aware during this time that a child from a one-parent family that lived in poverty on public assistance didn't have much status. This was especially apparent at school. Nowhere else would I experience the level of discrimination I encountered at school. The children whose families invited the nuns to dinner in their homes or brought them presents for the holidays were treated better. They were given special privileges. The nuns were not discreet in their rude comments about my shoes or my clothes or the fact that I didn't have the supplies I needed. I felt invisible as they talked about me and my family. Maybe it was because I was so quiet, or that I was a mediocre student, that the nuns felt they could ignore me. I was not a trouble maker. I worked hard. I tried my best, but I was much too worried about the dramas at home to be able to focus on school.

We were all dealing with the challenges of growing up without any real guidance and adjusting to our lives which included a high level of stress everyday.

CHAPTER FIVE

THE TEENAGE YEARS

There was no stopping life. I was growing and maturing and was now in middle school. School was becoming harder each year for me. I had attended a K-8 school, so there was no trauma about leaving the security of my elementary school to go into middle school. I just moved next door to the sixth-grade classroom.

What I noticed was that my school work became more and more difficult. I was not a good reader; I had trouble comprehending what I was reading. Reading was so painful. For reading instruction, each student took a turn at reading out loud. I never attempted to understand what was being read because I spent every minute trying to figure out which paragraph would be mine to read out loud, by counting the number of kids before me. As the other students read out loud, I practiced my paragraph. I would panic if I saw words I didn't know. I would try to ask someone sitting next to me for help. Sometimes I would mispronounce a word and everyone would laugh. I remember mispronouncing "depot"; I said DEPOT. It seemed like the whole world was laughing at me. I'm sure it was just a few students snickering, but I was so fragile that it seemed everyone was making fun of me. I developed a phobia for reading out loud. If the teacher announced that we would be reading a story out loud, I knew that I would not comprehend the story.

Another situation that caused me great pain in school was going to the chalkboard to diagram sentences. We took turns. I always prayed that somehow I wouldn't get called to go up there. I hid behind other kids in the hope the teacher wouldn't see me. Standing in front of the group made me so nervous that I couldn't concentrate. The nun gave each of us a sentence to diagram, which we would write on the board and then draw lines to indicate the parts of speech. I worried about not remembering the whole sentence, about spelling the words wrong, about how to diagram the sentence, and finally, about putting the words on the right lines. I must say though, by eighth grade, I did get somewhat proficient at diagramming sentences. I needed confidence but I had none.

Reading was hard for me, but math was even more difficult. No matter how hard I tried, I could not remember my times tables. I needed strategies for remembering them. I knew my 2's and 5's by heart but that was all. I did, however, invent a way to compensate for not being able to remember them. I had a notebook filled with white lined paper. On the back of this cardboard notebook was a grid with the times tables and all the equals measurements. I cut out the times tables grid and carried it with me for years, sneaking a look at it when needed. Keeping track of the grid wasn't as difficult as you might think. We wore the same uniform (navy blue pleated skirt and white blouse) every day. As we had only one uniform each, it was always in my pocket!

Nothing in middle school, however, was as painful for me as the spelling bee. I practiced my spelling words every week and did pretty well on spelling tests because I was better at knowing the word was right if I could see it, but spelling bees were too much pressure. I was so shy that feeling everyone look at me while I tried to figure out how to spell a word was torturous. I needed to write the word down to see if it looked right. Lined up with all the kids in my class, I almost always misspelled the word on the first try, and was humiliated to have to sit down first.

Another absolutely impossible situation occurred in eighth grade. Our class assignment was to memorize a poem during the first half of the year and, in the second half, to memorize the Preamble to the Constitution. Memorizing anything seemed impossible to me; I had no clue about how to do it. I told every teacher that I couldn't memorize. I must have been pretty convincing because they all let me get by with not doing it. One teacher did insist that we ALL had to recite a poem she had chosen. I kept telling her I wasn't ready to get up in front of the class to recite it. Finally, the whole class had done it except me. She finally told me privately to recite my poem to one of my classmates instead of the whole class. I was ecstatic that she let me off the hook, but then I realized that she had also excused another student who was obviously "very slow." I decided that I must be just as dumb. The classmate who listened to me recite the poem was very smart and, wanting to show off, she recited whole lines for me instead of making me do it myself.

My penmanship was excellent; I figured I got that talent from my Mom because she had excellent penmanship. I was always proud of the notes she wrote to my teachers. Learning how to write creatively was the difficult part. I remember begging Mom to help me. One assignment was to write a thank you letter to a friend; I had to make it up myself. I sat in the kitchen and cried. Mom felt sorry for me and, in total frustration, finally told me exactly what to write. She was angry that I couldn't do it by myself and complained that I should be able to write something that simple. I had convinced the whole world that I was helpless and not capable. I had learned helplessness, and everyone came to my rescue. During this time I also became a master at copying. I did not hesitate to copy anyone else's work. My classmates knew this and covered their work so I couldn't copy, but I still tried. I had totally convinced myself and everyone else that I was not able to do the work myself. I had no reason to believe anything else.

Another tragedy, involving my best friend, Donna, occurred during my middle-school years. She told me she had a "dreadful" secret to tell me. Every day before recess, the whole class walked single-file down to the basement to go to the bathrooms. My friend and I planned to be last in line so she could tell me her secret in the bathroom stall, where no one else would hear. Her parents were getting divorced, and she was moving away with her Mom and her siblings. I was devastated! How could I lose my best friend? What would I do for a friend now? She was my *only* friend.

I rationalized this loss by saying to myself: Donna is popular and probably wouldn't like me much longer because she was starting to get interested in boys. The boys teased her a lot. Yes, it was best for her to leave. BUT, it was another loss. She was so much fun and the one person who could make me forget my problems. I completely forgot who and where I was when we played together.

The year before she moved away, Donna threw a Halloween party. The day before Halloween, we went straight to her house after school to prepare the basement for the party. She and her older sister and her Mom were there with all the supplies. We filled a big tub with water and tested it to make sure the apples floated on the top. We hung scary things all around. We cooked some spaghetti and put the bowl behind a curtain, telling the kids they were feeling "slimy dog guts." We were having so much fun that I totally lost track of time. When I heard my friend's Mom calling me from the top of the stairs, her voice had a pitch that alarmed me. I ran up the steps to see my mother at the front door. She was very angry with me. She said she was worried about me; she didn't know where I was and it had gotten dark. I told her I was sorry, but I got involved in helping Donna get ready for the party. All the way home she yelled at me for not being responsible. I must come right home every night! Didn't I know that she had four other children at home alone? Didn't I know she needed to be cooking dinner for us, instead of running around to all the neighbors, asking if they had seen me? I don't actually remember the Halloween party. All the fun was gone for me because I was an irresponsible bad girl. I decided at that moment that I should not have a good time, but instead be "responsible."

One of the last things we did before Donna moved away was to play together in a field down the road from our house. She was a free spirit and loved doing things that I knew would get me into trouble if Mom found out about them. That is what made her so much fun. When we both needed to go to the bathroom, she said we could just pull our pants down and go right there. I knew I could get into a lot of trouble for doing this, but Donna said that there was no one around and she would never tell anyone, so we just pulled down our pants and peed together. We were in a neighbor's field because Donna wanted to ride his horses. We were trying to catch them, pet them and see if we could ride them. Of course, I was afraid of the horses, but she was determined to ride one of them. In the end, the horses ran away, so we just lay down in the middle of the field on the green grass.

While lying there in the grassy field, we saw a plane high in the sky leaving a trail of white vapor. We tried to guess where that plane might be going. We decided that we would grow up to be stewardesses and travel the world. I felt that there was a chance I could actually do that—when I was with my friend. She let me dream and she believed that it would happen for us. But Donna was leaving me, and I didn't know when I would ever see her again. My heart was heavy.

Another issue that I started to deal with at this time was my teeth. My father didn't have a single cavity when he died, but my Mom had lost all her teeth to false teeth in her early 40s. We never had toothpaste at home and were not taught to brush our teeth regularly. As a result, my siblings and I all had really bad teeth; we didn't brush often and, when we did, we used baking soda. Secondly, we didn't go to the dentist because we couldn't afford it, unless we had a toothache. When I did go to the dentist, I never had Novocain, either because our dentist didn't believe in it or it cost too much—and I was afraid of shots. Years later, I learned that one of the issues around my decaying teeth was that, because I never had Novocain, the dentist was not able to drill deep enough to get to the bottom of the decay. As a result, my teeth rotted underneath the fillings.

During these years, my two brothers really missed out on experiencing all those things that required a father. However, even with no father figure, Paul and David were stepping up to the plate to be "the men in our house." They were learning how to take apart the lawn mower, fix what was broken and put it back together. They were learning how to fix the car when it broke down and how to do plumbing and electrical work. Actually, anything that needed to be fixed was fixed by them. One day Mom decided that an old tool shed needed to be taken down; Paul, David and Colleen took the shed down. There was nothing they would not tackle.

My sisters and I were suffering too from not having a male figure around. I was so shy around boys, I couldn't even look at one in my class. I was so scared of them. They teased the other girls in class, but they rarely said anything to me. I felt too uncomfortable to talk to them. My friends were starting to have crushes on the boys, but I watched it all without having any idea of how to relate to or like them.

After Donna moved away, I looked for a new best friend, but there was nobody that I wanted to befriend. I tried to be friends with a girl up the street who shared the same birthday. One of the things that hurt me the most during this time was that she had a birthday party but did not invite me. It was my birthday too! All my classmates were there. I was devastated. I even asked her why she didn't invite me. She said that the invitation must have gotten lost in the mail. I didn't fall for that excuse. I knew she didn't like me. The problem was that I had to walk by her house every day on the way to school. Often she was coming out of her house just as I went by, so I frequently ended up walking with her.

I had been babysitting since sixth grade for the neighbors who lived up the street. Every year they had another baby. By eighth grade I was already dealing with three babies at one time. I earned 35 cents an hour and saved every penny I made. I would fall asleep as soon as I got the babies settled, and when the parents arrived home, I was sound asleep. In fact, they had a hard time waking me. I did wonder if they were concerned about my sound sleeping, but I was so exhausted from the day's work that staying up late was out of the question for me.

In eighth grade I also became a nanny for a small baby who lived in a house up the hill from my elementary school. I climbed the hill after school, taking charge of the baby so the Mom could have time to herself. The house was beautiful. The view from their home overlooked our small town. I took the baby out in the carriage for a walk and a nap in the shade under a tree in the backyard; the Mom instructed me to put a net over the baby so mosquitoes or flies wouldn't bite her. My job was to walk the baby until she fell asleep; then I did my assigned cleaning chores. I dusted, mopped, vacuumed and cleaned the bathrooms. This was my chance to see how the other half of the world lived. It looked like a wonderful life.

One Saturday evening I was minding the baby after spending the day by the river with some friends. We had laid out all afternoon in the sun. I had fair skin and I knew I had gotten burned. I put some lotion on my burned skin. I had the chills, but as soon as I got home I left for my babysitting job. It wasn't long before I started feeling sick. I was trying to take care of the baby and throwing up at the same time. I was dizzy and fainting. I just sat down with the baby when I felt faint. Never once did I think I should call my Mom. I needed the money, so I would stay there no matter how sick I was. The next day I told Mom how sick I was. She said I probably was experiencing a sun stroke.

During my eighth-grade year, I also got my first real job—at "Ray's Drive In." My older sister worked there too, as a carhop, but I was so shy, I just wanted to work in the kitchen. I was very excited to get this job. We had regular working hours and, every night after our shift, we ordered anything we wanted off the menu. That was the best part of all. Although it was only open during the summer, I was ensured of having something to do all summer long. I always worked the night shift, guaranteeing that I would get home late and that Mom would let both my sister and me sleep late. (We were always required to get up early, until we had this excuse.)

The first night that I officially worked at Ray's, I was assigned to washing dishes in the back room. My duties included ensuring a constant supply of frozen mugs. First, I washed the mugs in the sink, rinsed them in the rinse water and then put them on a rack in an opening in the wall. When they had dried, I moved them to the freezer so they would be cold and frosty when used to serve the root beer. After I had washed my first set of dirty mugs, I started to pile another set on top of the first set. Somehow, one of the mugs fell off the rack and straight down into the cooler, which was inconveniently open, where it shattered into a million pieces. The whole cooler had to be turned off and defrosted, while all the frozen mugs were washed again to remove the glass shards. I was mortified. How could I go back to work the next evening? I wasn't even capable of washing dishes without creating a huge problem! I went home thinking that they surely would never have me back. I did go back the next night—and for all four years of high school—ALWAYS being extra careful when washing those mugs.

My very favorite items to order at Ray's were beef tenderloin or a fish sandwich with fries. Both were deep fried. I just couldn't bring myself to eat a hamburger because I cooked at least a hundred of them each night. I prepared coleslaw and potato salad when we weren't busy. I also made the batter for onion rings. They were so good but, even then, we knew they weren't very good for us. After we closed for the evening, we ordered our food and ate as we did the closing chores—sweeping the floor, cleaning the catsup and mustard bottles, filling the salt and pepper shakers, and scrubbing the grill. That was by far the worst job; often Ray or his wife, Peg, would do it. Then they drove us home, as we basked in the knowledge that we made some money and ate some good food.

The drive-in also had an inside cafe, and I waited on those customers too. That was, for me, the hardest part because I never felt comfortable making change. The old-fashioned cash register didn't calculate how much change to give back to the customers. Sometimes, I would be cooking an order when fifteen people arrived, expecting to be served quickly. The owners were great about covering the cooking while I waited on the inside customers. They probably thought they would be served faster if they didn't have to wait for a carhop.

As I matured, the changes in my body began to frighten me. I was embarrassed because my breasts had started to develop. One of them was normal but the other was not developing properly. Mom insisted I start wearing a bra. I didn't want to wear a bra. I remember always wearing something over my blouse. Even if it was very hot, I would wear a sweater. I will never forget the first day I wore a bra. Some kids in school teased me about it. From that day on, I slouched forward to mask the fact that I was developing breasts. I could tell how uneven they were. I imagined that the whole world was gossiping about the fact that my breasts were not developing at the same rate.

One time when my Mom's sister, Aunt Agnes, was visiting, she had me show my breasts to her. They both stood there looking at me like I had five tits instead of two. They agreed that my lack of development had something to do with the fact that I had suffered from malnutrition when I was a baby. I had almost died when I was a baby, spending days in the hospital while my doctor attempted to find a formula that I could keep down. I was allergic to a number of formulas but they finally found one that worked.

Getting my period was traumatic. It arrived at the absolute worst time: I was in the middle of getting ready for a style show at the county fair. I belonged to a 4-H Club, and that year we were studying sewing; my mom helped me sew a dress for the fair. I was on the program to model a dress I made. Mom had never said a word to me about the momentous event of getting my period. I only knew about it because of that incident that had happened in the orphanage. I had already decided that I would not tell my Mom when I got my period because she had never talked to me about it. The night before the style show, I was awakened by a rumbling in my stomach. I thought I had wet my pants so I ran to the bathroom, where I discovered a huge clot of blood. I was panicked. I stuffed toilet paper in my pants and raced to the back closet where Mom kept all the rags. I knew that was what I had to use, but I had never walked before with a rag balanced between my legs. What if it fell out of my pants when I was modeling my dress at the county fair? What if the rag wasn't big enough and blood stained my dress? This, however, was not bad enough. Yet another style-show disaster awaited me.

Mom had sent me with her friend to Monticello to buy a pair of shoes for the style show, as I didn't have any good shoes. She dropped me off in front of the only shoe store in town. I had never shopped for shoes before in my life, so I didn't have a clue about my shoe size. The salesman measured my feet, but I definitely walked out of that shoe store with a pair of white patent leather shoes at least one size too big. I could not walk in them without my heels slipping out. I tried to hold them on by gripping my toes together. When I showed Mom the shoes I purchased, she was horrified. How could I have bought a pair of shoes so obviously too big? What was I thinking? It was too late to return to town, so I had no choice but to wear them. I guess Mom figured I might grow into them in a year or two. Maybe that was what I was thinking too.

I went to the fair with my 4-H leader. I knew I was acting strange. I was so fearful that when I sat down the blood would show through my outfit, that I tried to hold myself up off the backseat of the car. The kids I was with didn't seem to notice. When we arrived at the fair grounds, I went straight to the bathroom, not real bathrooms but cement stalls set up just for the fair. I went so often that the leader asked me if I was feeling okay. I replied that I really didn't feel good, but she was so preoccupied with getting the others and their outfits ready for the show that she didn't pay much attention to me. That was good because I spent most of the time going to the bathroom to check my make-shift pad. I had no idea what my body was doing, but it sure was inconvenient and messy. I didn't like it at all.

Finally, it was time for me to model my dress. It was a light shade of blue organza with darker blue flocked flowers on the see-through material. I was proud of the dress I had made, but I knew that my Mom had helped me way too much. She had become an excellent seamstress. She made me rip seems out as many times as needed to ensure the dress looked really good. However my new shoes slipped on every step as I climbed the stairs to the stage. I slid them as I crossed the stage so they wouldn't come off as I walked. Judges were scoring us not only on our outfits, but also on how we walked. I walked carefully then climbed down the steps on the other side on the stage—all without falling. It was over. I didn't care what score I got or if I got a blue ribbon. I had only one thing on my mind: I had my period and I needed to get back to the bathroom to check on things.

My biggest problem was that I didn't want Mom to know. I was obsessed with hiding this from her. It took a lot of vigilance for me to hide all the evidence and make sure she didn't see any clues, including taking the rags to the trash to burn. I didn't sleep well during my periods; I was worried I would get blood on my pajamas or, even worse, the sheets. Well, I hid it successfully for over a year. Mom started to fret and threatened to take me to the doctor because "You should have gotten your period by now!" I told her to be patient with me. I figured that if she didn't want to tell me about getting my period, she didn't need to know when I did.

Finally, one morning it all fell apart. We were doing the wash and Mom asked me: "Have you gotten your period?" I said "no". Then she showed me my pajamas. I told her that it had just happened but I didn't want to tell her. The secret was out.

When I reached ninth grade, my Mom and I went to register me at the new Catholic high school, built the year before for the five surrounding communities without a Catholic high school. Parents seeking a Catholic education for their kids were required to bus their children to this school. There was absolutely no question in my family that we would all continue our education at the Catholic high school. My older sister had attended, and I had heard lots of tales from her. I was very nervous about going to high school. Even though I always did my homework, worked hard and rarely missed a day of school in the last eight years, I already knew high school would not be easy for me.

I remember Mom helped me to fill out all the registration forms, which was followed by an interview with the principal. I was told that I would be assigned to the "C" class where the material covered would be "appropriate" to my abilities. At that point, I had no idea what the "C" class meant. It was just what my Mom expected; she was convinced that she had really dumb kids. When asked, "What are your hobbies?" I told the principal that my favorite hobby was to iron! Mom was mortified and yelled at me as soon as we got into the car. "Why did you tell her you loved to iron?" Honestly, I couldn't think of anything else and that was how I had spent most of my time outside of school. She told me that I must have some hobbies! I asked her what I should have said. What *were* my hobbies? I didn't know and neither did she.

My freshman year of high school, I finally made a new best friend. Her name was Marian. She lived in the country on a large farm, had a huge family—thirteen brothers and sisters—and her life seemed as difficult as mine. They had the tiniest house. Her Mom and Dad slept in the living room. To enter their house, we had to walk right through their bedroom. (I did wonder: how could they make so many babies with everyone walking through their bedroom? I figured out that, by the time the kids were coming home late at night, they had stopped making babies.) There was a large kitchen in the back of the house. It produced the best tasting down-home cooking you can imagine. Here bread was baked, delicious apple pies were made, and food from the garden was canned. A curious sight was a very tiny room off the kitchen, where the kids sat—and fought—while waiting to be called for dinner. With only two bedrooms upstairs, the boys all slept in one, and the girls in the other (two double beds and a couple of fold-up cots in each room—that was it for the house).

My new friend, Marian, and I had a lot in common. She was poor, although I thought she was rich because they had a large farm and lots of animals. She had to work hard, though, maybe even harder than me because there were so many kids and such a small space to live. We immediately became best friends. We talked for hours on the phone. This was a problem however because our one and only phone was on a small piece of furniture near the front door in the living room. There was no privacy. Everyone heard our phone conversations, including people on our party line up and down the road who could listen to our conversations too. Mom got exasperated with me because I stayed on the phone for hours. We saw each other every day at school, but we still had so much to talk about when we got home. We talked about our lives and tried to sort them out. Our little sisters gave us a great deal of grief. We both agreed that they should be doing more to help out, that they were both the youngest girls and were spoiled.

How I loved visiting her farm! I learned so much about life there. In fact, I learned everything I needed to know about life on this farm: how to make babies and how to drive! My friend and I talked about how you get pregnant; she kept saying that our parents did the same thing as the cows. I didn't know what the cows did! I had never noticed them doing anything like that before. I did not believe her, but she took me to the barn and showed me. She showed me other wondrous things such as: how to milk the cows by hand, how to separate the cream, and how the milk was stored so that the dairy company could pick up the milk.

Learning to drive a stick shift turned out to be a huge challenge for me. First, we had a very old car—a 1947 stick shift Chevy born the same year as me. Mom did not let me drive it out of the driveway, so all I did was drive forward and back in the driveway. I never got out of first gear and reverse. BUT my friend's house was a different situation—an old car and acres and acres of land to drive on! I must have killed the engine a hundred times as I tried to shift from first to second gear. Her whole family watched this crazy scene, starting, going forward, coming to a jerking stop and then starting over. I could not stop laughing as I attempted to coordinate one hand on the wheel, left foot on the clutch and right hand on the stick shift. It took a long time and much patience from Marian before I was able to drive successfully across the fields. She was lucky, she had been driving a tractor and watching her older brothers and sisters learn, so she seemed to have no trouble acquiring this skill.

My new friend, Marian, had friends in her classes. So we created our own little clique. We were not popular. Even though we didn't quite fit in, we had lots of fun together. Our little group of five girls was wild and silly and crazy. We laughed uncontrollably about the simplest of things. One of us would start laughing and then we all would go crazy laughing. We had one thing in common: we all had problems that we needed to escape. One of our friends had "crazy" parents, seven brothers and a baby sister called the caboose. Another friend had wealthy parents who gave her material things, but never what she needed. Another of our friends had an alcoholic mother who got too drunk to care for her seven children.

During my freshman year, I took a job (volunteered by my Mom), to take care of the mother of one of my Mom's friends, who was in the advanced stages of Alzheimer's disease. She did not want to put her mother in a nursing home. My Mom's friend was single and had devoted most of her life to taking care of her Mother. She needed to get away so she hired me to assist her on Saturdays. She picked me up early every Saturday morning. I was always exhausted from hanging out with my friends late on Friday night or working at the Drive-In. At her house, I sat with the Mother who was confused. When the noon whistle blew, she thought it was a fire and tried to escape from the house. Often it was so hot in the house, and quiet for such long periods of time, that I would fall asleep. When a noise awakened me, I would jump up and race around the house searching for the Mother inside and outside. My main job was to ensure she didn't wander away. I was petrified one day when I couldn't find her. When I finally did locate her, I had to coax her back to the house by promising to fix her lunch even though it wasn't lunch time. It was a constant battle to stay awake; the quiet and the heat, paired with nothing to do, ensured I would nod off. One time when I fixed her lunch, she couldn't find her teeth. I looked everywhere. Then I found her teeth in the freezer. This job lasted a year. We needed money so I never turned down a job. Eventually the woman died, and I was free again to sleep in on Saturday mornings!

I also babysat for a young couple with two small children. I particularly liked going to this house because I found a booklet on the bookshelf that explained the facts of life. Every time I went there, I would read and reread it after I got the children to bed. I read that sexual intercourse was required to get pregnant. I wasn't quite sure what that meant. I also read that if you missed a period, you were probably pregnant. I knew mine should be coming. In fact I thought I should get it that very night since it was the last day of the month. All night I kept checking. I was sick from worrying about it. I didn't think I could be pregnant, but I didn't have my period. What could I do? I figured that I would just have to wait to see if I was pregnant.

My older sister, Shirley, and I were not close because we were so different. She was outgoing, loud and smart, won the leads in the class plays, was a cheerleader and was good at everything. She took all the upper-level classes. It seemed that I was just the opposite. She did try to help me. She encouraged me to go out for cheerleading, and she tried to teach me the routines for the cheers. She encouraged me to try out for plays. I was too shy to even work backstage as the prompter. She tried to help me with projects.

One time I entered a poster in a contest. I won the contest, but all my friends said: "Shirley drew that poster, didn't she? You should not have accepted the prize because you didn't do the work! We know this is your sister's work. This is not yours." I was humiliated and decided not to ask her for help again. She was good at everything except one thing—getting along with people. She was accustomed to being in charge, something that worked well at home but not with her peers. When she would tell them what to do, they got mad at her.

Even though we weren't particularly close, Shirley did save my life many times, and to this day I am especially grateful for her help with one particular situation......... One morning I was running late for school, and I forgot to go to the bathroom. As I left the house I remembered that I had to use the bathroom, so I decided to just go to the out-house instead of going back inside. That would have been fine, but that very day my older sister had asked me to return a friend's Mother's diamond ring to her at school that morning. I was wearing the beautiful diamond on my ring finger. (My sister had the ring because my friend was on the same cheerleader squad. They had cheered a game the night before and had given the ring to my sister because she was afraid she might lose it while she was cheering.) My sister had given me specific instructions about making sure I returned the ring as soon as I got to school. As I was wiping my butt, the ring fell off my finger and disappeared into the dark piles of shit far below. I panicked. What would I tell my friend? What could I tell my sister? Where would we get the money to buy another ring? The worst of all—now everyone in my class would know that I was still using the outhouse!

I ran into the house and told my sister what had happened. I was hyperventilating. She told me to calm down and go on to school; she would deal with it. I did what she said, but all day I was sick with worry. How could I admit that I had lost the ring? I didn't want to talk to anyone; my friends asked me what was wrong. I was too embarrassed to tell anyone what happened. I felt like crying all the way home, but I did not cry. I saw no way out of this dilemma.

As soon as I walked into the house, my sister informed me that she had found the ring! I couldn't believe what I was hearing! HOW? She told me that after I left, she went out to the garage, found an old fishing rod with some wire and used a flashlight to look down the hole. Once she spotted the ring, she was able, after many attempts, to fish that ring right out of the pile of shit. She had cleaned it up and told me that SHE would deliver the ring to my friend. After that she often joked about the "diamonds in the privy!"

I did date during high school, but I was very nervous on every date. I would literally stop breathing. For me, it was never about having a good time. I was uncomfortable being with any male; it didn't matter who it was. I was nervous about how I looked, what to talk about and where we went. A movie was the best choice, but I was always afraid my date would want to hold hands; mine were always cold and clammy. Eating out was difficult too. To combat my fears, I always ordered the same thing: shrimp, fries and a Coke. Shrimp was easy to eat, and I found I could eat both the shrimp and the fries quickly with my fingers and then focus on what I should be saying. I didn't like it when my date looked at me. I felt self conscious. Finally, I always worried about having to kiss my date goodnight. I almost always responded by suggesting that we should wait to have our first kiss. (I am not sure what I was waiting for....) I once asked a friend what she said when she didn't want to kiss a guy. She said "we should wait" so I said the same thing! I later heard that my nickname with the guys in our class was "icebox." It certainly fit me.

One Sunday I was up in the church choir loft with other kids, preparing to sing for a Mass. There were no adults up there to supervise us. Of course, we were all messing around, laughing and tickling each other and falling off the bleachers. When Shirley heard us, she marched right up there and told us all to be quiet. She said that if we couldn't be quiet, we should just leave. Some of the girls (the nuns' favorites) got mad and told the nuns that next day that Shirley had yelled at them. One of the nuns took my sister out of class and marched her to each classroom to apologize to the kids for her behavior. Shirley refused to apologize—so they just stood there. She believed she had nothing to apologize for and refused to do it. It was very bold, even unheard of, to defy a nun. I was so embarrassed by her defiance. I had certainly learned my lessons well: we were to be seen but not heard. We were to do exactly what the nuns told us to do. I was the good girl and did exactly what I was supposed to do because that would keep the peace and not make trouble for my Mom.

Shirley believed the nuns treated us differently because we were poor. She complained bitterly to Mom about it.

One really happy memory from this period of my life was that I had a couple of friends who loved to dance; we would practice at their houses between school dances. During the dances we simply didn't care what anyone thought. We danced every dance. Dancing was fun, and if boys didn't ask us, we danced with each other. We did this shamelessly.

I would say my high school years could be divided into two "periods." The first two years were spent trying to figure out how to be popular and well liked. I watched the other girls and tried to imitate what they did so I could be popular too, but that never worked. I had a very bad feeling about myself being in the "C" track along with all the kids who were labeled "slow" or "not very smart." I fought this designation from the beginning because I wanted to take Latin and Algebra. The nuns said no. I kept worrying about how I could get a good education if I couldn't take certain classes. In my sophomore year, I persuaded the nuns to let me take both Latin and Algebra. All my friends had taken these classes the year before so I was with the freshman class. I had no friends and nobody to talk to or help me when I was struggling. I barely made it through both classes. I never won this battle throughout high school because I was always a year behind with the classes I was taking. I did get to take Geometry, but no other higher-level math classes. In the end I graduated with the lowest group. I was never able to convince anyone that I didn't belong with this group of kids. In fact, at this school, it seemed that once you got placed in the lowest group, there was no way to get out of it.

The second period of my high school life began around the start of my junior year. I sensed a very distinct difference with how I felt toward life. I had now seen for years the hopelessness of living a life of poverty in a small town. There was no chance of getting a date with the boys in my class who were popular and had money—and no way to escape the unwritten "caste system." I began to think about what I would do when my eighteenth birthday arrived and I would no longer be eligible for AFDC assistance. As I searched for a way out of this closed system, one thing I knew for sure was that I had to leave and never come back. How could I possibly do that? My family was still there. At this point I shut down as a person. I gave up. I stopped wanting to go to dances. I just wanted to work so I didn't have to deal with the rejection I felt. My friends noticed that I had changed. I stopped laughing, as I had during my first two years of high school. I stopped thinking everything was funny. In fact, very little seemed funny. It was hard to keep going, but I did arrive at one decision, one that I shared with no one.

I had been told that there were few options for my future. Expectations were low for what I might be able to accomplish. I could become a hairdresser or a secretary, or marry a farmer. None of these options sounded appealing. I decided that there was only one way available to me to escape my life: I would go to the convent. It was a brilliant decision even though I didn't realize it at the time. I believed I was being called to the religious life. In an Irish/German Catholic community, having a vocation was an honor. How did I come to this decision? I felt too ugly to get married; I could never have children because I was too frightened by doctors and hospitals, plus I never wanted them because "children made your life even more miserable." The main reason the convent sounded like a great option? I could get an education. I believed that God is very unpredictable and hard to satisfy. Surely I wouldn't go to hell if I dedicated my life to Him? I had reached this decision when I was a junior but I needed to get through high school first.

CHAPTER SIX

THE CONVENT YEARS

I was the tender age of seventeen when my Mom started to pressure me to make some decisions—about what I would do when I turned eighteen. The cause of her distress was that my Aid to Families with Dependent Children (AFDC) check would disappear when I turned eighteen, plus she knew I needed a plan. She could no longer afford for me to live at home. I turned eighteen in January but didn't graduate until June, and I wouldn't leave until September if I went away to school. I had been working during high school, saving all my money. I wasn't making much money; my jobs paid so little. (My regular babysitting job paid 35 cents an hour.) I could have helped my Mom with grocery money, but we never had that discussion. I put every cent in the bank because I knew I needed to be on my own as soon as I finished school.

This decision was pretty simple. I used a process of elimination to sort it out. My decision to go to the convent was finalized on our senior class retreat. As part of the retreat, we were required to meet with the priest to discuss our post-graduation plans. I announced that I thought I was being called to the religious life. We discussed how one would know this. He directed me to pray about it. I didn't really feel the need to pray about it. I was certain. I had this gut feeling that it was the right thing to do; God was calling me to enter into His service. I also thought I would bring honor and respect to my family—Catholic families that had a religious vocation were special. Secretly, I was desperate to run away from this life, to completely escape both my hometown and my family. The convent, with its strict rules, was the perfect answer to my need for a complete break with my family and everything I had suffered. I could start over, and recreate myself into a totally different person, once I left all this behind.

The next step was to get signed up for the convent. I turned for help to my friend, Peggy, who had a sister in the convent who knew exactly how to get enrolled. Her sister was on a mission in a small community not far from where I lived, so Peggy drove me to the convent where we met with her sister. She asked me why I believed I had a vocation. I repeated the same reasoning as I had told the priest. She told me that she could arrange for the Franciscans to send me the paperwork. She also asked me to visit the Motherhouse and talk to the postulant mistress who would tell me all I needed to know. I went with Peggy the next week and met with the Sisters who answered the door. They gave me all the paperwork for embarking on my new life: get a physical; fill out the application; order the trunk with all the clothing needed for my life as a nun; and report to the Motherhouse by 3:00 pm on September 3,1965.

The biggest hurdle was figuring out how to get a physical when I was scared of doctors and had never voluntarily gone to a doctor in my entire life. I asked my friend, Marian, to go with me. We had to walk across the street, through a small park, to the only medical clinic in town. I had walked BY there a hundred times but never walked IN there. (I did remember standing there in a long line that stretched out the door and down the street, with my siblings, when the polio vaccination came out. I was throwing a fit because I was so scared to get the vaccine. I know my mother was angry with me because I was irrational; all we had to do was suck on a sugar cube that had the medicine in it. I did put the sugar cube in my mouth and gagged.) Although my friend walked me over there, she did not come in with me. It would be embarrassing to me for the doctor and nurse to know how scared I was, so she went back to the park to wait for me.

My hand was shaking as I filled out the questionnaire. I couldn't focus or comprehend what the questions were. The doctor asked me the same questions over and over as I tried to answer. He asked me why I needed a physical. Never good at lying, I told him that I was planning to enter the convent. It was the first time I had said it out loud to anyone other than Marian. He didn't seem to be shocked. He commented, "It is such a blessing to have the gift of a vocation in your family. I bet your Mom must be so proud of you." (The truth was that I hadn't even told my Mom.) I had to get into a hospital gown, me who had never taken off my clothes in front of anyone before. He listened to my heartbeat, took my blood pressure, felt my glands and peered down my throat. I worried that he might inform me I had tuberculosis, or something even more dreadful. What if I didn't pass the physical? What would I do with my life if my *one and only plan* didn't work? Fear gripped me. I was eighteen years old but as insecure as a small child. He finally signed the paperwork, attesting to my physical fitness and soundness of mind to make this decision.

Informing Mom of my plan was a conversation that I put off as long as possible. I had made the decision six months before but didn't want to tell her. I wanted to keep it close to my heart for as long as possible. But Mom was becoming more and more frantic, worrying about what I would do when I graduated. I finally told her that I had a plan. She was visibly relieved. I told her that I planned to enter the Franciscan Order in September. I told her that I already had signed up and been accepted. My Mother had never supported a single decision I had made, and this was no exception.

She let loose with one of her worst tirades ever: "Do you know that these caring pillars of love treat some kids so badly? You know how badly you have been treated by the nuns. They profess to love everyone yet they play favorites. They give so much attention to the rich kids and ignore or abuse the poor kids." Did I plan to be part of a life that was truly a farce? Did I know that the nuns lived a lie? They took vows of poverty, but they ate better and lived better than us without any real concerns. They never went hungry. They had plenty to eat. They did not know real poverty. If I really wanted to take a vow of poverty, I should stay right where I was because I WAS living a life of poverty.

I knew she wouldn't be happy, but I was surprised at her anger. After all, she was the die-hard Catholic who never missed a Sunday mass, said the rosary daily and read out of her Catholic missal every morning and night. She constantly prayed that God would save her. She had required all of us to take part in all the Catholic rituals, yet she violently opposed my spending my life praying as she had taught us. My only thought at that moment was: this is exactly why I want to go away and never come back.

So, my life finally had some direction. I felt relief to know that I would soon escape this small town. I started to withdraw a bit from both my friends and my activities. I found myself wanting to work instead of going to dances. I used the excuse that I had to work, but the truth was that dancing and dating seemed meaningless activities, now that I was planning to leave this secular world behind.

I made one exception to this dating rule. His name was Francis. I decided to "go steady" with Francis that summer. It felt safe for me to be with him. Yes, we would neck on country roads, but as soon as he got more serious, I asked him to take me home. He was always respectful of me, and we had many conversations about me entering the convent. He asked, "You enjoy me kissing you, and yet you are going away to a place where you will never be kissed again or go out on another date? Don't you ever want to get married or have kids?" I answered all of his questions with one pat answer: "I know you can't understand this, but I am being called to the religious life. It is too hard to explain, but it's a gut feeling that this is what I am supposed to do." How could he argue with me? Having a religious vocation was not something that could be explained! So we dated and talked, and I felt comfort in knowing that I was going to get away from everything I had known for the past eighteen years. I was excited and fearful at the same time!

My friends planned a huge going-away party for me and my friend, Marian, who was also going to the convent. It was held in a large room above The Corner Tap, where, as children, we had performed at the St. Patrick's Day celebration. The party was set for a Friday night the week before I was scheduled to leave for the convent. My friends asked if I wanted "one last date" with a guy that I had been crazy about all during high school. They would make the arrangements. I said "YES" even though I was going steady with Francis. I knew Francis would be upset, but I did it anyway. It was a terrible night for me— I showed up with a guy who really didn't like me, and Francis drove around all night, trying to sort out why I would do such a thing to him.

My friends went with me to shop for a dress for the party. I had decided to use some of my money to buy a dress, instead of wearing something my Mom had made. I had few clothes because we wore uniforms from the first grade through high school. I also planned to wear this store-bought dress the day I entered the convent. Never having shopped for a dress before, I had no idea what was in style, what size I wore, what I liked or what looked good on me. I finally chose a purple and green plaid empire-waist dress. I thought I looked as good as I could. Marian bought the same dress in a different color of plaid. We essentially wore the same dress to our going-away party.

All of our friends were invited to the party. We had cake and ice cream, and a record player played music. Even though I loved to dance, I had no fun at this last party. I came with a guy who was with me only because my friends asked him to take me; my real boyfriend was not there. I did not feel comfortable being the center of attention, and I couldn't wait for the party to be over, but the night seemed to go on forever.

The night before I left for the convent, Francis asked me out on our last date—to Cedar Rapids for dinner and a movie. That sounded innocent enough. Francis came to pick me up, spoke briefly to my Mom, and then we were on our way. We ate at a restaurant, and I, of course, ordered the same thing I ordered on every date I had ever had (Shrimp!). After dinner, Francis said we should go see a new movie that had just been released—*The Sound of Music*.

I had seen very few movies in my life. I had no idea what the movie was about, but it sounded interesting from what Francis told me. We had watched only a few minutes when I realized I was in big trouble. I started to cry and I couldn't stop. I had rarely cried in my life and certainly never cried with a guy. What was I going to do? I had no Kleenex. I cried and wiped my tears on my sweater all night long. I couldn't stop crying. The story hit too close to home. The main character, Maria, went into a convent to escape falling in love with a man. She was a lively, beautiful girl who loved life. The mother superior realized why Maria had entered the convent, and she sent her away to deal with being in love with a man. I cried because I realized that I wanted to be like Maria, but I would not be sent home because I had come to the convent for the wrong reason. I believed I had been called to my vocation, and nobody was going to save me from that fate.

September 3, 1965, arrived bright and sunny. This was the day I entered the Franciscan Order of the Holy Family of Jesus, Mary and Joseph. It was a typically beautiful fall day in Iowa. The leaves were saying goodbye to their beautiful green, giving way to the next coat of equally beautiful yellows, reds and oranges. I, too, was saying goodbye to "what was." I hoped my transition would be as easy as the leaves changing color. It was wishful thinking. That morning, Francis came to say goodbye. I walked Francis to his car. He gave me a kiss and a present, a beautiful white pearl rosary. My brothers and sister went to school as normal that day. I don't remember saying goodbye to them. Two nights before, I had given away everything I owned. Most of my clothes, however, stayed right in the closet because my younger sister would inherit them. My only piece of jewelry, my great aunt's black onyx ring, I gave to my favorite cousin, Eileen. I used the couple of hundred dollars inherited from my grandparents to buy my convent trunk. I withdrew all the money I had saved since I started working and gave it to my Mom. I asked her to buy a new washer and dryer. I knew she would miss me the most on Saturdays, when I did the washing and ironing. Mom and I ate lunch together and then got in the car. Mom was quiet. What was there to say? I knew how much she didn't want me to leave. She was alone in her pain that day.

We drove the twenty-five miles to Dubuque. About halfway there, we stopped to say goodbye to a friend. He was planning to enter the seminary the next week and perhaps knew better than anyone else what I was doing. We got to the Motherhouse about 2:30 pm. I was assigned the number "1442." (I was the forty-second woman to enter the convent that day. There would be forty-eight before the day was done.) As Mom completed some paperwork, I was led away to a bathroom—to take off everything and replace my bra, panties, slip, nylons and dress with the simple black garb of the postulant (black tights, blouse and skirt, a big cloth bra and white bloomer panties). I was instructed to fold up all my possessions into a neat pile; then I walked down the long corridor to hand them all to my mother and say one last goodbye. I did all this without any emotion; my Mom was equally emotionally distant. After I said goodbye, I was escorted into a large room that would be our recreational area. Many of the girls were still crying. I just sat there, wondering what I had gotten myself into. It did not take long to find out that this life was going to be very different from what I had imagined.

After everyone had arrived, we all introduced ourselves and shared a little bit about ourselves, including our home parish. Most had come to this life as a result of a Sister who had influenced them. We proceeded to the chapel for Vespers and then, the dining room for dinner. The dinner was good. I was not choosy about what I ate; I was just happy to have food. After dinner we had our first meeting. This is the moment when I started to find out what I had signed up to do. We were told what our new life would look like: Yes, we would be up at 5:00 am to meditate. We would go to chapel at 6:00 am for Mass. Breakfast at 7:00 am, then chores. College classes would begin after our chores, then more chores from 3:00 to 4:00 pm, and a period for recreation from 4:00 to 5:00 pm. After evening prayers (Vespers) in the chapel, we went downstairs to dinner. We had a small dining room right off the main dining room. The main dining room was filled with many Sisters, all dressed in their habits. We sat quietly eating while we listened to a Sister at the lectern reading from scripture. After that we were free to talk to our new friends.

After dinner we all went into the common recreation room where we found out our bedroom assignments. (They were called "cells.") There were four women in the "J" room. All of our names started with the letter "J": Joleen, Judy, Jeanie and Janice. Each had a white curtain that pulled around her small space. In my space, I had a single bed, a small wooden dresser with all the clothes from my trunk, and a pitcher and bowl. Group recreation was from 7:00 to 8:00 pm; no talking was allowed after 8:00 pm. When we passed someone in the hallway, we had to look down and say, "Praise be Jesus Christ." The other person would respond, "Now and forever, Amen." There would be NO talking in our bedrooms, ever! Most of us were eighteen years old.

It was hard to conceive that we could possibly honor these rules, but no one ever questioned them. It was just the way it was, and we had all signed up for this. Suffering, denial and sacrifice would win us favor with God. We were informed that it would be a good idea to spend time with the Lord in the chapel before bed. We learned that we would not be receiving any phone calls, but we would have a chance once a week, on Sunday afternoon, to write to our families. We could receive mail every day during our recreation period, but every letter we received would be opened and read before we got to read it. Our first visiting day was at the end of our first year, when we received our postulant veils. We would not go home for three years. We would not leave the grounds of the Motherhouse except to see the dentist or doctor. We would not watch TV or listen to the news.

To be truthful this routine looked pretty good to me; I was used to a disciplined life. The most exciting thing for me was that I no longer had to worry about my Mom's depression, not having enough money, or food, the car breaking down, not fitting in with my family, or not belonging to the "in" clique at my high school. I thought I could create my own cool clique in the convent. When I told my classmates how much I was enjoying this new life, most looked at me like I was crazy. They were crying, missing their families, and missing the lives they had left behind. I, on the other hand, felt like this was the best life I had experienced so far. I was on a new, exciting adventure, and it all looked so much better than the life I had left behind.

One of the things that made me the happiest was that I was going to be able to attend college, but I was concerned that I wouldn't be able to make it in college. I asked the nuns what would happen if someone wasn't smart enough to pass the college classes; they said that person would have to become a *cook*. In this teaching order, everyone became a teacher. They said there would be special classes for those needing extra help. I knew right away that I would be one of those taking remedial classes while most of my classmates studied Shakespeare. I envied those kids, reading the classics and putting on plays. I learned that my older sister, who was attending college a few miles from the Motherhouse, had the lead in *Much Ado About Nothing*. She was starring as Beatrice, and I was studying remedial reading. It didn't seem fair, but I was so thankful to have the opportunity to study. But first, I had to learn *how* to study. Determined to become a good reader and make it through college, I studied all the time. Every free period found me in the library studying. I read things out loud. I kept reading things over and over again until I understood them. I did not give up. After a rough start my first semester, I did better every semester after that.

The class that I remember most vividly was Music Appreciation. Sister Marie Therese taught this class and she was the best, setting high expectations for every one of us. She was determined that we would be able to recognize the music of all the great composers. Standing by her old record player and a pile of black records, she set the needle on any part of the record, asking us to identify the work and the composer. Some of the postulants in our class, who had taken music lessons before, invented words to help us remember the themes. This helped all of us do better in that class.

We had a large institutional bathroom, with lots of toilets; it was right across from our bedroom and it was warm. The showers were in another smaller room down the hall; we each signed up for a time to take showers. We used a pitcher and washbasin in our rooms to wash up daily, but we could take a shower once a week. The shower room had very little light, and there were no mirrors. I wondered how we would take care of our periods, but that was handled like everything else: in the supply room. The supply room was opened once a week to get personal items we needed.

Those first nine months passed by quickly; our routine kept us very busy. Every Sunday we spent the afternoon writing letters to our families. My letters to my Mom were long and detailed. I heard nothing from the outside world, so all I could relate in these letters was my daily convent life. I spent hours recounting all I had learned about the Catholic Church. My family thought I was becoming brainwashed. My older sister was so upset by my letters that she started leaving books, magazines and newspapers for me to read on the doorsteps of the main convent. I never saw any of these materials and only found out about them when I saw a thesaurus in the library with my sister's name in it. My postulant mistress told me that my sister had dropped it off for me to use. Since we were in training to take a vow of poverty and everything was communally owned, it was put in the library for everyone's use.

During this year, a few of our classmates decided that this life was not for them. Others were asked to leave. When someone decided to leave, she was not allowed to tell anyone. She simply disappeared. Whenever we noticed that someone was gone, we ran upstairs to the attic to see if we might be able to see our friend leaving down the front driveway—but we never saw anyone leaving. Were they shuttled away in the middle of the night or when we were all in the chapel praying? The mistress just made an announcement that so and so had decided that the religious life was not for her. It was so hard, not getting to say goodbye to our good friends. One day they were there and the next day they were gone. During my first year in the convent, I did not question whether this was the right decision for me or if I could do this for the rest of my life, even though some of my friends had left. Since we were not allowed to talk to any of our departing friends, we never knew how they decided to leave.

The first year, we were called "postulants." We wore a black mid-calf woolen skirt, a black polyester blouse, black tights and black shoes with "granny heels." Our schedule consisted of attending classes, recreation, praying and doing our chores. Our college classes were held in classrooms on the second floor of the Motherhouse. We had lots of different types of chores: dusting, vacuuming and scrubbing floors, working in the laundry room, and helping in the kitchen to prepare food or setting up the dining room or doing dishes afterwards. After nine months of this schedule, we had a ceremony to receive our postulant veils—our first step in a long, eight-year process of committing to the religious life. We wrote the words of the ceremony that spoke to the symbolism of getting our veils. During the ceremony we each received a small black nylon veil that covered our heads. The veil had a stiff white band; bobby pins were used to hold the veil in place. It was just large enough to cover our heads. Its main purpose was to get us used to wearing something on our heads. It certainly made us look "nunlier"! I was definitely ready for this first step.

During this time I was still receiving letters from my boyfriend, Francis. Our mail was opened and read by the postulant mistress. After a couple of months of letters from him, the postulant mistress told me that I could no longer receive letters from him. I was ordered to write to tell him that he should no longer write to me; I was not to mention that the nuns made me write the letter. I did as instructed, writing, "I am committing my life to Christ and I can no longer have the distractions of the worldly life, so please stop writing to me." That was the end of that part of my life. I later learned that Francis signed up with the Navy for seven years on the day he got my letter. That sounded drastic, but then I realized that I had signed up for the convent for the rest of my life. Seven years didn't sound so bad!

The nuns also read every letter that we wrote. We left our letters un-sealed on the mistress's desk. We did plan to send letters out on visiting day, but there would be no visiting day for a whole year. By then it really didn't matter.

Were we ever allowed to leave the Mount? Yes, but mostly NO! We did take the bus to visit the doctor and the dentist. I had some cavities and made a number of visits to the dentist, who turned out to be our postulant mistress's brother. We always went on these trips with at least one or two other postulants. These trips were scary because, having been locked up for more than six months, we felt uncomfortable being out in public. People stared at us.

What was the hardest thing about being in the convent? For me it was music depravation! During high school I had LOVED music and danc-ing. I grew up listening to the radio that sat on top of the refrigerator. I actually danced with the refrigerator to the music coming from the radio. So when I realized that I would never again hear any rock and roll music, my heart was heavy, all the joy taken from my soul.

Like a number of my classmates, I had smoked a bit during high school but never could get the knack of inhaling. Truthfully, I didn't really want to learn because I had heard how bad it was for your lungs. In our first days at the Motherhouse, I saw a couple of the girls pick up butts discarded by local hired hands, and smoke them. I had the good fortune to be in the same dormitory with Jeanie, who had smoked a lot in high school. One day she received a package in the mail. (The rule about receiving packages was that any food must be put in the recreation room, for everyone to share.) Her package contained a whole box of fudge, the best fudge I had ever tasted. She snuck it up to her room, and for at least a week we sneaked into her "cell" to eat the fudge. With no utensils, we just grabbed huge chunks of it with our fingers. It was so much fun to eat.

The biggest bonus, however, was hidden deep in the box. To this day, I am not sure how that package passed inspection. When Jeanie discovered the cigarettes, we immediately began plotting how we would sneak away to smoke them. There were four of us in this adventure. Surely, if we went far enough away from the Motherhouse into the fields, no one would ever know what we were up to? We swore each other to secrecy, but could we trust each other? This was a big risk for us because if even one person cheated, we would all be in serious trouble. The next day we met as agreed, out by the Stations of the Cross. We wanted it to appear as if we were going for an innocent walk, so we didn't leave together. When all four of us met up, we were excited. We walked quickly. When we felt that we were far enough away from the building, out into a hilly field far from the Motherhouse, we lit up our Marlboros. I tried to inhale. It didn't work, but I was so happy to be part of this group. At least that is what I thought at that moment. It felt fun to be doing something risky and daring.

We couldn't be gone too long, for fear we would all be missed, so after smoking a couple of cigarettes, we headed back to the convent. It was at that point that I started to freak out. What if the nuns could smell the smoke? What if they had noticed we were missing? What would happen to us if we got caught? My mind began to race. I was sure that God would punish me for such a blatant violation of the rules. I was always the good girl. I couldn't even think about getting kicked out of the convent. Why had I taken this risk? Was I addicted to nicotine? I vowed I would NEVER do this again. I went straight to my room and brushed my teeth, then joined the rest of our class as they were going into chapel. They wanted to know where we were. Our response: we said we had taken too long of a walk and lost track of time. I never found out if the other girls finished that package of cigarettes, but I was never again a part of it.

It was Christmas time, and somehow one of our classmates found out that *White Christmas* was on TV. We all knew there was a TV in the basement. After recreation, we were supposed to go to chapel, say our night prayers and head upstairs to our bedrooms. The word spread that we were going to sneak to the basement to watch *White Christmas*. We knew we would be in serious trouble if we got caught, but we were willing to take the chance. We plugged in the TV, found the channel, and settled in on some wooden chairs we found at the other end of the basement. The movie was just getting good when the postulant mistress surprised us, stood in front of the TV with her arms crossed, and very sternly demanded we return upstairs immediately!

You can be sure we got quite a lecture that next morning! We learned quickly that the pain inflicted was not worth the price of disobeying the

rules. Since we went to confession every Saturday, we would have to confess this infraction. Actually, I was relieved to have something to confess.
It was so hard to come up with something new to confess every week. I
stood in line outside the confessional, waiting for the priest to hear my
confession, in anguish over what I would say. I usually confessed that I
had been unkind to a friend or had disobeyed the mistress or had taken
something that didn't belong to me. I repeated these "sins" week after
week for years, even though I had not committed any such sins.

During recreation, in winter time, we went tobogganing and skating. Both activities were great fun, but we didn't have the right clothes to
keep warm in the cold Iowa winters. We needed heavier mittens, scarves
and boots to venture outside in the below zero weather. Pants were out
of the question, so our legs got very cold. We must have looked frightful
(and cold!) in our habits, climbing onto the toboggans for a ride down
the hills near the Motherhouse. Skating was also cold, but somewhat
more manageable in our habits.

I had been in the convent about ten months when the postulant mistress called me into her office. As I waited, I wondered if she found out
that I had been smoking. Was she going to ask me to leave? My mind was
running wild. My worst fear was about to be realized. She came in, closed
the door and announced, "Your Mother has had a heart attack. We think
it is important for you to visit her in the hospital. I have arranged for
your parish priest to take you to Monticello where your Mother is hospi-
talized." My first reaction was to ask myself, "Do I have to go see her?" I
was so scared to see Mom. I hadn't seen or talked to her in ten months; I
hadn't seen any of my family. None of us had left the Motherhouse. We
had not yet even had our first visiting day. Everyone was envious that I
was getting to leave for an overnight. I was scared. The priest picked me
up, and we went straight to the hospital. He planned to visit with me and

my Mom, and then take me to a local convent that was owned by our Franciscan Order. After Mass he would come for me, take me for another short visit to the hospital, and then return me to the Motherhouse.

I remember being shocked to see my mother looking so frail. She was in intensive care, hooked up to all sorts of tubes. I didn't know what to say. I really didn't have to say anything because she was too sick. It had been almost a year since I had spoken to her. The priest filled up the empty spaces of our conversation. I remember him saying that she had better get well quickly because Colleen, my younger sister, was "acting wild and running the streets." "You know, Helen, it is not going to be good to leave your daughter alone for any length of time." It was a sobering experience for me because I had all but forgotten about my brothers and sisters who were still dealing with the life I had so gladly left behind. I just wanted to leave and go back to the convent; this was too uncomfortable for me to deal with. On the way back, I didn't say a word to the priest. He, in turn, talked about many innocuous things.

Upon returning to the convent I found a situation that I could never have imagined. Everyone in my class was infected with chiggers, the result of a long hike! Everyone was itching and uncomfortable. I was the only one without chiggers; I felt alone and left out. They were all jealous of me getting to see my family. They were suffering from the constant itching. Nothing else mattered at the time. I wanted to tell them how painful it was for me to see my mother in the hospital, hooked up to all the tubes, but this was not going to happen because they were all preoccupied with itching and wishing THEY could go see their mothers.

Our first summer in the convent presented some problems for me and my classmates, especially adjusting to wearing those long black dresses with black tights and black granny shoes all summer long. Gone were the shorts and tops and sandals of past summers. It was hot and humid all summer long, and it rained a lot. That year, the Mississippi River was flooding our city. We could only imagine the destruction as the river overran its banks. We were all safe, out of harm's way, because we were located on a huge cliff overlooking the Mississippi, but the river was rising every day and many people were affected by the flooding. I wished that we could fill sandbags or do something constructive to help.

One day during recreation time, several of us went up to the attic where the elderly nuns' trunks were stored. It was a rainy day with nothing interesting to do, so we started exploring some of the old trunks. Somehow the postulant mistress got wind of our activity. She immediately assembled the entire class and sternly informed us that she knew we were doing things we shouldn't be doing. She required each of us to make an individual confession to her in her office of our wrongdoings. She said we should include in our confession *everything* that we were doing that was wrong.

We were not allowed to talk to each other, so we couldn't compare notes. As I waited in line to go into her office, I saw my friend come out. She rolled her eyes and looked down. I wondered if she had confessed to the smoking or the food in our rooms. No, I decided, I would not bring up anything except the most recent incident. I admitted that I was in the attic but I, personally, had not taken anything out of the trunks. (Some of my classmates, however, had been fooling around and dressing up with things they found in the trunks.) She told me that I was guilty by association, that I had no right to look in anyone else's trunk. She ended by asking me to personally assess whether this religious life was for me. (Later we found out that she asked this question to every one of our classmates!)

The summer went by quickly because we had not only attended summer school, but also had lots of work in the garden. The garden was huge and located in back of the Motherhouse. Working in the garden was part of our chore assignments. Our first visiting day finally arrived. I was so worried because my Mom might still be quite weak from her heart attack; she might not be able to come. Everyone was excited to see their families but I was worried. First, I didn't know if my family would come if my Mom was not able to be there. If they did come, what kind of shape would my mother be in? I felt distant from my brothers and sisters. What would I say to them? I felt my relationship with my family was different from my classmates' families.

Well, the day turned out okay. Mom arrived with all my siblings. We took pictures and talked about general topics. Shirley said that I was being brainwashed. My siblings were all distant. It was clear they thought I was crazy to be choosing this life, and this one day confirmed their suspicions. They could no longer relate to anything I was saying or doing, even though they were still entrenched in the Catholic Church.

My postulant year was now coming to an end. Did I ever look back and say that I needed to get out of there? Never! Not once did I question my decision to enter the convent. I felt there was no turning back. It had been a year of clean sheets, good food, warm nights and new friends, and I was working on getting closer to God. Where was God? How could I get in touch with Him? If I prayed hard enough, would I eventually get to know Him? I had been taught that if I sacrificed everything for Him, I would be rewarded with a close personal relationship with God. So far, I saw no evidence of this happening.

One of the activities aimed at helping us get closer to God was a ten-day retreat at the end of our postulant year. I was appalled when I heard that we were required to remain silent for the entire TEN days! I had no idea how I was going to do this. I loved to talk to my friends. How could I go ten days without talking to anyone? I feared this would push me over the edge. I didn't have the tools to entertain myself for ten straight days. At the end of this retreat, we would become canonicals and begin our second year of convent life. Somehow I made it through those ten days. It was not as hard as I feared. Part of each day was structured for prayer and meditation. During our free time I read a lot and walked outside around the beautiful grounds of the Motherhouse. At the end of the retreat, we were ready to move into a new stage of convent life.

We were told that we would have to change our names when we became novices, so I started to ponder which names I should submit to the Mother Superior. She would make the final decision, but I could submit three requests for the Sister name I wanted to be called once I became a novice. My first requested name was Sister Vincent, after my Dad. My second request was Sister Tara (where I got that name, I do not know). My third choice was Sister Sara Marie. I predicted she would choose Sister Vincent because there was a sentimental reason for that name. Sister Tara sounded too much like "Sister Terror." I thought Sister Sara Marie would be a good name for me because I loved the name Sara, and Marie was my middle name.

In the ceremony we would become brides of Jesus Christ. One morning after class, the postulant mistress asked us to meet her on the third floor of the convent in front of a room that was always locked. When she opened the door, we saw a rack of old, faded wedding dresses. I tried on a few but none seemed to fit me. Finally, one of my classmates handed me a dress that was too small for her. It fit me, but I sure didn't feel like a beautiful bride. I didn't really know what it should feel like to be a "Bride of Christ," or any kind of bride, for that matter. Maybe it was because I was wearing black granny shoes under the bride's gown? I would also be carrying something strange: instead of flowers, a brown habit (the only clothing I would have for the rest of my life). I would take the vows of

poverty, chastity and obedience. Even though I would take these temporary vows for three years in a row, I had to treat them as if they were final
vows. After I took final vows, I would have to petition the Pope if I ever
wanted to leave the convent.

The day of the ceremony was a hot, sunny, humid Midwestern day.
My family and friends arrived. We were lined up one by one in our
bridal gowns. The large chapel was packed with our invited guests. I
did not look for my friends or family as we marched, single file, down
the center aisle, carrying the brown Franciscan habit. It felt strange to
be dressed in white and carrying a heavy brown habit. I would go in as
Janice McDermott and come out of the chapel with a different name.
During the vows ceremony, I learned that Mother Superior had chosen
Sister Sara Marie for me.

During the ceremony we left carrying our habits, and came back
dressed in our habits. My habit consisted of a floor-length brown dress
with a scapula (a long, flowing piece of material with a hole in the middle
to put my head through) that covered my entire body, both front and
back over my dress. My dress had three-quarter length sleeves; under the
sleeves was a see-through black sleeve that had elastic on one end to hold it
up under the sleeves. The idea was to cover the entire arm. I wore a white
veil that covered my head except for my bangs, a large, heavy black rosary
around my waist, and a medium-sized cross around my neck. We also
would get a ring to wear on our left ring finger when we took final vows.

So my life as a novice began. This second year was far more intense.
It was a year of strictly religious study; we did not take any college classes.
Only in our third year were we allowed to read any secular newspapers,
books or magazines, or to watch TV. Shirley continued to be upset about
how I had been cut off from the world, so she brought me more things
to read. Although she had not seen me, she could tell from the tone of

my letters that I was becoming more steeped in the deeply-held doctrine of the Catholic Church. How could this not happen? We spent all day studying religious doctrine.

Shortly after we became novices, a new group of postulants arrived at the Motherhouse. They immediately informed us that we were totally "brainwashed." One member of the new class was a beautiful woman named Joanne. She was especially vocal about us not knowing anything that had happened over the past year. (We told her it would happen to her too!) We often snuck into the closet to listen to her stories and to hear her play the guitar and sing Simon and Garfunkel and Beatles songs. She knew the songs by heart and had such a beautiful voice. She sang many songs, but my favorite was *Bridge Over Troubled Waters*. We knew she would get in trouble if she were ever caught singing outside of recreational time. She eventually did get in trouble, and her guitar was locked up except during recreation. I remember those times in the closet listening to her sing as some of my happiest moments in the convent.

It was during this year that I got called into the canonical mistress's office. She said she had some serious concerns about me becoming a sister. She said my laugh was too loud and unbecoming, that I had to be very careful of how I sat. She said that if I couldn't control my laugh and sit properly "as a sister," I would need to seriously look at whether this was the life for me. I hate to admit it, but I never took that threat seriously. I continued to laugh loudly. I had always been flexible and could sit cross-legged easily. (I did try to sit properly when I was around the mistress.)

The topic of sex in the convent is not easy to talk about. I grew up feeling so uncomfortable with being touched. Being in the convent was perfect for me in that respect. We were not expected or allowed to touch each other.

One night, right before the eight o'clock rule of not speaking to each other, one of my fellow classmates asked to come to my room to give me a back rub. (She was the only one in our class who was studying to be a nurse.) As part of her training she was to learn the technique of massage, so she was practicing on her classmates. She came to my room and started giving me a great massage. It was not long before I was totally relaxed and had an orgasm. I was very nervous and upset about this. I wondered if she knew what had happened. I decided that it was just too dangerous for her to practice on me. From that day forward, I never again let her come to my room to practice her techniques. Later she said to me, "I guess you didn't like the way I gave you a massage." I didn't say anything. How could I say that I thought that her giving me an orgasm regularly would lead me down a road that was too scary and sinful for me to get involved in? We were told our bodies were sacred. We were brides of Christ. We took a vow of chastity. We would take no pleasure from our bodies. I knew it was wrong.

What I observed and experienced the next four years would open my eyes to a whole new meaning for the word "sex". During our weekly meetings, the mistress talked to us about what she called "particular friendships." Much later in life, I was able to identify the meaning of "particular friendships" as lesbian relationships. At first we didn't have a clue what she was talking about because we had never heard of "particular friendships." She was so vague in how she described these friendships, to the point we all wondered if we had one. We were told that these friendships were a mortal sin and must stop immediately. Over time I began to notice that many of my classmates had paired up with another sister, spending a great deal of time together alone. The same thing happened to me. I had become infatuated with another sister who was a year ahead of me. I wanted to be with her all the time. She was pretty, lively and smart, and she played the guitar. I was nervous around her. I felt different around her. I worshipped the ground she walked on. Every chance I got, I would try to sit by her. I never talked to her about how I felt, so I never knew if she realized how crazy I was about her. I hardly realized what had happened to me. It was only after she left the Motherhouse, at the end of my second year in the convent, that I realized how deeply attached I was to her. I felt terribly alone and depressed. It was my first experience with this kind of loss. Even though I never saw or engaged in any sexual relations during my five years in the convent, I thought certain relationships might fall into the category of "particular friendships."

It was during this time that I had my first concerns about living my whole adult life with only women. Since there were no men around to love, might I find myself falling in love with a woman? I wondered if I was a lesbian. I found myself wishing that I had a rich, loving family that would drive up to the front of the Motherhouse and whisk me away, like one of my classmates' family did for her. I started to have strange thoughts about what I was doing in this place. I started having some fleeting thoughts: "What have I gotten myself into?"

During our canonical year we concentrated on deepening our religious life. We learned to sacrifice as much as we could to atone for our sins. One of the practices that we used to get closer to God was a posture that symbolized our surrender to God. After evening prayers we would go to the chapel and hold our arms out and up, as if we were being arrested. This posture, which was held for long periods of time, showed that we were willing to suffer for Christ and surrender to His will. We also said many prayers during these periods of arm holding. I tried to hold my arms up as long as the older sisters, who would sit in the chapel for hours. I would plead with God to come to me, to speak to me, to let me get to know Him. I was willing to give my life to Him. All I needed was a little word from Him. I was beginning to feel somewhat desperate. Other sisters advised me to persevere, and I would eventually find God.

Another convent practice that was dying out by the time I entered the convent in 1965 was the "chapter of faults." We were not allowed to confess actual sins, but we did confess "imperfections" and minor faults. We lay flat, side by side on the floor in a large room, prostrating our bodies, confessing our faults and begging for forgiveness for all our sins.

Our second year ended with another silent ten-day retreat. This one was a bit easier because we had so many books to read and passages from the bible to meditate on. We were instructed to think much more about what vows would mean to us and how we were dedicating our lives to Christ. At this time, two classmates were asked to leave. We had started two years ago with forty-eight women. We were now down to forty-two classmates.

In our third year we were the oldest group at the Motherhouse, most of us just turning twenty. We resumed a full load of college courses. We went to classes, prayed, worked and studied. We settled into a routine. We had adjusted to this austere lifestyle, and when the next group of postulants arrived, we didn't have much interaction with them. For the most part, I remained happy that I was in this safe haven. The sacrifice of not going home, talking on the phone or seeing my friends or family rarely bothered me. In fact, most of my friends stopped writing me during this third year. I was still happy to be totally consumed by this new life.

College seemed to be getting easier for me. I wanted to feel smart so I studied as much as I could; I had lots of time so it was easy to study. I was proud to be doing well in my college classes, but I was still required to take a remedial class in my third year at the Motherhouse. To my dismay, I was not allowed to take the Shakespeare course with my classmates because it was offered at the same time as the remedial reading/grammar class. My classmates were learning famous lines from Shakespeare and acting out scenes from his plays. My older sister had played the lead in *Much Ado About Nothing*, and I longed to talk to her about her role as Beatrice—if only I had taken the class. My classmates learned calligraphy while I attended a lab for the remedial class. I refused to get discouraged. I asked my friends to teach me calligraphy. I borrowed their pens and practiced right along with them.

Even though Shirley was in college only a few miles away, there was no way she could contact me. But her life still impacted mine. She was getting a degree in Drama, and I guess she thought she was an expert about being a nun because she had a sister in the convent. One evening, she and a friend went into the costume department and took what they needed to dress up like nuns. They proceeded to take a taxi to a local high school that was operated by my order and tried to get into the play for free, pleading that they had no money. Of course, they were caught and punished. The news made it to the Motherhouse, and I was sufficiently embarrassed.

During this third year in the convent, Shirley graduated from college. That day should have been a big event in our family. She was setting the standard for all of us. She had led the way. She had endured. My father had an eighth-grade education and my Mom, a high school education. No one else could have realized how much her graduation meant to our family, but it was out of the question to even think about attending her graduation.

Shortly after she graduated from college, she married her college sweetheart, Roger. He was a mechanical engineer who had taken a job in Los Angeles with Martin Marietta. Shirley planned to move to California after the wedding. The wedding was only a few miles from the Motherhouse, but I wasn't allowed to attend. Colleen was her maid of honor. They were permitted to visit me after the reception so I could meet my new brother-in-law and see my sister dressed in her wedding dress. I waited all day for them to come. It got dark. Finally, I got a call to come to the front parlor. There, I saw my sister, dressed in a beautiful wedding gown with a mink collar. Her long beautiful hair was pulled up into a French bun. Colleen and her cousin, Eileen, were maids of honor. My mother looked exhausted and overwhelmed; she surely missed having her husband there to give away her oldest daughter. I am not sure if she found any consolation in her daughter marrying a kind, loving Catholic man from a good family who would give her daughter the life she was programmed to want.

I was shaken for a few days after this event. It brought home to me so vividly how removed I was from my family. I hadn't even known that my sister had a serious boyfriend or any of the details of the wedding. Now she was married and moving to California with her new husband.

My family's life was moving forward, but I had no part in it. My brother had graduated from high school and entered the Air Force. That left only Colleen and David at home to carry the responsibility of taking care of Mom, and only two siblings receiving Aid to Families with Dependent Children meant less and less money for my Mom. How was she making it? I, however, had only momentary concerns about my family. I continued to feel happy that I no longer had to worry about my Mom's mental or physical health or never-ending financial problems. During this time my Mom got a teaching position in the public school. She would finally have a short amount of time to accrue a retirement pension.

There was another concern that started to bother me during this third year. If I was supposed to become the bride of Christ, why were there no signs that God was pleased with my dedication? Could I dedicate my whole life to something or someone so silent? Feeling that I needed some signs that God was pleased with me, I prayed and prayed for any sign. I got nothing. When I asked my classmates about this, they said that is where faith and trust enter the picture. I just needed to trust that God would be there for me and that I was his beloved child with whom He was well pleased. I was not yet really questioning whether I should do this. Even though I had some fleeting doubts, I was sure it was the right decision.

Life continued outside the convent. The Beatles were recording new songs. Neil Armstrong walked on the moon. Robert Kennedy and Martin Luther King had been assassinated. Momentous events were exploding around us, but we were oblivious to most of them. We were frozen in time, busy focusing on learning how to pray and dedicating our lives to God. I did not give a thought to life outside the walls of the Motherhouse. We were totally isolated, and that was fine with me. We did hear news of one event that would affect us greatly. The Vatican Council was meeting in Rome. Pope John XXIII was making sweeping changes for the Catholic Church—changes that would move the Catholic Church into modern times. As part of these "sweeping changes" we were given permission to go back to our secular names. So, instead of Sister Sara Marie, I could be called Sister Janice. We were given the choice of making either "vows" or "promises." I chose to return to Sister Janice, and I had no problem deciding to take vows because I was sure I wanted to commit my life to Christ. However, things at the Motherhouse became more unsettled as each of my classmates tried to decide what she wanted to do. We were confused. We had signed up for a specific life, but now all of that was drastically changing. The changes were for the better, but they created a lot of uncertainty.

I had now lived in an institution for three years, and I started to wonder what it would be like to go home for the first time in three years.

Who would I see? Would people look at me funny? How would my family react to me? I had seen them only twice in the past three years. Would my friends come to see me? What would I say to them? What would I say to my family? Would they be able to attend my vows ceremony?

My Mom continued to struggle with her health. During this third year she had another heart attack. I was not allowed to visit her this time. I wondered if she would be strong enough to attend my vows ceremony. After the ceremony, I would be permitted to go home for five days, until it was time to travel across the state on a train with my classmates to finish my last two years of school. Immediately after graduation, I would be assigned to my first mission. The next couple of years were well scripted, or so I thought.

As we were preparing for the ceremony, one of my closest friends disappeared from the convent. The skill of the nuns in sneaking our classmates out of the Motherhouse always amazed us. She, of course, was not allowed to say goodbye. I am sure she was sworn to secrecy about her plan to leave. The other possibility was that, once the decision to leave had been made, that person was immediately shipped off. She never told a single person that she was leaving. She was just gone. I was so sad because I wasn't sure if I would ever see her again. (She was the friend who was so much fun, who gave me the fudge, the brownies and the cigarettes.) I was sure she had decided that smoking, dating and having a good time with her friends was too much to give up. She was from a wealthy family who could drive up in their mobile home and take her away.

The day of my vows dawned sunny, hot and humid. It was August 10th, 1968. I had invited a number of extended family members. My father's brother, Uncle Cyril, would represent his side of the family. My aunt and uncle came from Chicago. My siblings were there. Mom did come, but she was weak and tired. My Uncle Walter, who had taken care of my smallest brother for a year while we were in the orphanage, was there. He was very talkative, and excited to be part of this "magnificent ceremony." I got the feeling that he was more excited about the ceremony than in me, his niece who had just taken her first vows. The day passed quickly. There were many visitors. Forty-two of us had entered three years ago; now thirty-four of us had taken our first vows. We all left with our families at the end of the day—to make our first home visit in three years. We also said goodbye to the Motherhouse. It was an emotional time for us. We had grown and changed, but lots more changes were to come. I was twenty-one.

My first visit home after three years was a shock. I can't describe it in any other way. I knew I had grown even more distant from my family, but this visit confirmed the gulf that had widened between us. I had seen my family twice in the past three years, but their lives had changed completely. I felt uncomfortable being outside the convent walls for the first time. It felt like I was standing on quicksand; everything had changed. My high school friends were gone. Paul had graduated and was in the Air Force; Colleen had graduated and was living with an aunt and uncle while attending beauty school; Shirley had married and was living in Los Angeles. David was my only sibling still at home, attending our Catholic high school. He was bright and asking too many questions in his religion classes. He had gotten into trouble with the priest during religion classes and incurred his wrath. David was not in a mood to deal with my blind faith in the Catholic religion.

That left my Mom and me to interact with each other. I had imagined that things might possibly be different between us because I had witnessed other families interacting, but she was as distant as ever. She was grieving the loss of her daughter to a system with which she deeply disagreed, but had followed so faithfully for so many years. My vows had sealed my commitment to my "new life." It seemed that absence had not made the heart grow fonder.

Some of my friends did come to visit. I felt shy and embarrassed about the way I looked, and I couldn't carry on a conversation about the normal things people talk about—current events, TV shows, movies, fashions. More than anything, I was overwhelmed by how small our house felt. I had been living in an institution, and now my house felt like a doll house. When the week was over, I was more than happy to board the train and head west to the opposite end of the state, to finish my junior and senior years at Briar Cliff College, a private Catholic college. My Mom drove me to the southern part of Iowa, about 100 miles away, to catch the train.

I was excited to get on the train. I was embarking on a new adventure! Soon we were to learn that we would have a lot more freedom. Here we would attend classes with students our age, even males, because the campus had become co-ed the year before.

Most of my classmates were already on the train. Others came on board as the train passed their towns. They talked about how their home visits went. I didn't say a word. We spoke to some of the passengers on the train about being Catholic. They said they weren't Catholic, but were Methodist or Lutheran. I thought to myself, "I wonder if they know they are going to hell?" I was beginning to question this whole idea—how could a loving God send so many people to hell, simply because they didn't belong to the Catholic Church?

The trip west was wonderful. I loved every moment of the click clack of the steel wheels hitting the rails. Every mile was taking me to a new adventure, and farther away from the life I had known in eastern Iowa. I had never even been to western Iowa. In fact, I had only ever travelled about 90 miles from my home in one direction. I never closed my eyes during the trip. I was twenty-one years old, beginning my fourth year in the convent and moving across the state. I loved this new adventure.

We arrived at our station at 10:30 pm in Sioux City, Iowa, and were picked up by two young Sisters who came in habits that looked more relaxed than anything we had seen at the Motherhouse. They wore veils but not the long, heavy kind. They were talking to us as if they didn't have to observe that rule of silence. After all, it was 10:30 at night! It was two and half hours after they were supposed to be silent. They assured us that life would be very different for us at the "Cliff." We were quickly shown to our rooms in a new dorm called Noonan Hall. We each carried one black suitcase; our trunks would arrive later.

I was very excited to see one of our convent classmates—one of those who had "disappeared" in the middle of the night. Her family lived nearby and we had already heard that she was attending our college. (She was my friend with the illicit cigarettes.) I was so excited to see her! She came right over and offered to take me to dinner, accompanied by her boyfriend, Russ. It made me feel even more self-conscious. How had she changed so dramatically in such a short time? When I saw her, I began to wonder what it would be like—to wear regular clothes, apply makeup, smell so good and have a boyfriend. We had little to say to each other, except that I told her how much I missed her. She announced that she was getting married soon and wanted to know if I would be in her wedding! She would sneak me out of the convent, buy me a bridesmaid's dress; she would pay for everything. I laughed. There was no way I could do that. I would be breaking all the rules! It was way too far out of my comfort zone to even imagine how I would look in anything but black.

Life here, indeed, was very different from life at the Motherhouse. The first thing we discovered, to our delight, was that we would each have our own room! Each room had a single bed, a small area for a sink and toilet, and a desk with a shelf above it for our books. It was actually possible to go to our room and *close the door*. We did share a large institutional bathroom. The large building, which was shared with the priest, was multipurpose. We were on the second and third floors, and the priest's quarters, on the first floor.

The large reception area near the front entrance of our building was used by the students. One afternoon when I was returning from the library, I was surprised to find a party in the reception area for young college women. The purpose of the party was to introduce them to a line of fine china, options for flatware and a luxurious line of pots and pans. I stopped to watch and listen. This was all foreign to me; never had I even dreamed of owning such beautiful items. I watched the women picking out patterns, ordering the necessities for their married life, a life I had never even imagined. I went to my room and sat there for the longest time, wondering about this life that was so foreign to me. My family had inherited old pots, pans and dishes from our Great Aunts Winnie and Gertie. We had a few good dishes and some silverware that we used on special occasions, but I had never imagined picking out my own silverware or dish patterns.

At the Cliff, we were bombarded with many new things we had never experienced at the Motherhouse. Each floor had a TV, where we could watch the news or other educational programs. The older nuns who taught at the college shared the two floors with us, so they decided what we watched. I spent very little time doing that, since I didn't like TV and did not feel comfortable socializing with the older sisters. I started to wonder how I would survive when I was sent on a mission with mostly older nuns.

Classes began shortly after we arrived. I jumped full speed into my studies. I wanted to make sure I stayed on top of my classes. I studied endlessly in my room, but as a result of a lifetime of lacking confidence, I continued to worry that I might fail a class. At first, classes seemed harder. There were so many students in our classes, and they all seemed smarter than me. I put so much pressure on myself to succeed. I was a nun; I HAD to do well.

Very soon, I was faced with the decision to declare a major. The truth was that I never thought I would ever graduate from college because I didn't think I was smart enough. Now I had to plan for the last two years, taking courses in my major. What should I major in? I didn't feel like I could "major" in anything. I had no confidence that I could be a teacher, but I had joined a teaching order, so that was our only option. Would they ask me to leave if I informed them I didn't want to teach? I knew I was required to teach but felt that social work would be something that suited me better. I felt strongly about the way my family had been treated during those years when social workers were regular visitors to our home. I had even stronger emotions about how we had been treated by our teachers when I was a child. I wanted to be the kind of teacher/social worker that my family had desperately needed during those crisis years. So I made the decision to major in Sociology with a minor in Education. The college did not yet offer a major in Education.

I found my sociology classes to be the most interesting of all my courses. It was 1969. In class we discussed the future of the "leisure class" and how the many new labor-saving devices would ensure the freedom to relax and have fun. The big dilemma we discussed in class: what would we do with all our free time? We would have electric mixers, electric dishwashers, automatic washers and dryers, etc. We all tried to fantasize about what we would do with all of our leisure time because we had so many devices to save us copious amounts of time.

The best part about majoring in sociology—we were required to do field placements. My first placement was at the Indian Center in downtown Sioux City. We visited Indian family homes to help families with whatever they needed. I vividly remember washing an aging woman's hair. We did painting, housecleaning, errands and other chores. The field placements provided an opportunity to get to know some of my fellow classmates. During our work together, they asked me questions that were disturbing to me, such as, "Why did you go to the convent? Are you happy there? Are you sure you really want to do this for the rest of your life? Have you ever thought about leaving?" They countered with, "You don't seem like the 'nun type.' It doesn't seem like you are very happy. You laugh so funny; you do seem like you are having a good time."

I didn't have good answers to these questions. No, I never thought about leaving, but I could not explain why. They could never understand the way of life I had learned to accept. They didn't know what I had been taught—that once you have made a decision, you act on it without questioning it. "You made your bed; now lay in it" was a saying my Mom repeated regularly. My life was focused solely on living the decision I had made. However, these students helped me to start thinking about the decision I had made when I was seventeen.

At this very same time, something happened that was pivotal to determining the route my future would take. I was in charge of preparing the chapel for Mass every morning. This entailed getting up early every morning to lay out the chaplain's vestments, light the candles, pour the wine and open the Bible to the day's readings. One morning on the way to the sacristy, the chaplain asked if I had ever thought about leaving. I answered emphatically, "NEVER." He replied, "You are more at risk for leaving than almost anyone." I was, of course, quite shaken by this statement. I asked him why. He said that an unexamined life is a sure sign that you will wake up at some point and decide that you want to be somewhere else. He said it was important to ask that question often. He gave me permission to ask myself the question, "Do I want to leave?" I quickly answered, "Of course not. I have chosen this life for many very good reasons." In any case, there was no way to turn back, and I should not entertain such a thought. This was hard to reconcile because it WAS a priest who asked me to ponder this baffling question. I was confused so I decided to ignore his advice.

This first year at the Cliff went very quickly. When the school year was over, our class stayed at the college over the summer, taking courses and preparing to renew our vows. It was a fun time, but also a tumultuous one, because a group of young nuns who had been out on a mission, but hadn't finished college, returned to study for the summer. These young missionaries introduced us to new ways of looking at the Catholic Church. Some had embraced "speaking in tongues" and the Pentecostal Movement, and they encouraged us to speak in tongues. It seemed we were getting into some dangerous stuff, but it was exciting and interesting. The older nuns were very suspicious when they caught wind of us doing the "Pentecostal thing." They accused us of being Communists, and they became more and more hostile and suspicious toward us. More and more of my classmates were talking about leaving.

More unsettling changes came about that summer. We were informed that we were no longer required to wear habits; we could wear simple blouses and black skirts. Again we were given the choice to renew vows or to take promises. I put all these doubts behind me and decided to take vows again. At the ceremony in the college chapel, all of us who were taking vows stood up to recite our vows.

I had just one visitor from my family during this year, my younger sister, Colleen. She had completed beauty school and was on her way to

California to live with my older sister, Shirley, and her husband, Roger. Colleen was dating a cute guy from a well-to-do family that owned a trucking company. He had driven her across the state in one of his family owned semi-trailer trucks. She visited briefly. I arranged for her to get to the train station to travel to L.A. I questioned her about why she had decided to say goodbye to this cute guy with a lot of money. She explained that she had higher aspirations in life, that because she was able to make it through beauty school, she believed she could also graduate from college. The truth was that being a beautician didn't suit her; she didn't like the gossip in beauty shops, so she took a job in a wig shop and in funeral homes. No gossip there!

The fall season came quickly. Western Iowa was as beautiful as eastern Iowa. The trees were dressed in the most beautiful colors of reds, oranges and yellows. Students returned to the campus. I was now twenty-three; it was my senior year in college. Getting back to classes made me nervous and excited: I was on the verge of having a dream come true. I didn't allow myself to get too excited yet because it still seemed to me an impossible dream. I couldn't believe I was going to graduate from college. Did anyone else know what a miracle this was?

During my senior year, in 1970, many students on college campuses were protesting the Vietnam War. Our campus was no exception. I participated in the protest marches, where emotions ran high. I was scared, but also excited that I was speaking up against a war the United States should never have gotten into and desperately needed to get out of asap. Even though my brother, Paul, had been drafted, he was safe in Thailand, working as a jet mechanic. However, he was working on the planes that were dropping bombs all over Vietnam. He too believed that we should not be there.

That last year at Briar Cliff brought so many changes to my life. A young woman, named Barb, from my home town entered the convent and came to the Cliff my senior year. I had known her since we were children. We took a couple of long talks, and one day, she said something that completely shook me: "If I was as unhappy as you seem to be, I would do something about it." No one had ever said anything like that to me. She suggested that I talk to the school counselor. I had no idea how that decision would so radically change my life. I walked by the counseling office a few times before I gathered the courage to go in and make the appointment. I learned that there was only one counselor, and he was a MAN! What could he possibly know about what I was going through?

I made the appointment and immediately began to feel better. I didn't know what would transpire, but at least I had hope that someone might help me sort out why I felt so unhappy and unsettled. The unhappiness had snuck up on me during my two years at the college. I didn't know why I was so unhappy; I wasn't even able to give it a name until Barb said it.

This counselor turned out to be the best. I am sure he could tell how nervous it made me to talk to him. He instructed me to sit down and suggested that I take some time and relax for a few minutes. He then encouraged me to talk about my life. I told him about my growing-up years and how I had decided to go to the convent. He came to the conclusion that I was trying to decide whether I should leave the convent. I violently disagreed with him. He asked me, "Do you want to leave?" I said, "No!" He instructed me to think about that question and return in a week. I went back to my room and I thought about it. When I went back the next week, he asked me the same question, "Do you want to leave the convent?" I told him that I didn't believe I wanted to leave. He told me to think about this question and come back in another week. I did this again. This time I admitted to myself that I would like to leave BUT there was no way I could leave. The next week, I told him just that. Again, he told me to think about it for a week. That next week, when I returned to his office, I admitted that I wanted to leave. He replied, "YOU CAN LEAVE."

That was all it took. He had given me permission. Right then and there, I decided I would leave the convent. Immediately I felt a huge weight had been lifted off my shoulders. I went back to my room, and I lay on my bed for hours. In fact, every minute I had free, I lay on my bed and thought about leaving. Life seemed to be pouring back into my body. My heart was so happy. I tried to imagine what it would be like. I decided not to tell anyone. I needed to live with this decision for a while. It was so radical for me! It went against everything I had been programmed to believe about how I would live my life. What would I do? Where would I go? How would I pull this off? I had no money, no clothes, no possessions, and no job. The first thing to do was tell my Superior. Amazingly, she seemed resigned. She didn't even act surprised. So many of my classmates were leaving or had left. She did ask me if I was sure of my decision. I said, "YES."

I asked her for the money to purchase a ticket to take the train across Iowa to give this news to my Mom. I was sure she would not be happy about my decision because she had never been happy about anything that I had done. In this case, however, I really underestimated my mother's reaction!

I never went back to see the counselor after I reached this decision in late November and made my train reservation in early December. I would depart on the Friday before Christmas, spending a week at my Mom's house over Christmas break. This would be only the second time I had been home in five years. My married sister, Shirley, was visiting. I really needed her to be there because I thought she would support my decision more than anyone else; she had been the most vocal in opposing my decision to go into the convent. I was now counting on her to help me get out of the convent.

That train trip was actually quite eventful. It was 1969 and this winter was one of the coldest, snowiest on record in Iowa. After I boarded the train in Sioux City, it wasn't long before word started circulating that the train might not make it to its destination because of the snow and severe cold. The windows of the train were completely frozen. It was cold inside the train. I wondered if someone from my family would even be able to come for me. Although several hours late, we finally arrived, and my mom and sister met me at the train.

I have no memory of that Christmas, what gifts I got or even if I gave anyone a gift. I do remember telling Shirley that I needed to talk to her—alone. There was still no privacy in our home. In this cold house we all lived in the only two warm rooms: the kitchen and the living room. She suggested that we take a walk. What a crazy idea that was! Mom was immediately suspicious. With the snow piled high everywhere, the road was the only path where we could walk. As soon as we got away from the house, I told Shirley that I planned to leave the convent. I just blurted it out. I had been waiting for days to tell someone, anyone.

We walked and talked until we couldn't stand the cold another minute. Shirley, once again, came through for me; she helped me make a plan. I loved my sister for her support. She didn't ask me if I was sure; she didn't question me about how I was going to make it. She just took charge. I told her that I wanted to stay until I graduated. She immediately decided to attend my graduation; afterwards she would load up my few possessions and bring me back to Denver with her and her husband. She said I could stay with them as long as I wanted. The plan was set.

The happiness I felt was overwhelming, but it was very short lived. We broke the news to Mom as soon as we returned to the house. She was furious, even more upset than when I announced I was going to the convent. She kept repeating, "Good Lord, God bless you." She bombarded me with questions. How could I possibly make it in this world that I had not known for five years? Where was I going to live? How would I support myself? She tried to talk me out of my decision. She possibly feared that I might want to return home. But I never once considered that. I wanted to see the world!

I had been resilient to go to the convent and stay there for five years, but when I decided to leave, I felt even more resilient. I refused to adopt my mother's fears. I had plans to make and places to go. On the train I dreamed about what my future life would be. I knew that when I returned to school, I needed to apply myself to finishing my last semester of college. I had a new lease on life. I decided on that train trip that I would never again let myself be depressed. I couldn't imagine getting married or having children, but I did think about the freedom ahead for me. I could go where I wanted. I could eat what I wanted. I could wear what I wanted. I could shop for clothes. I could live where I wanted. I could deal with God on my own terms.

I didn't know how to process my relationship with God. I had tried hard during those five years to get close to God. I wanted Him to show up in my life. I was making this extreme sacrifice, but God seemed totally silent. Where was He? Why did I feel so abandoned by Him? The Catholic Church seemed archaic to me. I wondered why the older nuns stayed in the convent. Perhaps they were too afraid to leave. I wondered why anyone would choose this life. I went to the chapel to pray, but I had nothing to say. I felt totally abandoned by God. I remember thinking to myself: I have prayed enough these five years to last me the rest of my life. I am taking time off from God. In maybe fifteen or twenty years, I will get back to dealing with God. For me it was the deepest crisis in faith. I could hardly wait to not have to go to Mass or any service. I would leave the Catholic Church for good. I had seen it from the inside and I didn't like it. These were some of my thoughts on that long train ride back to school.

That last semester of college was the most exciting one of all. I had a new lease on life. I was going to graduate. My dream of graduating was coming true. The most amazing fact of all—I was leaving the convent. I whispered to myself in my free time, "I am leaving! I am leaving!" When not studying, I spent time in my room thinking about what my new life would be like. I told only a few people that I was leaving. One of my classmates, Beverly, was an only child from a wealthy Chicago family. When her parents came to visit, Beverly told them about my decision to leave, and my complete lack of resources. Her Mom offered me all the clothes she no longer wanted—a number of beautiful outfits from Marshall Field in Chicago, and twenty dollars in cash. I stared at the clothes. I couldn't imagine wearing a single one of these sophisticated, adult clothes from the North Shore boutiques, not when my classmates were all wearing bell-bottoms and halter tops. How could a twenty-three year old possibly look good in clothes made for forty-year-old women? After I tried them on, I packed them in my suitcase. At least I would have some color in my black suitcase when I left.

During this last semester of school, I student taught in a fourth-grade classroom at a Catholic elementary school near the campus. This was a totally frightening experience. I was so ill prepared for student teaching that I spent most of my time just watching my supervising teacher. Each time she told me it was my turn to teach a class, I begged off. I survived the whole semester in this way. I believe I taught only one class during the semester, the day my college professor came to observe. The students were so good; all I had to do was figure out what to teach during that one period. The supervising teacher helped me by telling me exactly what to say. I practiced it over and over again. The whole experience was unsettling. Teaching didn't feel right to me. I had made my decision to become a teacher in fourth grade, when I longed to become the kind of teacher I so badly needed myself. Not one teacher in my years of schooling had encouraged me, seen through my shyness, assured me that I would make it, insisted that I was smart enough or said that I would be successful in life. I wanted so desperately to hear that. Now, I wanted to do that for my students. My student teaching didn't give me a chance to give this message. I thought it might be different when I had my own class, but I didn't know if I could teach a class all day every day! I put this concern on the "back burner" because I had to graduate, leave the convent, find a place to live—and land a job.

The truth was that teaching was the only thing I was prepared to do, and yet, I wasn't really prepared. I decided to start applying for teaching jobs, but where? In Iowa? At a Catholic school? About that same time, I learned that one of my closest friends, Ann, who was already out on mission, planned to leave. I asked her to share an apartment with me in Cedar Rapids. This was a great idea because we had both led such a sheltered life, and we could now help each other find out about the world—together. The best thing of all: she was funny and made me laugh. We could laugh together as we adjusted to our new lives outside the convent. She said, "Yes!"

I applied to several nearby Catholic elementary schools, insisting to them that I was planning to leave the convent, but wanted to teach in a Catholic school. (I wasn't able at this point to admit that I had become totally disconnected from God.) I got a call from the principal of a Catholic school with about 300 students, in need of a fourth-grade teacher. That was the grade I had "student taught." The principal interviewed me over the phone. She said she was interested in me because, even though I was leaving the convent, Sisters make the best teachers! The pay—$4,300 per year—sounded like a lot of money to me. She suggested I visit the school when I got home. (She didn't say: "when you leave the convent.") She called me "Sister Janice." I wanted to remind her that she would be calling me "Miss McDermott," but I would deal with that later.

The day before graduation, I met with the Mother Superior. She gave me forty dollars and reminded me that my vows were still in force until August; even though I wasn't in the convent, I must live in poverty, chastity and obedience. In August I could sign the document terminating my affiliation with the Franciscan Order. I was also informed that I must pay back my tuition expenses because I had failed to go on a mission. This news upset me greatly as I had just given five precious years of my youth to the Order. I did, however, feel indebted to them for my college education and vowed to make regular contributions to the Motherhouse or the college. I informed them of my intention to make regular contributions to the Order.

Graduation day arrived. I was thrilled. I had accomplished a huge personal goal. My whole family attended the ceremony. They were there as my name was announced with those students receiving a BA in Sociology and Education: Sister Janice McDermott. That would be the last time I heard that name. The day before the ceremony, my family enjoyed a picnic in a nearby park. Shirley and I had already finalized the plan for my "escape." In my trunk I had stored my habit, shoes, rosaries and prayer books, and the small hand-made booklets with poems and quotes from friends that I had saved over the past five years. I would not need anything in that trunk; I would pick it up when my vows expired in August. How would I make it in the outside world? I was about to begin that journey, and discover the answer to that question.

Resiliency is the ability to adapt and bounce back when things don't go as planned. I had not planned to leave the convent, but there I was walking out the door. I could not wallow or dwell on this 180-degree turn in my life. I had to acknowledge the situation and just move forward, embrace this change and remain optimistic. I needed to stay tough and keep growing. I had developed problem-solving skills from all the situations we experienced as children. I, somehow, knew I needed to keep picking myself up as many times as it would take to get the life I had imagined.

CHAPTER SEVEN

TOTALLY UNPREPARED

After my graduation ceremony, I said goodbye to my siblings and my Mom. They were traveling back to Iowa. My sister waited for me in the car while I went to my bedroom one last time, to pick up my black suitcase. I took off my habit and changed into one of the outfits that my friend's Mom had given me. As I put it on, I felt both apprehensive and excited. What surprised me was how scared I felt. At this point, I did not worry about whether the clothes I was wearing were in style or even matched; I was focused solely on the amazing fact that I was being set free—and about to embark on a whole new life. I didn't take time to say goodbye to anyone. While my classmates were celebrating their own graduations with their families, I slipped quietly down the back stairway for the last time. This was it: goodbye to my five years of convent life. I had not revealed to any of my lay classmates that I was leaving, but I did regret that none of them would know how they had helped me to discover that this commitment no longer felt right, and how grateful I was to them for that. I figured that no one would suspect I was leaving because the President of the College had just presented me with my diploma, in front of everyone, saying, "Congratulations, Sister Janice McDermott."

So now it was time to execute the plan Shirley and I had concocted last December when I confessed I wanted to leave the convent. She lived in Denver, where she had moved two years earlier when her husband took a job with Martin Marietta. She lived in a red brick house a few blocks from Washington Park. She offered to bring me to Denver so I could decide what I would do next.

When she pulled her car up to the loading dock, I slipped out the back door with my suitcase. Our drive to Colorado was long. I started out driving the car, even though I had gained only a little experience in driving while in high school, and none the past five years. (I did have enough foresight to apply for an Iowa license once I realized that I was going to leave the convent.) Physically and mentally exhausted, it wasn't long before I told Shirley I couldn't drive any further.

Shirley drove through the night, and we arrived safely in Denver sometime after midnight. At one point we stopped for dinner. This was the first time I realized that I now needed money. I offered to pay for my dinner, but my sister said she would get it. (She was married to an electrical engineer, so money was not a concern for her at that point in her life.) She seemed pleased to have been instrumental in extricating me from a situation where I was "constantly being brainwashed." Shirley lamented that one of the biggest mistakes she had made was failing to stop me from entering the convent. Now she was helping me out of a situation she deemed intolerable. She said I could stay with her and her husband for as long as I needed. This offer was a god-send; to this day I am grateful to her for that help.

I had never been to Denver. This was as far away from Iowa as I had ever been. The first thing I wanted to do on my first morning in Denver was to see the mountains. I walked down the street, feeling free, but scared. I walked only a half block before I came back to the house. My sister asked me if I had seen the mountains. I shrugged, "I think so." She came over to me and asked, "Why aren't you sure?" I didn't want to tell her that I was too scared to go a full block to the end of the street so I could see them for sure. She must have known because she urged me to walk over to Washington Park after breakfast so that I could see them "for sure." We went to the park later that day, and there I got my first glimpse of the mountains. They still had snow on them. They were breathtakingly beautiful: "What a beautiful place to have landed after all my years living in Iowa." The air was cool and fresh, and the sun was shining so bright. This place was a little bit of heaven.

It was the summer of 1970, and there were many young people in Washington Park. Most were there as a couple; very few young women were there by themselves. The guys who were alone seemed to be "stoned." I was fascinated by all the young women in tie-dye halter tops and short skirts or cut-off jeans, their long, straight hair parted in the middle. Many had a ribbon tied around their head; others wore red handkerchief scarfs rolled up right above their eyes. Some wore the same red handkerchiefs as halter tops. Most of the men were shirtless, wearing only dirty cut-off jeans. Few wore shoes. In fact, everyone looked kind of dirty. I had heard my brother-in-law talk about the "hippies" in the park. Even their dogs looked shaggy and not cared for. This world was completely foreign to me!

This whole scene freaked me out: how was I going to fit into this life? I was shocked by the contrast of my hand-me-down polyester pant suit from a boutique shop on the North Shore of Lake Michigan vs. the hippie scene I had observed in Washington Park. This was when I suffered my first doubts about whether I could fit into a world so totally different from the world I had left only five years before. I decided I did not want to go back to the park again. I would deal with these painful thoughts by ignoring them. Maybe that was the only way I could be resilient at this point in my life.

Looking back, there were ways that I could have identified with those young people in the park. They were close to my age; I had protested the Vietnam War on my college campus; I felt passionate about the United States getting out of a war that we could not win. I was already growing my hair longer, and parted in the middle, but it was still embarrassingly short for the times.

I may not have looked like these young people, but I did share their idealism. I wanted to live my life very differently from my parents' generation. Like many other young people, I felt a certain amount of superiority, based on my certainty that we were NOT going to make the same mistakes as our parents. Like them, I too shared a sense of optimism and a willingness to think differently, but that day I did not think of such things. I only felt terribly strange and different.

I think my brother-in-law sensed how out of place I felt. That afternoon he drove us to Colorado Springs to see the chapel at the Air Force Academy. It was a fun day, and I kept thinking how thoughtful it was of him to choose a chapel—something I could relate to, in the midst of all the changes I was experiencing. Another weekend he drove us to Central City, an old mining town that took us on a trip back in history. The shops on the main street brought back memories of my Iowa childhood, with their wood-burning stoves and the antique furniture that were still part of my Iowa home. Rocky Mountain National Park was another weekend destination. These trips were wonderful; I felt safe, tucked in the car with my brother-in-law and sister, taking in the beauty of the Rocky Mountains. As I enjoyed these quiet drives, I wondered, "What is going to happen to me? How can I make money in this big city? Where should I go to look for a job?"

My sister was working at a Denver radio station at the time. Her manager knew she had gone to retrieve her younger sister from a convent and asked if he could interview me on the radio. Just three days after I left the convent, I found myself nervously answering his questions about my life in the convent. I answered each question carefully, wanting to tell the truth about my convent experience, without condemning the Catholic Church. After all, I had voluntarily entered the convent and was able to leave when it no longer felt like it was my life path.

The interviews were taped in the KBTR Studios in Denver by a man named Larry. It ran on the radio in five segments. During each segment Larry asked me a question. He asked me questions such as: "After being in the convent for five years, can you adjust to life outside the convent?" I said I was about to find out if I could make that adjustment, but I thought I could. Others had done it before me. He wondered what kind of training I received? I told him I had been able to graduate from college, and that I attended an extra year, called a canonical year, to do an in-depth study of the Bible. He wanted to know how I decided to leave the convent. I told him it took a lot of courage to even think about leaving; I did not bring up my brief therapy sessions. He wondered if I had been affected by the nun's changing role in society. I told him that I believed that was why so many of my classmates were leaving and why I felt so unsettled in the convent. When Larry asked why I left, I said, "I left because I was not happy in the convent any longer. You can't be of service and make a contribution to society if you are unhappy. I wanted to do more but felt restricted by the role that society expected of me as a nun. If you can't find happiness and be yourself, then you cannot stay, so I had no choice but to leave." There was so much more I could have said. When Larry asked if I would marry, I said, "It is probably the last thought on my mind at the moment. There is so much to adjust to, living outside the convent." I didn't tell him how monumental an adjustment I was facing; I hadn't heard any music, gone shopping, attended a movie, driven a car, earned money, been gainfully employed or visited friends and family for five years.

I was overwhelmed with the bounty of choices that lay before me. My only way to cope was to take one day at a time. During these first days at my sister's home, I became obsessed with finding a job for the summer. In order to stay in Denver, I needed work. My biggest problem was that I didn't know how to get around; I needed a car or to learn how to ride the bus. Both of these options felt overwhelming. Everyday I searched the "Help Wanted" ads in the newspaper and finally found an ad for a telephone marketing job located in a woman's home. I had little self-confidence, but I thought I might be able to do that job. I applied and was hired the same day I went for the interview. The job was so boring. I read from a script all day long; most people were angry and hung up right away. My sister drove me to and from work for a couple of days, then told me I needed to start riding the bus. The thought of riding the bus was so scary that I quit after the third day. More importantly, the owner of the business had said something that bothered me, "Where have you been? There is something strange about you."

The fact that the job was so boring, and I couldn't figure out a way to get there, plus the lady's questions, made me too nervous. I came home and told my sister that I just couldn't do that job and thought I should go back to Iowa. I never planned to go back to my home town. My friends had moved away; they had their own lives. My mother had no faith that I could survive in the outside world, so I knew I couldn't go there. ("Dear child, what ever is going to become of you? You will never be able to adjust to life outside the convent.")

With no options and my sister not really encouraging me to stay, I decided to move back to Iowa, but not to my mother's house. I went to Dubuque, Iowa, where the Motherhouse was located, and twenty-five miles from where my Mom lived. I rationalized that I needed to be close in order to sign the convent release papers when the time came. My high school friend, Marian, lived there too. She had gone to the convent with me and had left the year before. I asked if I could stay with her. She had a small apartment, which she shared with her boyfriend, but offered me the couch. So I, and my black suitcase, moved in to her tiny apartment.

Marian was preoccupied with her new life and boyfriend, so she had little time to help me with the problems I was having. Perhaps it was too painful for her to focus on me, having gone through her own adjustment to secular life the year before.

That summer, eastern Iowa set a record for one of the hottest and most humid summers ever. Every night we sweated while we hung around outside on the front stoop, waiting for our apartment to cool off enough to go to bed. That couch was hot and smelly. Had I made a bad decision moving into her apartment? This definitely was not how I had imagined my life. Reality has a way of making one come to grips with life; again, I needed to find work as soon as possible.

I looked for a job every day, but I had no car and little experience working, other than cooking and waitressing at Ray's Drive In during high school. Plus, I would be moving to Cedar Rapids at the end of the

summer to start my first teaching job. I finally landed a waitress job at
Mr. Steak. I met the manager in a bar and convinced him that he needed
to hire me because I needed a job badly. I started work the next day, but
he turned out to be a bad boss! He terrorized us, yelling at us for anything that came into his mind: "Have I yelled at you lately?" or "Don't
stand by the booths talking to the customers. Take their order and GO."
(That was good advice.) Once he yelled at us, "If you have no customers you MUST stay busy. Wash those windows or sweep the floor. Do
something. Don't just stand there." He told us that if he caught us eating
any food he would fire us on the spot. I was hungry, but I dared not eat
anything! I could not afford to lose this job. A couple of times, I grabbed
food from a customer's plate when I was cleaning the booth. I put it in
my pocket and then went to the bathroom stall to eat it. He treated us
so poorly and paid us only minimum wage; we thought we could take
anything that fit in our bags. I took some silverware that we could use
when we set up our apartment. Later I realized this behavior was not in
line with the life I wanted to live.

Despite the heat and the crummy summer job, I had fun that
summer. I hung around with a couple of friends who recently left the
convent. They understood what I was going through, and we shared
the sense that we had to both party and play hard to make up for the
years we had been locked away. One place we visited regularly was East
Dubuque, Illinois. With a lower drinking age and lots of bars, it was
renowned as a place of sin and ill repute when I was young. No good
Catholic girl should be seen in East Dubuque! Well, we went there regularly—just because we could.

One night I was with my friend, Ann, at a bar in East Dubuque. We
had been drinking beer and talking to two friendly guys. One of them
mentioned that his parents owned a boat that was docked near the bar.

Did we want to take the boat out on the Mississippi River? I thought that sounded really fun. Ann was a bit cautious, but I pointed out that we had never had that experience before, and it would be fun to be out on the river in the middle of the night. So we left with them, went down to the river and climbed into the boat.

Neither Ann nor I had any idea what this boat trip would entail. I had grown up only twenty-five miles from the Mississippi, but never had been on a boat on the river and certainly not in the middle of the night. We could see very little in the darkness. The best part about that 1am boat ride: no one else was crazy enough to be driving a boat around the Mississippi in the middle of the night!

I started worrying because the guys were still drinking, and I was desperate to go to the bathroom almost from the moment we left the shore. Only weeks since I left the convent and one of the first times I actually was hanging out with guys, and all I could think about was peeing my pants. That boat trip seemed like it would never end. I pretended to be scared, but the truth was that I had to go to the bathroom much more than I was scared. When we finally docked the boat, I ran into the bushes to pee. We thanked them for the experience and went on our way.

That summer was filled with lots of new experiences. Because I was sleeping on my friend's couch, I often stayed with my friend, Ann, whom I planned to live with in the fall. She lived with her parents in Dubuque. Like me, Ann was waiting for her vows to expire. How lucky we were that her parents welcomed us and fed us. Her mom was a very loving, devout Catholic. From her I learned the real power of holy water and candles! One night when a couple of us were staying at her parents' house, sleeping on the living room floor, a nasty wind and lightning storm came up. Ann's mom rushed out of her bedroom and sprinkled holy water on us, then lit some candles, praying for the storm to pass quickly.

Another night at Ann's parents' house, I woke up in the middle of the night, gasping for breath, something that had never happened to me before. My first thought was that, just as I finally had the courage to leave the convent, I was going to die! Ann's Mom heard me coughing and wheezing and came to investigate. I was sitting up in bed and couldn't breathe. She thought it might be an allergy attack; I told her I never had any allergies. She suspected it was due to the dogs that she was taking care of for the weekend. I had never had a pet as a child, and there were no dogs or cats in the convent. This was the first time that I had stayed in a home where an animal lived. Ann's Mom gave me an allergy tablet and I went right to sleep.

By mid-August I was ready to leave this city and start my teaching career. I was excited about the next stage of my life, but first I had to go to the Motherhouse one last time to sign my exit papers. It felt so final and that felt so good. Signing the papers and getting my trunk, and saying goodbye to this part of my life turned out to be uneventful, taking less than fifteen minutes. I loaded my trunk, containing all my memorabilia from the past five years, into my friend's car and I was on my way. I loved that trunk and was glad to have it with me; it still lives in my office today.

Ann and I searched for an apartment in Marion, a suburb of Cedar Rapids, and found a small efficiency apartment for ninety dollars a month. It was perfect; it had a main room with a tiny kitchen and a sitting area, one bedroom off the hallway with a small shower in the closet, and a tiny closet in the hallway. (This was not a problem for us because neither of us had many clothes to hang in it.) The best part was that it was furnished—a bed and a couch in the sitting area and a tiny table for two where we could eat. The owners of the apartment lived in the main part of the house, so we walked only a few steps across our front porch to deliver the $90.00 rent check each month.

We moved in a few days before I started my teaching job. There was little to move because we owned almost nothing. My mother did not have any extra money, but she did buy us a dish pan and drainer for our apartment. She gave it to me when we stopped to see her. I had not spent much time with her that summer. She still didn't believe I could adjust to life outside the convent. I had my own doubts and didn't need her reinforcing them.

I was thrilled at the prospect of teaching, or at least having an income. Ann found a job at a radio factory, not far from where I taught. She took this job, not only because it was the first job she found, but because she could smoke at her desk. (She had started smoking right after she left the convent.)

Neither of us had money, but we knew we needed a car. Ann and her brother found a shoddy, bluish-green 1963 Plymouth with a push button transmission. It worked well initially, but quickly started to act up. It was unpredictable, often stalling at random intersections. Men would often stop and ask if we needed help. We always said we were fine and knew what to do. Actually, Ann knew what to do. She got under the hood and I sat in the drivers seat. We always managed to get it started again. Luckily, I carpooled to school, so I didn't have to deal with our car every day.

Despite our less than reliable vehicle and tiny, sparsely furnished apartment, Ann and I were happy. I was adjusting and happy to be teaching fourth grade. Fortunately, the fourth grade was departmentalized, so I didn't have to teach everything; students moved to another room for science and math. I taught Reading, Writing, Art and Religion. I worked hard to prepare lessons for my students. The other fourth-grade teacher was a tremendous help. I had heard it said, "You are only as good as the teacher next door." That was true for me. The other fourth-grade teacher next door was experienced and helped me deal with discipline issues, organize my lessons and figure out homework assignments. My students came from upper middle-class homes, with so many advantages and material possessions; I found it difficult to relate to them. Having grown up in poverty, I felt jealous of their lives and their possessions.

In addition to the day-to-day challenges of being a first-year teacher, I also dealt with the issues that arose from teaching Religion at a Catholic school. I was angry at God; I left the convent feeling abandoned by the God to whom I had dedicated the past five years of my life. How could I teach my students about a loving, forgiving God when I was so conflicted myself? The liturgy no longer had meaning for me. I had stopped praying. I was confused, and this was obvious to me with every Religion class that I taught. Luckily, fourth graders don't ask deep philosophical questions, so I used the rote answers that I learned as a child in my own Catechism classes.

Another issue became apparent to me almost immediately. The nuns at the school seemed to feel that they were "responsible" for me, as if the Mother Superior was still watching over me. Even though these nuns were a different order from my order, they seemed overly concerned about my welfare.

This was 1971 and female teachers were required to wear dresses. At one point, the principal called me to her office to correct me for wearing my skirts too short. She was concerned, not only for the students, but also for the male teachers on the staff. She mentioned that one of the male teachers seemed to be very interested in me. (I did not tell her that I had already had a couple of dates with this teacher.) His attention was unsettling to me because the last thing I wanted was a boyfriend. I had to first figure out how to adjust to my new life.

However, I figured that going on a few dates would be helpful for adjusting to the "real world." On one of our first dates, he took me to a Grateful Dead concert at the University of Iowa. I had never been to the university or to a rock concert. In high school, I always dressed up for a date. So the night of the concert I set my hair in rollers, and put on a dress and heels. When we arrived at the concert, I was surprised to see everyone else dressed very casually—in jeans, flannel shirts and Birkenstocks. We had to climb to the top of the bleachers in the auditorium to find our seats. I was mortified by how different I looked, and how difficult it was to climb bleachers in high heels and a dress. Plus I had never heard of the Grateful Dead. Their music was so loud, and everyone was shouting, screaming and singing along to the words they all knew by heart. I was so relieved to finally have the concert over and to be back in his car heading home.

I wasn't prepared for what happened next. My date became extremely "passionate" after he parked his new Charger in front of our apartment. He professed how much he loved me and wanted to be with me. I was confused. I was simply being myself, and I didn't think there was anything really lovable about me at that point in my life. I had so much to learn and explore. Learning about men was not a high priority for me.

This surprising confession of his love had serious implications for being myself at school. I became more quiet and shy. I stopped going to the staff lounge or even walking in the hallways. I stayed in my classroom and concentrated on learning to become a better teacher. I worked hard every day and most evenings to reach this goal.

I was feeling stressed about teaching, and about my admirer, as I prepared for the fall parent-teacher conferences. My students had created a mural to be hung in the classroom for the conferences. My classroom had a back door that opened to a courtyard. Although no one ever went into the courtyard, it was a way to let in fresh air and cool off the classroom. The day before conferences, I had the back door open; a strong wind blew the mural down and ripped it in a few places. I held myself together until the end of the day, and then I started crying. I could not stop. I cried all the way home. My roommate found me later, still sobbing uncontrollably. All the stress from leaving the convent and trying to become a good teacher had caught up with me. This type of emotional breakdown was something I had never allowed myself to do before. It scared me because I felt out of control, but I did eventually stop crying. My roommate persuaded me to go to a movie. I can't recall the name of the movie, but it did the trick. I allowed myself to focus on something other than the stresses of teaching and learning how to date again.

There was always one bright spot to every week, even though this first year out of the convent was challenging. Ann and I went out every Wednesday evening, no matter what. There was never an excuse for not going to the bars on Wednesday night. We called it "hump day" but we often said we should have called it "sanity night" because going out drinking and dancing allowed us to make it through the rest of the week.

I needed to blow off steam because I was so nervous about my teaching during this first year. Ann, on the other hand, was dealing with the boredom of her factory job. Then, after just a couple of months at her job, she got a pink slip. She worried about how she would come up with her half of the rent. We both pushed our worries aside on Wednesday nights.

We usually went to a place called The Star Lite on First Avenue. There we drank beer and danced. If "Proud Mary" was playing, we were out on the dance floor. It was "our song" and we never missed dancing to it. Both of us loved to dance, so this was the best part of going out. Drinking, however, was not easy for me. I was thin and could not drink much liquor before I felt woozy. Ann seemed to hold her liquor better. We both acted silly and took risks driving home after drinking. It was as if we were making up for the "lost years" we had spent in the convent by acting like teenagers now.

That first Christmas out of the convent was exciting. I had no money to buy gifts. It was not part of our life in the convent, so I was used to not giving gifts. Our family decided to drive to Denver to visit Shirley and her husband. It gave me a chance to escape the pressure of my first year of teaching and the guy who "loved" me.

Why did I keep dating this teacher? Honestly, I had never learned to say "no," so it never entered my mind that I had a choice. I thought I could learn about guys and dating by going out with him. He made a big deal about the Christmas gift he was giving me and often had me guessing what it might be. I was hoping he would NOT be crazy enough to give me a ring or something too expensive. I was blown away when I finally opened his gift. It was hot electric rollers! He also gave my roommate a gift—a very nice bottle of perfume. She can still tell me the name of the lovely perfume she received from my boyfriend. With all the things I needed in my life, hot electric rollers would have been near the bottom of a long list! Some beautiful perfume might have been first on my list. Shirley's high school boyfriend gave her Chanel No. 5; that is what I wanted.

Our trip to Denver was wonderful; it felt like I had a family again. We stayed at my sister's house, ate delicious food, and explored Denver and the mountains together. This trip was much more relaxing than the one only seven months earlier, when I had just left the convent. I now had a job, and I felt I wasn't so "green" about the ways of the world. My younger sister, Colleen, had graduated from beauty school but, since she did not enjoy working on people's hair, she got a job in a wig shop; wigs were very much in style in the early 70s. She gave each of us a wig for Christmas. I liked the light brown, short, conservative hair style she chose for me; it felt modern and nothing like the veil that I had worn for five years. I was beginning to feel like a normal person. The habit and the religious life no longer separated me from my family. It felt wonderful. We spent Christmas Eve in Central City. I found great pleasure in the small glass of wine offered to each of us in one of the stores. I finally felt all grown up.

It was during this visit to Denver that my allergy to cats and dogs was confirmed. Shirley had a huge sheep dog and a furry gray cat. They were there when I came to Denver from the convent, but I don't remember being bothered by them. However, this time, the first night I was there I had trouble breathing; it got worse each night. By the third night I was sitting up wheezing and coughing and could not sleep. My sister came to the rescue with allergy medicine. This confirmation of an allergy to dogs and cats was not good news because my mom had recently rescued a cat. I knew I would have problems if I stayed with her.

After Christmas, Ann found a job at General Mills, so she could relax about paying the rent. With fewer money worries, even mundane tasks like cooking and going to the grocery store were fun. Actually, everything was fun. We loved just driving down the street. Everything made us laugh. We would look at each other and shout, "WE ARE FREE!" We were thrilled to be able to come and go when and where we wanted.

We managed to feed ourselves even though neither of us was fond of cooking. We both had major responsibilities in the kitchen when we were growing up. I had not cooked for five years, but Ann had taken the "cooking route" in the convent. She had actually cooked for all the Sisters on her first mission. It was one of the reasons she decided to leave the convent: she couldn't imagine spending the rest of her life cooking. We loved that we could eat whatever we liked, even if it was just half of a grapefruit!

Grocery shopping was especially fun because the store gave out S&H Green Stamps, so we came home each week with stamps to paste in our book. We could get all kinds of items for free after we had filled a certain number of stamp books. We talked about what we needed the most. Ann wanted a ring more than anything, but there were no rings in the catalog. I wanted a dictionary—and that is exactly what I ended up getting with those Green Stamps. Ann bought a black onyx ring with her first pay-check. She still wears it today, and we still use the dictionary I got with the Green Stamps.

I used my first paycheck to buy contacts. I thought I needed contacts more than anything else in the world. I was sure they would make me feel more attractive, hip and worldly. I had worn glasses periodically in high school but, with all the studying in the convent, I needed glasses. I had "granny glasses" in the convent, but now, they screamed "convent," even though they were popular with the hippies. I wanted to get rid of them as quickly as possible, so I went to the eye doctor as soon as I got my first pay check. I felt much better with my contacts but was able to wear them only at school. My eyes hurt so much by the end of the day, I could not wear them in the evening. When we went out at night, I chose impaired vision over my granny glasses.

On one of our Wednesday night trips to the bar, I met a rather hand-some guy. (I had finally decided to stop dating the teacher at school.) He seemed to be interested in some of the same things as me. On our first date he asked me about my roommate, Ann. When I told him she was not going with anyone, he said he had a friend that he thought she might like. He was so convinced they would be a good match that we decided to return home early from our date, pick up my roommate and take her over to his friend's house. Ann had already gone to bed—with huge rollers in her wet hair! We persuaded her to change her clothes and come with us. I insisted she remove the rollers, but she said she would look even worse with wet hair. She was a good sport and, when we arrived at the friend's house, she made lots of jokes about being pulled out of bed late at night to meet this special guy. He saw that she had a great sense of humor; she did make us laugh about how silly she looked. He called her a couple of days later. They married within a year and are still together today.

Ann and her boyfriend began dating. Soon, something happened that made it clear that I wasn't going to stay with the guy I had been dating. We attended an evening yoga class. I loved yoga and thought it was cool that he wanted to go with me. But I got really scared on the way home from our second yoga class. That snowy winter night, his van stalled in the middle of an intersection. He immediately "lost it," screaming, shouting and banging his hands on the steering wheel. I was scared; his temper frightened me. I had a flash of what my life would be like if I stayed with him. I was good at paying attention to these "intuitive hits." I didn't tell him that his temper frightened me. He was only the second guy I had dated since I left the convent, and he, too, seemed way too obsessed with me. I was still not emotionally mature enough for a serious relationship, with yet another guy clinging to me.

He could sense I was pulling away, so he tried even harder to impress me. He learned that I had never been on a plane, so he bought us tickets to fly to Chicago to visit my friend, Marian, the same friend that I had lived with the previous summer. She had moved to Chicago with her boyfriend. Again, too many people were in the apartment that weekend. Her brother and his wife were visiting, and she had a couple of friends living with her as well. Whether she couldn't say "no" or she felt obligated to let us visit, it felt like an intrusion. In the middle of the night, Marian's brother and his wife started arguing. We strained to hear what they were saying. We were laying in the middle of the living room floor on cushions. It seemed a safe place to me; with all the "traffic" coming and going, I didn't have to worry about what I might be expected to do with this guy who was much too interested in me.

The true highlight of that weekend was meeting Marian at the Drake Hotel in downtown Chicago. The hotel was beautiful, and I was delighted to sit there in the hotel lobby, dreaming of the day I could actually stay at the Drake. After staying in that crowded apartment all weekend, I was happy to get home to my cozy little efficiency apartment with Ann, where we could laugh about life and my Chicago adventures.

The school year was progressing. I could see that my students were learning. I had been observed a number of times by the principal, who thought I was doing a good job. She was pleased with how hard I worked and my desire to improve. I asked lots of questions of the staff, especially the young sixth-grade teacher who was a strong disciplinarian and a stickler for grammar, spelling and punctuation. She taught us by telling stories about how unhappy she was when her students made silly grammatical errors. I started paying more attention to my students' writing so they wouldn't make the same mistakes.

The grammar stickler taught us more than just teaching tips. She was newly married and quite open about everything related to her sex life. We asked her lots of questions, and she told us stories about her married life. She was never shocked by the questions we asked. Since I carpooled with her, we had lots of time alone to talk. While I appreciated her openness, I knew I would never be like her, keeping nothing about her sex life sacred or private.

During the spring I decided I would not stay at this school for another year. I had dreams, and it was clear that these dreams weren't going to happen in Iowa. I wanted to live in a big city; Chicago was the closest big city, so I started sending out resumes to every Catholic school in the Chicagoland area. I got an interview at a Catholic school in Joliet, Illinois, southwest of Chicago. The teacher from the school whom I had dated volunteered to take me to Chicago for the interview. I met with the school principal at a restaurant along the expressway. She interviewed me for an hour and a half and then offered me a fourth-grade teaching position. I found out later that she favored hiring ex-nuns and ex-priests, which explained why it seemed she liked me even before we met. She said I needed to be flexible because the school was being remodeled, and we would be housed temporarily in an orphanage. That was a bit frightening to think about—that I would be spending a year in the basement of an orphanage, as I had done when I was eight. I signed the contract, returned to Iowa, and told the principal there I would not be returning the following year.

I was so excited about this new adventure that I went back to smiling and being myself again at school. I was leaving Iowa and my first teaching job. I felt free again. After signing the new teaching contract in Joliet, I yearned to do something exciting and daring. I dreamed of hitchhiking in Europe. Shirley had already been to Europe; she loved France and could speak fluent French. I was dying to travel and to prove that I would never again be stuck in Iowa like my Mom.

I thought of Sis, a convent friend, who had left the year before me. She spoke fluent French and had traveled to Europe. I wrote to ask if she would be interested in hitchhiking with me in Europe over the summer, and I told her about the American Student Exchange Program that I had read about in a teacher travel magazine. This program placed students all over Europe in businesses that needed workers. The students worked for free, in exchange for room and board, in six-week increments. She said it sounded great, so we both applied to the program, were accepted and received our placements within weeks, and started planning our trip.

Our work assignment was in the Swiss Alps, at a French restaurant on top of the Jungfrau in South Central Switzerland. We found that the only way to get to the hotel, called Jungfraujoch, was via a cogwheel railway that climbed to the Eiger Glacier station. The train continued through the Eiger tunnel for two and half hours, pausing to allow passengers to take in the spectacular views on the way to the highest railway station in Europe. The Jungfraujoch, over 11,000 feet high, featured some of Switzerland's most breathtaking scenery. We would live and work there for six weeks in the middle of the summer. It seemed like a placement directly from the gods. Sis and I had saved enough money to hitch through Europe in the weeks before and after our work program. We planned to stay in hostels, which were very reasonably priced. It all seemed doable, and even though I had made less than four thousand dollars my first year of teaching, we were sure it would all work out. This was another dream come true! I was going to Europe for the summer, and I had a new teaching position near Chicago. This WAS what I thought life would be like once I left the convent.

There were, however, a couple of glitches to the plan. First, my roommate, Ann, and her boyfriend planned to marry that summer and she wanted me to be in her wedding. Luckily, they were willing to change the date to the end of summer so I could be in the wedding.

The other glitch was that we needed to leave for Europe before the end of the school year. I had not taken any sick leave, so I asked for and received permission to use my leave the last two days of school. Before leaving, I had to close up my classroom, even though the students would be there two more days, and also find a good sub for the students. This might have been an unprofessional thing to do, but I was able to convince everyone, including myself, that this was an opportunity I could not pass up.

As a child I had never traveled farther than two hours from home. Now I was going to another continent. I was following my dreams even though it sounded scary. I did not let any fearful thoughts enter my mind. I wanted to go to Europe and I was doing it.

CHAPTER EIGHT

HITCHING THROUGH EUROPE

I packed the few possessions I owned and brought them to my Mom's house. My Mom was worried about me going to Europe, but she quickly acknowledged that nothing she said would change my mind. She was concerned that it would be too dangerous; after all, I was "an inexperienced young woman who had been in a convent for the past five years." She couldn't imagine me navigating another continent, even if I was going with a friend. This never crossed my mind. I was on my way and more excited than I could ever put into words!

My Mom reluctantly agreed to drive me to the Dubuque bus station, where I caught a bus to Chicago's O'Hare Airport for my flight to New York. I met Sis at the North Terminal of La Guardia. For my trip across the ocean, I had chosen to wear a skirt and blouse. Having no experience with traveling, I didn't know it was more important to be comfortable than to worry about how I looked. We took one look at each other and started laughing because we each had two suitcases. How did we have enough stuff to fill two suitcases less than a year after leaving the convent?

The long flight to Amsterdam, in nylons, skirt and blouse was not relaxing. I was too excited to sleep. I realized I had to stop "dressing up." It was no longer the 60s; it was 1971, and life had changed dramatically in the past six years. I had been on only one flight before, and now here I was flying to Europe. It felt surreal. I knew virtually nothing about Europe. I had the sensation that I was going to another planet. I had no idea of how to visualize this strange place.

When we landed in Amsterdam, I remember being surprised that it had grass, trees and buildings, just like in America. Soon after we landed, Sis heard her name being paged. Her brother, John, wanted to spend some time in Europe on his way home from a tour in Vietnam and had arranged to fly to Amsterdam's Schiphol Airport to meet us. He had arrived four hours earlier and was impatiently waiting for us in the terminal. This arrangement turned out to be a great advantage as John planned to travel with us for part of our hitchhiking adventure. John made it clear from our first hello that he did not want to talk about his Vietnam experience, so we honored his request. We were glad he had survived and was able to join us for part of our journey.

We took the twenty-minute train ride into Amsterdam. When John saw our four suitcases, he said, "You can't hitch around Europe with all that crap!" We knew he was right. What were we thinking? We decided to deal with our "crap" later because we had a hotel where we could leave our suitcases for the two days while we were with the American Student Exchange Program, the organization that found us a work site. We hung out with the other twenty students who were part of the program, and we met at a fancy restaurant for dinner. I was not hungry and could not force myself to eat; I felt tired because I hadn't slept on the plane. (I knew nothing about jet lag, but I was about to find out.) My legs and arms felt heavy. I barely dragged my body back to the hotel after dinner.

The next morning I struggled to get up, still feeling exhausted from the flight and the stress involved with finding a new job, closing up my classroom and saying goodbye to my life in Iowa. Sis kept reminding me that we had to meet the rest of our group for a full day of sightseeing: a bus tour of Amsterdam, a canal trip, an excursion to a diamond factory, a Chinese dinner and a night in the bars of downtown Amsterdam. Youth being on my side, I rallied and felt only elation about this exciting adventure. Seeing Amsterdam and drinking espresso at a local cafe was a dream come true. Despite my inexperience with travel, I imagined my European experience would include sipping coffee at sidewalk cafes and having wine, bread and cheese in the park while we people-watched.

The Amsterdam bars were filled with loud, unintelligible music, flashing lights and lots of handsome men. Sis was very cute and enjoyed more than her share of men asking her to dance. I was fascinated by the scene—I loved dancing, the music and seeing lots of beautiful European men at the bars.

The next morning we said goodbye to the students we had met through the exchange program. Our second day in the city, we were on our own, so the three of us decided our first adventure would be to visit the Rijksmuseum, where we fell in love with Van Gogh's *Self Portrait* and many works by Rembrandt and Vermeer. After the museum, we retrieved our bags and moved to a cheaper hotel—the dingy, depressing, low-priced Kabul Hotel in central Amsterdam, chosen for its low rates and location. We later learned it was located in the heart of the Red Light District where, more than once, John attracted the interest of young women sitting on the ledge of a window looking for business. We climbed to our room on the fourth floor, lugging our bags all the way. We were ready to crash, still tired from our flight, and our full day of sightseeing. We had just settled in when the most amazing thing happened.

That same day, Holland had won the European Soccer Cup. I had barely even heard of soccer. This was a night for all of Holland to celebrate. Sis, John and I hung out our rusty, dusty, fourth-floor window as soon as we heard the noise, music and commotion. We were already in bed, but jumped up and swung the windows open to watch the celebration. Below us was the Amstel River; just beyond was the expansive main street of Amsterdam. People were flooding into the street from every direction, blowing horns, screaming, shouting and moving in droves down the street. It was a party like none I had ever seen. We decided to watch from our wonderful vantage point instead of joining the throngs of people in the street. The partying went on late into the night, but we closed our windows and fell into a deep sleep from pure exhaustion.

The next day we roughly sketched out a plan to hitch for the next couple of weeks. John and Sis had already done some research, so they knew which museums and other places they wanted to go. I agreed to their plan because they knew Europe.

Amsterdam is a relatively small city so it was easy to get around on the tram. Trams went on all the main roads, stopped regularly, and were fast and easy to ride. After three days of exploring Amsterdam, we planned to ride the tram to the edge of the city to start our hitching adventure. We were giddy as we embarked on our journey. But first, we had to get rid of one suitcase each. Where could we ditch them? We had no idea. The Universe was quick to give us an answer. John struck up a conversation with an elderly gentleman on the tram. We asked him what we might do about our suitcases. He offered to store them at his house for the summer! So, instead of heading to the edge of the city, we got off at his stop. We carried them to the second floor of his bungalow and then consolidated the clothes we absolutely needed into one small suitcase. (I left all my dresses behind.) That would be all we would have for the next two months. The elderly, kind gentleman wrote his address so we could reclaim our belongings at the end of the summer. As we left his house, we looked at each other, smiled—and wondered if we would ever see our things again. We weren't really attached to them; Sis and I had lived for five years with a vow of poverty, so we were used to owning nothing. We got back on the tram and headed to the edge of the city, where we set up our first hitching positions.

Sis picked up a brown piece of cardboard in the street and wrote our desired destination, "Utrecht." We had hardly settled in at our spot when an old van stopped for us. We thought, "Wow! This is going to be easy!" We hopped into the back and settled in for the trip to Utrecht. The driver spoke English, so we had a congenial conversation, and he willingly dropped us off at the outskirts of the city. We were excited, but our excitement waned as we sat for almost an hour waiting for a ride into the city. During that hour, a huge dust storm rained dirt and debris on us from every direction. My contacts quickly filled with dust. My eyes hurt badly; I started to cry. I didn't have glasses, so I needed to figure out how to get the dust out of my eyes without losing my contacts. Sis was dealing with her own problems because she discovered that one of the lenses in her glasses was broken. Maybe hitching wasn't going to be quite so easy. I stepped into an enclosed storefront, took out my contacts and stored them in their container. When we finally got a ride into the city, we had to immediately deal with Sis's glasses.

On top of our vision challenges, my feet had developed a number of blisters in just the few days I had been in Europe! I definitely didn't have the correct shoes for walking long distances. Both Sis and John insisted I buy a pair of tennis shoes. I did not want to get shoes because I was concerned about spending money so early in our trip. However, there was no choice; I needed to keep up with Sis and John. Sis got her glasses fixed, and I got Band-Aids for my blisters and a pair of cheap tennis shoes that were somewhat comfortable. After dealing with our emergencies, we explored the fourth largest city of the Netherlands, Utrecht.

Then we were on to Antwerp, Belgium. We were lucky with hitching to Antwerp. One ride took us all the way there, and we headed straight to the only hostel in town. Staying at hostels was a fun part of our trip; we loved meeting people from all around the world. All three of us liked to talk, so we got to know people wherever we stayed. Some of the hostels reminded us of our convent life, with just a bunk bed and a place to shower. The hostel opened at dinner time; we could bring food to eat and socialize with the other guests, but we were promptly herded to bed at 9 pm, lights out by 10 pm. Guests had to leave by 7 am the next morning. Often we were awakened by the song, *Guantanamera*. Sis could sing it, and I loved it, so I asked her to sing it over and over again.

The next morning, after getting shuffled out of the hostel, we found the town square and waited there for the rest of the world to wake up. At a small market we bought coffee, a baguette, a sausage link and some Laughing Cow cheese. We had a grand time sitting in the park, eating breakfast. Antwerp is a beautiful city located along the Scheldt River and is one of the largest seaports in Europe. We marveled at the large ships sitting in the port as we rode our rental bikes along the river. We stayed only one day in Antwerp and then made our way to the edge of the city and held up our sign for Brussels. This time an older man picked us up and took us all the way to our destination.

We went to the city center and started to look for one of Brussels' most famous landmarks, the Manneken Pis. This small brass fountain sculpture depicts a naked boy urinating in the fountain's basin. There are many legends surrounding the statue, built around 1618. The one we heard involved a wealthy merchant who, during a visit to the city with his family, lost his young son. The merchant hastily formed a search party that scoured the city until the boy was found, happily urinating in a small garden. The merchant, as a gift of gratitude to the locals, paid to install the now famous fountain. It was small and located on a side street; we would never have found it without the exact address.

After exploring Brussels we headed to Paris. Our hitching luck seemed to run out in Brussels. We stood outside the city for hours. When no one stopped, we decided to go back into the city and catch the train to Paris. Maybe we weren't meant to go to Paris, but we wanted to see the Eiffel Tower and experience everything French—the fashion, the food, the language.

Before we boarded the train we bought bread, cheese, sausage, apples and a bottle of wine at a small grocery store near the train station. As we rode the train to Paris, we shared the wine, drinking it straight from the bottle, and enjoyed the delicious food we had purchased. Nothing went to waste. We ate and drank everything by the time we arrived in Paris. Both Sis and John spoke French, so we were not worried about navigating our way through France.

Paris was expensive. Both Sis and John were worried about money. John had arranged to have money wired from home, but it hadn't come. He kept borrowing from his sister, which made her very nervous. It was hard to find a hostel with a vacancy because every young person staying in Paris needed a cheap room. The first night we stayed in an expensive hotel near the Champs Elysees. The next night, we ended up at a dumpy hostel on the outer edge of the city. We spent our days sightseeing: visiting the Eiffel Tower, the Louvre, Sacre Coeur and other museums in Paris, so it was fine to crash at a cheap hostel, asleep before our heads hit the pillow. When we returned to the hostel after our third day, something awful happened. Sis had stored her wallet in a locker but when we returned, her money was gone. Their money situation immediately went from bad to dire. Now, neither of them had money. How could they stay in Paris without money? We kept checking Western Union to see if John's money had been wired. I couldn't help because I had so little cash.

Finally, money arrived and we all relaxed. We sat at the sidewalk cafes, drank delicious French coffee and watched the young, fabulously dressed French women make their way to work. We wondered what life was like for them; we decided they surely must live at home and spend all their money on clothes.

It was such fun sitting in the park where the pigeons waited for any crumbs we might drop, but we were always hungry, so the pigeons didn't fare too well. Even though it was exciting to be in Paris, Sis was ready to leave after she had her money stolen.

On our last night in Paris, we treated ourselves to the famous French fish stew called Bouillabaisse. John said, "We simply CANNOT leave Paris without trying Bouillabaisse!" I had never heard of it, but both Sis and John insisted that despite the cost, we couldn't leave Paris without eating it. This fish soup was only served at fancy restaurants. It was good, but my palette was not trained to appreciate great seafood, so I was not impressed with the subtle tastes of the variety of fish in the recipe.

We headed to the south of France, to Fontainebleau, Lyon, Avignon, and Marseille. Sometimes we had to wait a long time for a ride, while other times our rides happened quickly. There was no rhyme or reason to how quickly we got picked up or how long we waited. On several occasions I started a conversation with someone at a restaurant or a rest stop while we waited. These conversations often turned into rides. Getting a ride right away was pure joy. Other times, we just gave up, went back into town and bought a bus ticket.

We were on our way to Nice, for the next leg of our journey. A young guy near Toulon picked us up. Sis got in the front seat while I climbed in the back with John. The guy evidently assumed that we were a couple, so he started touching Sis's leg and getting way too friendly in the front seat. Before long she was yelling at him in French. The guy got mad when he realized he was not going to get anywhere with Sis. He veered the car off the highway and onto a country road, where he made us get out in the middle of nowhere. Then he sped off, leaving us stranded.

We had absolutely no idea where we were. It was dusk, and our only choice was to start walking. There was not a single car on this country road. We walked and walked and soon it became completely dark. We could see lights in the distance, so we kept walking. As we got closer to town, we heard dogs barking. It was 9:00 pm when we finally arrived in the small town. There was only one hotel. We banged on the windows and doors for someone to let us in. Finally we heard a lady yelling at us in French from a window on the third floor, telling us there was no room and to go away. So we walked down the street to the town square; nothing was open. We sat there, tired and hungry, wondering how we could get ourselves out of this predicament.

We were sitting on swings in the town square when a couple of men appeared from a side street. They were carnival workers who were staying in campers at the park. They must have heard us talking. We told them of our problem. They felt sorry for us and said we could sleep on a bunk in one of their campers with one stipulation. We had to get out as soon as the sun came up so they could get moving to their next event. We agreed, and all three of us climbed into one small compartment. John laid on the floor, and Sis and I shared the bunk. I somehow managed to get my

149

contacts out in the dark without losing them; we fell asleep immediately. We had only a few hours before sunrise, but it was much better than sitting up in the town square all night. I secretly thanked God for this help. I believed that I was being Divinely protected this entire trip. These carnival guys were sent to help us. I felt grateful.

Morning came all too quickly. One of the guys pounded loudly on the camper door. John got out first, then Sis and I quickly scooted out of our bunk and waved goodbye to the workers as they pulled the camper out of the park. We didn't even get a chance to thank them. Back at the town square, we wondered how we could get out of this wretched little town. People stared but no one spoke. We waited for a couple of hours along the only small road through town. One guy stopped and offered us a ride to a larger city, but he had no room in the cab; we could ride in the back part of his REFRIGERATED truck. We said, "No, thanks." Finally someone gave us a ride to a busy highway, where we stood with our sign: "NICE!"

We waited a long time before getting a ride to Nice, but it was worth the effort it took to get there. Our first order of business was to find food. We went to a small cafe and, after eating, we started to relax, and enjoy the beauty of southern France. It took our breath away—warm, sunny and stunningly beautiful. I had a fleeting thought that if I ever got married, we would take a Mediterranean cruise for our honeymoon.

That afternoon, walking by the water, we came upon a young American woman sitting on the sidewalk, crying hysterically. I asked her if I could help. She couldn't stop crying long enough to talk. She just shook her head, "No." I wondered if she was lonesome, or if she had just found out she was pregnant, or if her boyfriend had left her. She continued sobbing, as we walked past her. I wanted to go back to offer help again, but Sis and John said we should leave her alone. Her crying made me appreciate our grand adventure; I couldn't imagine being that distraught in such a beautiful place. I felt immensely grateful for this trip and the incredible experiences we were having. However, we had been on the road for a month and were starting to get weary. We had washed our clothes in a sink so many times they were starting to look grungy.

We were used to our routine: hurry out of bed, eat a quick breakfast at the hostel and head to the highway to start hitching. The hardest part of hitching was waiting and not knowing if we would get a ride. At one point Sis put a brown paper bag over her head, with our next destination, "GENOA" scribbled on it. The excitement of hitching was beginning to wane as we found ourselves in some tough situations. Some guys were great, but others were crazy, or very fast drivers. One ride we accepted was in a pickup with a door held closed by a rope. We were starting to tire of staying in hostels. We visited Genoa, Milan and Como in Italy; these are all beautiful places with great things to see, but we knew our hitching days were coming to a close because we had to report soon to our work placement in Switzerland.

Sis and I needed to get to Interlaken to catch the train to the top of the Jungfraujoch, where we would work for the next seven weeks. We were looking forward to staying in one place and not worrying about food or shelter or running out of money. When we arrived at Jungfraujoch, we knew we would have food and a warm bed. Little did we know how some other issues would become huge for us. In northern Italy, we said goodbye to John, who was heading home to Chicago. We were grateful he had been with us for most of our hitching days.

Outside Como we were picked up by a middle-aged, heavy-set man who told us he was driving all the way to Interlaken, which was exactly where we needed to go. This ride was a gift for many reasons—he was going exactly where we needed to go, and he had an air conditioned

Mercedes Benz (the reason I fell in love with Mercedes!). Neither of us had experience with traveling in the mountains, but we quickly realized that it was getting colder. We were dressed in shorts and sleeveless tops. The kind man stopped to allow us to take in some of the spectacular Swiss scenery and to change into warmer clothes, and he even bought us lunch. When we arrived in Interlaken, he took us to the tourist office, where we found the location of our hostel and the train that would take us to Eigergletscher, the midway point on our way to the top of the Jungfrau. We had to stay there one night to allow our bodies to begin to adjust to the high altitude (11,000 feet) at which we would be living for the next seven weeks. At Eigergletscher we had a toasty, warm room with a down comforter and incredibly delicious homemade food. It was heavenly. We slept better there than we had in all the hostels throughout our trip. The next morning, after a delicious Swiss breakfast, we got back on the train for the two-hour trip through a mountain tunnel to the top of the Jungfrau. We wondered: What were we getting ourselves into? One thing was certain: there would be no easy escape if we didn't like our placement!

When we arrived at the Jungfraujoch Hotel at the end of the tunnel, we were met by a middle-aged German man who showed us to our rooms. He told us to take time to settle in, that the altitude was an adjustment for most people, so we should take it easy. Our rooms were small but unbelievably warm and comfortable. My bed had a beautiful down comforter with a pristine white duvet cover. Out my window, we could see the magnificent Eiger Mountain right across the vast expanse of a glacier. Had we died and gone to heaven? A deep prayer of gratitude came over me as I soaked in this beautiful spot. Even though I was so angry at God for the past five years, I always felt a deep sense of gratitude for things working out so well.

We met our German guide in the large dining room on the main floor for dinner. He gave us a tour of both the very formal restaurant upstairs and the less expensive cafe downstairs by the train station. We would be assigned to work at either of these sites. During our tour of the Ski School and the Ice Palace, we were told we were not allowed to ski. That was a relief for me because the mountain looked way too steep to walk on, much less slide down. The views from these locations were surreal. Only two days before, we were in sunny, warm Nice, wearing shorts. Now wearing all the clothes we brought, we were in a mountain getaway with unparalleled beauty. How quiet it was during the day and how beautiful and bright the stars were at night. The only sounds were the crash of snow falling from an avalanche, a helicopter rescuing a fallen mountain climber or a dog sled bringing back a dead person who had slipped off the mountain. We could go out on the deck to view these events or watch them from the massive windows in the main dining room.

We settled into our rooms for our first night on the mountain and fell asleep immediately; the next morning we met in the main dining room to receive our assignments. Sis was assigned to the main dining room upstairs because she spoke French. Many customers were French-speaking. I was assigned to the cafe on the lower level. I loved this because the cafe was very busy, and I got to wait on and meet many young people who could not afford to eat upstairs in the formal dining room. The American students made me laugh. They consistently ordered "a Coke with ice" and a hamburger or hot dog. The busy cafe had long lines, but I was happy every day, enjoying this beautiful place with an international community. In the upper dining room, Sis waited on wealthy people who were much more demanding and difficult.

Many Europeans came up for the day, taking the last train back to Interlaken in the early evening. After the last train departed at 6:30 pm, the employees sat together in the main dining room to eat dinner. After dinner we played music and danced, sometimes ending up in someone's room laughing, talking and sharing stories. After dinner one evening, while we were all still sitting and chatting, one of the loudest English-speaking French guys at our table announced that Sis and I had just left a convent. He said, "If you have been in the convent for the past five years, that must mean you are virgins. Could that be true? Twenty-four year-old virgins!" He couldn't believe it. He told everyone who would listen. We were both so embarrassed.

One evening, after we had been there a week, we were all dancing when a handsome guy asked me to dance. His name was Elan; he grew up in Tel Aviv, and he had attended a famous French cooking school. He worked in the hotel kitchen, responsible for all the delicious food we ate each evening. He could speak four languages including English. We talked whenever we could and enjoyed getting to know each other. He was cute, and I was thrilled that he kept asking me to dance. Sis was receiving lots of attention from an English guy named Roger.

One evening we got off early, so Sis, Roger, Elan and I took the train to Interlaken. We went to dinner at a famous French fondue restaurant and then went dancing. It was really fun. Another weekend, we enjoyed a dinner in Grindelwald where we found the most scrumptious chocolate cake in the world at a local bakery. Elan was a chef and he knew where to find the best food. For me, the famous Swiss chocolate bars were the highlight of every trip we made down the mountain.

One weekend, Elan persuaded his boss to give him an extra day off, and to let him borrow his car so we could travel to Basel. Elan loved Basel and felt I should see this city before I left Switzerland. He said that Basel was Switzerland's third largest city and that many foreigners missed this city because it is so tucked away on the northern edge of the country, bordering both France and Germany. It was only when we were on the train going down the mountain that it occurred to me that this would be the first time I would be alone with Elan for a whole weekend. We felt so happy, singing songs in the car as we zipped along the Autobahn to Basel. I was smiling so much that my cheeks hurt. I looked out the window at one point and saw a billboard in French, reminding everyone to secure their seat belts. We did not have our seat belts on. At that moment, Elan reached down to change the tape player located under the dashboard; the "Age of Aquarius" was playing. He wanted to turn it up, but he also turned the wheel when he reached under the dashboard, and in that second he lost control of the car. It skidded out of control, flipped over and landed upside-down on the opposite side of the Autobahn, facing the wrong way.

I momentarily lost consciousness; when I came to, I heard gas dripping from the car. My only thought was to get out of the car! I climbed out the broken driver-side window and looked for Elan. I couldn't find him; he had been thrown into the back seat. My only injury—a cut on my middle finger, an outcome I immediately attributed to Divine protection. Elan had more serious injuries. The first people to stop spoke only Scheizerdeutch, the Swiss German language. They accused Elan of kissing me and not paying attention to his driving. He argued with them and said he was just changing the tape player. I couldn't understand what they were saying, but I knew, by the sound of Elan's angry voice, that they were arguing. The police arrived shortly. Witnesses repeated to the police the same story about Elan kissing me as the cause of the accident. Elan, again, argued with the police.

One reason the police may have believed the witnesses was because the borrowed car had a trunk full of *Playboy* magazines. When the accident occurred, the trunk flew open, and pictures of naked women scattered all over the Autobahn. Even though Elan was bleeding, we had to pick up all the magazines before the police would take him to the hospital. As cars whizzed by, I helped him pick up the "girly" magazines, as did several people who had stopped to help. The police officer said he would take us to the hospital as soon as the car was towed. The car was totaled, and it was towed to the junk yard. When we finally arrived at the hospital, I waited while Elan got stitches in his head and shoulder. He was in a lot of pain. The hospital staff released him after a number of hours. It was dark and late, so we walked to the nearest hotel.

We checked into our room. That night seemed endless because Elan was in excruciating pain, and there was nothing I could do but listen to him moan throughout the night. There was certainly no need to worry about what I would do all night alone with this cute guy! In the morning we went to the police station to file paper work for the accident. Then it was time to make the dreaded call to his friend who owned the car. It was a sobering phone call, and Elan wasn't able to recover after that. He was in pain; he had wrecked his friend's car; and our fun weekend was ruined. What more could we do? After filing the police report, we found the train station and made our way back to Interlacken and through the mountains to the top of the Jungfrau. This was not the way the weekend was supposed to unfold.

After the accident, Elan and I hung out together every chance we got. We felt really close after sharing such a terrible experience. We were grateful to have survived and remained close the whole time I worked on the Jungfrau. It was a safe relationship because I knew I was going home to the States; he talked about moving back to Israel, although he did promise to visit me in the United States.

I soon received a letter from my mother dated the day of the accident. She said she was worried about me. She had heard the drinking water in Europe was tainted. When I read her letter and realized it was written the same day as our accident, I speculated that my Mom might have some psychic abilities. However, it wasn't the drinking water that she needed to warn me about...... how about my careless, young, inexperienced driver traveling too fast on the Autobahn?

One of the very wealthy guests who stayed six weeks at the Jungfraujock was a German man named Herr Schmitt. We got to know him and love him. He spoke English well, was thoughtful and asked us intelligent questions about America. We decided to throw a going-away party for him on his last night on the mountain. It was a fun evening of drinking, talking and dancing. We all loved him and were grateful for how special he had made our stay on the Jungfrau.

On our last night, the staff planned a going-away party for us. We had great food; we talked and danced late into the night. Our new friends gave us a charm bracelet fashioned out of European coins. (I still wear it occasionally.) Our hearts were filled with the love we felt from the Jungfrau staff and the new friends we met on top of the Jungfrau.

The next day we made one last visit to the Ski School and the Ice Palace. I paused at the top of the mountain and thanked God for giving me such an incredible experience. I was not sure how to pray, so I just said, "THANK YOU GOD. THANK YOU. THANK YOU." (Years later I thought that this trip was a "thank you gift" for giving five years of my life to His service.) Sis was exhausted and ready to go home. I was tired too, but felt blessed in many ways for the opportunity to live on this beautiful mountain for six weeks.

I returned to my room to take one last look when I ran into Elan. We had a moment alone to say goodbye. It was a sweet, touching moment. He promised to come to America to visit me. A maid was cleaning my room. I wanted to take a "Jungfraujoch Hotel" hand towel as a keepsake but decided that would be stealing. I had a lifetime of memories to take with me. We boarded the train for our last trip down the mountain through the tunnel. The train stopped twice for us to take pictures of the spectacular views. I jumped out each time to soak up the last of the amazing scenery. My heart was thrilled, yet sad, to be saying goodbye to such a fabulous time on the Jungfrau.

Elan's last gift to me was the best gift. Instead of our plan to hitch all the way to Amsterdam, he arranged for us to travel to Germany with one of his fellow restaurant chef employees. Not only did we secure a great ride all the way to Germany, but we got to stay overnight at her parents' home. The next day her parents drove us to the train station, where we bought tickets to Amsterdam. We met the rest of the American Student Exchange Program participants at the airport to fly back to the States together. We had fun comparing notes about our summer placements. (Sis and I believed we had the best placement.) When we arrived in Amsterdam, we went immediately to retrieve our bags from the elderly man's home. We thanked him profusely for safeguarding our bags.

We were out of money, but grateful for all the experiences. We spent the summer in Europe for much less than five dollars a day! It was a great adventure. Now I had something to talk about other than my convent experiences. I smiled all the way back to America, where I would start my new life in a new state, with a new school and a new roommate.

CHAPTER NINE

A New School and A New Life

I arrived home from Europe relaxed, tired and happy. I was proud of myself for accomplishing my dream of hitching in Europe. I felt ready for my next adventure: a move to the Chicago area to begin a new teaching position.

My former roommate, Ann, had spent the summer making wedding plans. I was thrilled to be her maid of honor. I had just one week to take part in her wedding, find an apartment, move my meager belongings to the Chicago area and get settled to start my new teaching job.

The wedding was fun; my friend was marrying a wonderful guy that she loved. I was proud to have played a role in helping her find him. My present to her was a black cow bell from the Swiss Alps that she could hang on the wall in her new home. She had borrowed a yellow dress for me to wear as her maid of honor. I was nervous about seeing my old boyfriend, but we barely talked during the reception. He told me he thought I might have lost weight hitching through Europe, but it looked like I had actually gained weight. That comment made it clear to me that I had made the right decision; I didn't need anyone making comments about my body.

After the wedding, I headed home to visit my Mom before I moved to Chicago. Mom had tried to contact me when I arrived back in the States, but I didn't get her message. (I was used to not being in contact with her during my convent years.) She was worried and unhappy that I hadn't phoned, and it was one of the few times she seemed genuinely distressed that I was out of contact with her.

My relationship with my Mom became more strained after I left the convent. I wanted her to believe in me, to trust my decisions, and to have faith that I knew what I was doing. She was not able to do this for me because of her own pain. It would be a long, painful journey to realize I could not get this support from my Mom.

Before I left for Europe, I had asked another convent friend, Ellen, if she wanted to move to Chicago with me. She had left the convent about the same time as me and had spent her first year teaching at a Catholic school near the Motherhouse. She wanted to get out of that situation, so she agreed to move to Chicago with me. When I was interviewing for my teaching position, I mentioned to my new principal that I had an ex-nun friend who was also interested in a position. When a position opened up, Ellen was offered the job. I returned from Europe to hear this exciting news. Ellen also told me she had fallen madly in love with a tall, handsome, fast-talking guy she met while working at Foley's department store where she worked as a store detective.

Despite being engaged, she was looking forward to our new living and working arrangement. We would be teaching in the same room with only a room divider between us. She had already rented furniture and an apartment for us! But almost immediately, I started to feel lonely because Ellen was absorbed in her new love. I started to worry about money since I had already spent the little savings I had from my first year of teaching. I was going to be making only a thousand dollars more per year than I did my first year of teaching. I knew things were going to be different, but I had no idea of how different life would be, living in a new city with a different friend.

We moved into a large apartment complex a couple of miles from school. We set up our one-bedroom apartment with rental furniture from Cort Furniture, so we had a monthly rental fee for the furniture on top of our apartment rent. We each had a single bed—not too different from our convent bedroom, except we didn't have white cotton curtains around our single beds.

We taught at St. Mary's Sacred Heart, an inner-city school in Joliet, Illinois. We spent most of our waking hours getting our classrooms ready. We loved our new principal; she inspired us to be passionate about our teaching. She said, "These children can't read and they can't write and they can't compute. We MUST teach them to read and write and do math. Nothing else matters." We submitted lesson plans every week to show how we would teach our students these essential skills. She approved our lessons or asked us to plan different activities to ensure the students' success. I was grateful for not having to teach a Religion class—there wasn't one. (Many of the students were not Catholic, so Religion classes were not required.) The only thing that mattered was to teach the students to read, write and do math so they could catch up with the other students their age.

After a couple of weeks, we went car shopping. I was nervous about owning my own car. I did not think I could afford one, but Ellen was sure that I could if I took out a three-year loan. So we went to a Chevy dealership in Joliet and looked for the cheapest new car on the lot. The salesman quipped, "Of course you can afford a new car. You are a teacher!" On the spot, I bought a dark green 1971 Vega. I was proud of myself and at the same time freaked out because it was the first large purchase of my life.

The first weekend after I purchased my car, I drove back to Iowa, excited to show my Mom and brother my new purchase. A couple of other convent friends from Chicago wanted to visit their Iowa parents, so we all went in my new car. I hadn't had much experience with driving the freeways of Chicago, so I was quite nervous. I did relax a bit after driving on the expressway for an hour. However, as we crossed the Illinois state line into Iowa, ominous storm clouds turned into a driving rain storm. I had been watching the clouds and praying that we would get to Iowa before the storm hit, but it was not meant to be. Before long, the wind was blowing so hard that my little Vega was being tossed around like a tilt-a-whirl ride at the carnival. I was having a hard time seeing and keeping the car on the road. All of a sudden there was a loud bang and a flapping noise—like something had come loose on the car.

One of my friends, Jane, in the backseat joked that my car sounded like a "tin box" and believed I was about to lose whatever was flapping on the car. I slowed down and pulled off the road. She volunteered to check out the noise. She got soaked as she retrieved the piece of metal flapping off the side of my car; part of the right side window had come loose. She put the piece in the backseat. All of Jane's joking made me feel both angry and mortified. I had borrowed a lot of money to buy this car and now, on its maiden voyage, it felt like it was a terrible decision. When we finally arrived safely in Iowa, my brother, Paul, a car expert, confirmed my suspicions. He advised, "You need to get rid of this car as quickly as possible. It is a piece of shit." I was devastated. I berated myself for not consulting him first because he knew so much about cars! My Mom did not say a word about my car, either good or bad. I knew she believed my brother. My brother fixed the broken piece of the back window and the drive back to Chicago with my friends was uneventful, but I no longer felt good about buying my car. I felt ashamed.

I did not tell my family that I was already feeling unhappy. I was living in a city with a roommate who was engaged and did not want to go out. I met a couple of teachers at school, but they were either married or engaged. I had just enjoyed such an exciting summer, but now, in a few short weeks, I started to feel trapped again.

There was one young female teacher at my school, Nell, who was unattached and not dating anyone. She was from Peoria, Illinois. She did not know anyone in the city, so we hung out together after school, often going to the "Dog n Suds" to have a Coke. We shared the same sense of urgency about finding a social life. One day we were sitting in one of the red plastic booths at the Dog n Suds when a guy in the next booth started talking to us. We talked back and forth for a while. He told us he was a pilot and worked for Motorola. He asked if he could join us. My friend did not think that was a good idea, but I whispered to her that he might give us a ride in his corporate jet. (He later told me that he had heard that comment.) He joined us and we talked for a long time. Before we left he asked for Nell's number. They began dating and eventually got married. After he and Nell were married, he took us up in a plane he rented from his company located at O'Hare. Nell already had enough of flying and didn't want to come with us. He loved flying model planes and was actually building his own plane.

Another teacher we had fun with was an upper-level science teacher named Colleen. She was engaged to her long-time high school boyfriend, Jerry, with whom she was planning a large Polish wedding. She grew up in Joliet and showed us her favorite places. One of those was a small Chicago-style hot dog stand close to school. I really wasn't crazy about hot dogs, but I loved going there with her. She was lots of fun, and I learned to love those Chicago-style hot dogs. We talked about school politics and how good or bad the kids had been that day, and she provided weekly updates on her wedding plans. We discussed who I might date. One time she said, "What about that young, male teacher at school named Luke?" But added in the same sentence, "Oh wait, he's already engaged. Never mind." I had not really noticed or thought of him because I knew he was engaged.

It was late October and I was feeling restless and unsettled. I felt that moving to a new school had not really helped me. My restlessness was due to many things. I wanted to start dating, but with no options, I felt isolated and alone. My lack of money was a constant source of worry. I wanted to get out of town.

I was in contact with Sis, my European hitching partner. She was always up for traveling, and she lived in the Chicago area. She suggested a trip to New York to visit Cindy, one of the students we had met in Europe. Sis called Cindy to tell her we wanted to visit. She said, "Sure, come to Allentown and we'll take the train into the Big Apple." We still had so little money, but that never seemed to concern us when we had a chance for an adventure! We considered hitching to Allentown, but decided it wasn't safe.

One day I was talking to some guys from our apartment building when they were outside working on their car. They said they were trying to get their car working so they could go back to the Philly area to visit their families for the Thanksgiving holiday. I said, "Wow! That is exactly where my friend and I want to go." So we made plans. They said we were welcome to come along if we were willing to help pay for gas.

They mentioned that driving to Philadelphia was always "a little dicey" during the winter months because of the weather. They had relatives in Pittsburgh whom we could stay with on Wednesday evening, and then drive the rest of the way to Allentown early Thanksgiving morning. They would leave us with our friend and continue on to Philly.

I was beginning to notice a clear pattern. As soon as I clearly defined something I wanted, doors seemed to open, pathways began to unfold. Things just worked out. No need to know how it would happen, just that it would happen. I was having my first glimpse of realizing that, if I didn't worry, things magically worked out if I trusted the process. The trick was to be clear about what I wanted, and then not worry about how it would manifest itself.

I was happy to have something to look forward to. I called my Mom to explain I would not be home for Thanksgiving. I felt no remorse for making plans apart from my family during the holidays because they were used to me not being home.

We loaded our bags into the trunk of the guys' car, which was in "good working condition." Our first day of travel went off without incident. We left right after school on Wednesday and traveled through Indiana and Ohio, arriving at the guys' aunt's house in Pittsburgh around 10 pm. We were tired but grateful that we had a free place to sleep. Sis and I shared a couch in the living room; the guys slept in the extra bedroom. The next morning the aunt mentioned that she had heard there was a big snowstorm making its way down from Lake Ontario through New York and was due to hit the middle of Pennsylvania on Thanksgiving Day! This did not deter us. We got our tired bodies up and headed out as soon as we had a delicious breakfast made by the kind-hearted aunt. Sis and I had one goal—to have a late Thanksgiving dinner with our friend in Allentown. If we were delayed, we just would eat leftovers when we arrived.

As the morning wore on, it started to snow and then it very quickly turned into a blizzard. We could barely see the road, but the guys kept driving. We were young, foolish and determined. We did not discuss stopping. There were few cars on the turnpike. Finally, the snow became so deep that we had to stop the car. We were stranded miles from an exit ramp. We sat wondering what we should do. Would we be rescued? Incredibly, I was more concerned about missing Thanksgiving dinner. I had learned from growing up in Iowa that you should never leave your car if you are stranded in a storm, so we sat quietly. I wondered whether I should have stayed at home, but this thought was quickly dismissed because I loved adventure, and this certainly was an adventure. I prayed that we would be rescued soon. Praying was my "go-to" mode when I was in trouble. "Dear God, please send someone soon to help us." Finally we heard the sound of a Highway Patrol jeep; a sheriff had come to rescue us. He gave us a god-awful look that said, "You might be the stupidest kids on the planet today." We said something lame like, "We really wanted to get home to be with our families on Thanksgiving." "Well," he said disgustedly, "You aren't going to make it. The turnpike is closed. I can take you to the next exit where there is food and lodging."

We didn't argue with the sheriff who was rescuing us and climbed into his jeep. He dropped us off at a local motel with an attached restaurant. The sheriff instructed the guys to leave the keys in the car and claim it after the snow plows went through the next morning. The sheriff assured them that nobody was going to steal a car stranded in one of the worst blizzards in recent memory. Sis and I rented a room and then headed to the restaurant which was ready to close. They had a little turkey and dressing left, but no cranberries or mashed potatoes or my favorite, green bean casserole. They didn't charge us for the incomplete meal. I think the owners felt sorry for us because we looked pathetic. We called Cindy, to say that we would not be coming until the next day. We asked, "Do you think we could still get to New York City?"

She said, "Sure. You have to get here first!" We discussed what we wanted to see in New York. Cindy suggested we take the train to Grand Central Station, see Times Square, Central Park and the Empire State Building. We considered seeing a play on 42nd Street or visiting the Metropolitan Museum of Art, but, with only a day in the city and so little money, we opted for free activities.

The next morning, we retrieved the car and were on our way. We arrived in Allentown later in the day on Friday. As planned, we got up early the next morning and caught the train into the city. It was a whirl-wind day but we loved it. We stood in Grand Central Station, staring at its beauty and grandeur. We walked through Central Park, amazed at all the people enjoying it on such a cold, damp, snowy day. My favorite part about being in New York was watching people; people were everywhere. We ran around all day, ate the sandwiches our friend's mom had made for us, and caught the last train back to Allentown late that evening. The next morning we met the two guys and drove straight through to Chicago. I woke up tired but ready to teach the next morning.

In early December my old Iowa teacher boyfriend called to say both of his parents had been killed in a car accident. He asked me to come to be with him during the wake/funeral. How could I say no? I couldn't imagine how difficult it would be to lose both your parents so tragically. I drove to Iowa and he picked me up at my Mom's house. I spent the next three days with him and his family. I found myself crying uncon-trollably at his parents' service. This was so unusual for me because I hadn't cried in a long time. My heart was broken, for him and his family. During those three days, his sisters asked me if I was in love with their brother. I said I wasn't sure what that meant. They assured me that I would know when it happened. After the funeral, he drove me back to my Mom's house, and on the way he told me how much he still loved me. He assumed I loved him because I agreed to be with him during this tragedy. I told him I came to be with him because I was his friend, not his girlfriend, that I had moved to Chicago and planned to stay there. I didn't tell him that I was lonely, isolated and desperately wanting to be in a relationship. I knew my story would not help him. I did know for sure that this man was not the man I wanted to be with for the rest of my life. I had so much more to learn and experience before I could commit to a serious relationship.

It was a very cold December in Illinois. I was feeling especially lonely. My roommate, Ellen, talked to her boyfriend every night, and in between, they wrote love letters. I was happy for her, happy she was in love, but wanted to be happy myself. I was tired of being alone, even if I wasn't sure about being in a relationship. One night I had a thought that put me back in touch with something I realized during our trip to New York: I must be clear about what I want and then release it to the Universe so it could come to me.

That thought changed everything—I needed to have a clear picture about the person I wanted to meet, in order to recognize him when he showed up. I made a list of the ideal qualities I wanted in a partner. Even though I had felt finished with God when I left the convent, I noticed that whenever I got desperate, I prayed. Now I asked God for help in finding a partner. I looked at my list daily, and then one day, out of the blue, I heard a voice in my head, *You already know the guy you will be with.* I smiled and answered back, "Sure!" The truth was that I hardly knew any men. There was only one male teacher at our school; he was engaged. I had never even talked to him.

There was a guy in the downstairs apartment we talked with whenever Ellen and I met him in the hallway. He had a PhD and was a professor at the University of Illinois in De Kalb. He started to hang out at our apartment, asking us to braid his afro. Both Ellen and I did this for him. One night he asked me to come back to his apartment. (He knew my roommate was engaged.) I was curious about a lot of things. I wanted to see his apartment, but I was also curious about sex. I thought he might want to kiss me or possibly do a little necking.

He had a lot more planned for that night. I was totally unprepared for what happened. He showed me around his apartment, and we ended up on a sheepskin rug on the floor in the middle of the living room. We kissed. I immediately felt like I needed to stop. I pulled away. When he started to take off my clothes, I said I needed to leave. He said emphatically, "Oh, no you don't. You are not going anywhere. You started this and now we are going to finish it." He wouldn't let me go. He grabbed me so hard that I didn't feel I could escape. He finished taking off my clothes as well as his own. He raped me. The penetration was the most painful part. After he was finished, he told me to come into his bedroom to get some sleep. He said he had to teach a class the next morning and he needed sleep!

I was so traumatized that I lay there on his bed as stiff as a board not able to breathe. I kept listening to his breathing. When I was sure he was asleep, I finally got the courage to leave and snuck out of his apartment. I was shaking and totally devastated and shamed by what had happened. My roommate was asleep when I got back upstairs. I decided that I would not tell anyone about what happened. I was convinced it was my fault. What had I done or said to make him think that I was interested in having sex with him? My fatal fault: I was curious about him because he was articulate, educated and a university professor.

I blamed myself. Why didn't I scream? Why didn't I try to escape? Why didn't I try to fight him off? Was I too stupid to know he had other intentions? Why did I trust this man? What did I do wrong to end up being abused this way? I never thought I would lose my virginity in such a violent, non-loving situation, where I was forced to have sex with someone I barely knew and certainly didn't love. I could not sleep and felt too ashamed to even tell Ellen. For days I walked around in a fog, feeling dirty and used. How could this happen to me?

My biggest worry was that I might be pregnant. One evening I arrived home at the same time as this guy. We parked next to each other and entered the building at the same time. I told him that I had not gotten my period. He said, "Don't worry. You are not pregnant. I have had sex with lots of women and have never gotten anyone pregnant." He assured me that I would be fine. How could I be fine? This one event would impact the rest of my life! How could I carry on with my life and trust men? The pain of being raped felt like the worst kind of pain because of the shame; I couldn't talk to anyone about it. I buried that shame and guilt.

Recently, on the front page of *The Denver Post*, the headline read, "Not ashamed." It was the story of a University of Colorado sexual assault survivor who was willing to reveal her identity and speak out to help others. She said speaking out helped her to take back the control she felt she lost when she was raped. This woman's courage gave me the courage to write about my own sexual assault. She said, "If it helps another person to not feel ashamed, that's all I want." It helped me.

After all these years, here is what I know is true about this painful event. I was young and I had no skills to fight off a large, imposing older man. I did not seek professional help to deal with this painful event. All my life, I had always done what I was told. I had been socialized to put up and shut up, no matter what was happening. My mother's wise counsel did not help me: "You made this bed, now you must lie in it." Recently I read an article that stated, "You don't have to lie in the bed you made just because you made it that way once." I now know I would fight back with every ounce of my life.

This was a time in my life that I was resilient because I did just keep going on with my life even though I felt deeply wounded. I had the ability to successfully cope on the outside; no one knew what had happened to me. However, I was not so resilient because I was not able to protect myself from the negative inner effect of that stressor. That event haunted me for years.

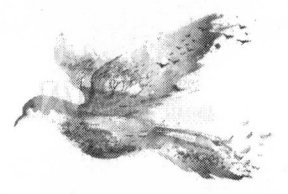

CHAPTER TEN

TOTALLY UNPREPARED, ONCE AGAIN

I spent the holidays in Iowa and returned to Illinois more despondent than ever. My friend and I were sitting in an East Dubuque bar on New Year's Eve 1971. I saw only couples. I wondered: What is going to happen to me? What am I going to do with my life? How am I ever going to meet anyone? I felt such a deep sense of sadness. I had left the convent feeling so optimistic about being in charge of my life, but here I was, thinking I was even more stuck now than in the convent. It was a low point in my life, but I knew the rape had not caused me to reject all men. I believed there were good men available; I was ready to meet one of them.

I had to also face the fact that I was unsettled in my teaching position, even though I had been there only a couple of months. I was sure of one thing. I had to get out of the Catholic school system—poor pay and no benefits. I decided that if I was going to teach, I needed to be in the public school system. That clarity helped propel me into the next phase of my life, although I didn't realize it. At that point it looked like I was floundering and in the midst of another bad decision.

Ellen was worried about me when I returned after the holidays. She could tell I wasn't happy and decided to plan a party for my 26th birthday, inviting all of our convent friends living in the Chicago area. She invited a few men we knew, including Luke, the young guy who taught with us and was recently engaged to a young woman named Cindy. I asked Ellen why she had invited him; she said that he was nice, and we needed some guys at the party. I secretly thought it wasn't too helpful to invite men who were already attached.

At the party, Luke and I talked, mostly about Chicago. I told him how much I loved the city. He revealed that he had taught on the south side of Chicago and knew the city well. He asked me if I wanted to go into the city with him. I said yes, but I was confused. Was he asking me out? Why ask me out if he was engaged? He called the next day to say he got tickets for a play at the Pheasant Run Dinner Theatre. I wasn't really excited about going out with him, because I didn't think he was available, but decided to go because I needed something to do. I was still worried about being pregnant, so when he called, I hesitated at first, but decided to go because I would have an evening away from my worries.

When Luke knocked on my apartment door that next Friday night, I was blown away. He looked so cute in his blue turtleneck sweater and black pants (Cindy had given him new clothes for Christmas). I wore my tall black boots, a short black skirt and blue sweater (also a Christmas present). At this point, I didn't have many clothes; I had at least given away all the clothes donated by my convent friend's mom. Luke drove an old Volkswagen that had to be pushed to start it. I suggested that we drive my new Vega into the city.

We talked nonstop and, at one point, I asked, "Where have you been? I have been looking for you my whole life." He seemed to understand and comforted me in a way that I had never experienced before. I wanted to know why he had asked me out when he was engaged. He said Cindy suggested they both date other people, to make sure they were perfect for each other; he was merely following her instructions. He also revealed that he had spent five years in the Christian Brothers. The Christian Brothers were a Catholic religious community whose main focus was the education of youth. He had left two years ago, the same time I had left the convent, and was trying to make his way in the world. He had attended a Christian Brothers high school and wanted to become a teacher; he thought he had to join the Order in order to accomplish that dream. After deciding to leave because he felt disenchanted with the Catholic Church, he felt, like me, that he had wasted five years of his life. We had so much in common.

Ellen was away with her fiancee for the weekend that we had our date. When she returned on Sunday night, I told her that I had fallen in love with Luke and wanted to marry him. She was shocked! She politely reminded me that he was engaged. I said it didn't matter. I felt this truth with my whole being. I was convinced that I would eventually marry him because the very qualities I admired in Luke were all on the list I had created only a few months before. I knew deep in my soul that Luke was the answer to all my imagining of what a future husband would be like.

A couple of weeks later, Luke and I decided to visit a psychic he knew from his job at the Hispanic Community Center. We asked to have separate readings. Luke went first. When it was my turn, I told her that I was in love with this man and wanted to be with him. She said I would need to be very patient. He needed time to get out of his current relationship which was not good for him. After we left the psychic, we compared cursory notes, but didn't reveal the details of our experiences. After that, I didn't see Luke again for two months. He called every once in a while from a pay phone. He had no money because he no longer taught at my school. He had only been working part time, teaching English to students from Mexico. However, during Christmas vacation, the Hispanic families visited their families in Mexico, and few of them returned, so Luke was let go.

During these "pay phone talks" Luke told me about Cindy. He told me about their arguments. I ended every conversation with the same wisdom: "YOU DESERVE BETTER." He said he couldn't leave her because her mother was dying of cancer. He needed to stay with her until after her mom's death which was imminent. I was totally patient during this period because the psychic told me to give him lots of space and time to heal.

At the end of January, both Ellen and I decided that we needed a second job. She needed money because she and her fiancee planned to get married. She didn't want to go out to the bars, so working in the evenings seemed a good solution for both of us. She began working in a department store as a store detective, and I applied in the shoe department at the same store. I was not interested in dating anyone else; I was patiently waiting for the love of my life to be free.

The months went by and Ellen decided to marry her fiancee over spring break. Either I would have to move out or she would move to another place with her new husband. Since I knew I couldn't afford the rented furniture and the apartment by myself, I agreed to look for another place. I didn't have a clue about where to go. I considered asking a couple of the married teachers to rent a room in their homes. Both unmarried teachers at school were now engaged and busy creating their own lives. Neither option seemed workable.

The only person I could think to ask was Luke. He had started calling more often, so I knew that Cindy's mom had passed away and he was no longer engaged. The next time he called, I asked him if it might be possible for me to live with him for the last six weeks of the school year. As soon as school was out, I planned to move to Oak Park, near downtown Chicago, with my high school friend and to work for the summer at a Volkswagen dealership on North Avenue. He said that I should first come to see if this was a place I wanted to live. He didn't seem to understand that I really couldn't be choosy. His apartment was closer to school but had only one bedroom—and nothing in the refrigerator but a six-pack of Lipton ice tea. I figured I could sleep on the couch for six weeks and maybe help him clean up his neglected apartment. We agreed that I would pay half the rent, which would help him a lot. He was looking for work and had applied for a job as an interpreter at an Illinois state employment office. If he got that job, he too would have to move.

Now that I had a place to stay, I relaxed—and planned another travel adventure! My friend, Colleen, in the middle of planning a summer wedding, wanted to visit Fort Lauderdale one last time before she got married. She went there every year during college, so she knew it well and loved the beach. I was thrilled with this offer; Fort Lauderdale was one of the experiences I had missed while in the convent.

Once again, I found myself chatting with two guys in my apartment building. They mentioned that they were driving to Florida for spring break. I asked if we could go too if we helped pay for gas. I was no longer willing to stand on the Expressway with a sign saying "Fort Lauderdale." It was illegal at that time to hitch in the States and definitely not safe. I had already moved my things into Luke's apartment, and it seemed a good idea to be gone as much as possible.

Luke was there when the guys came to pick up Colleen and me. He asked them all kinds of questions and acted very protective of me. When we got to the car, Colleen said, "What was that all about?" I told her, "I think he likes me and is worried about me taking off with some guys we don't even know." I was secretly happy that someone seemed to be concerned about my safety and well being.

Our trip from Illinois to Florida took many hours; my butt hurt. I wanted to complain, but we were merely passengers in two strangers' car. We had no say about where we were going or when we would stop. We stopped only long enough to get gas and use the bathroom. They wanted to make it to Atlanta, Georgia, where one guy's aunt and uncle lived. It was a ten-and-a-half-hour drive. We arrived there in the middle of the night and Colleen and I got a couch turned into a bed in the living room. Exhausted, we crashed as soon as we lay down. We dreamed of being in Florida, where we could walk the hot, sandy beaches, enjoy the warm weather and take a swim in the motel pool. Colleen had made reservations at the place where she always stayed.

We were up early the next morning, had a delicious breakfast and said "goodbye and thank you" to the guy's aunt. We were ready for the second leg of our journey, another nine hours. We arrived in Fort Lauderdale late the second day. The guys dropped us at our motel, and we agreed to meet them at the end of the week right where they dropped us off.

Immediately we put on shorts and halter tops and headed to the beach. I had never seen the ocean. My breath was barely audible as I took in the beauty and the vastness of the ocean for the first time. I was surprised that I felt so fearful; the wind was blowing hard, it was loud and the waves were high. I had always imagined it would be relaxing to be by the ocean, but the noise made me tense and unsettled. I was grateful that it was too late to go in the water.

College kids were everywhere on the beach—girls in bikinis, playing volleyball and laying out and riding up and down the strip. They were so mellow and having tons of fun. This scene made me feel old; we were no longer college kids. We were exhausted after the long drive, so we headed back to our motel for a good night's sleep. The next day we slept in and then had breakfast at Colleen's favorite breakfast place. On the way back to our hotel we bought food for a picnic and headed to the beach.

We both wanted a "tan" so we spent the entire day laying in the sun. The ocean was calmer, so I ventured into the water a couple of times to cool off. I was not used to sand, and didn't like how it stuck to my body. After a full day at the beach, we headed back to our motel. Colleen didn't feel good; she thought we might had gotten too much sun! I am all Irish and she was Polish. Both of us started the morning lily white. Before long we were both beet red! Colleen got burned the worst. As the evening wore on, she was in so much pain, she could barely move. We finally trekked to a drug store to ask the pharmacist what we could purchase to help with our burns. He said, "You kids are all alike.... You just don't take it slow, so you get burned and then you have to spend the rest of the week out of the sun."

And that is exactly what happened to us. We were too miserable to go back to the beach for the rest of the week. We went out only in the evenings. Colleen was engaged so she didn't mind retiring early. I was busy thinking about how I might create a life with Luke. I longed to get to know him, but I needed to remain disinterested and aloof. He needed time to heal after his broken engagement. During our stay in Florida, all I did was think about him and how much I wanted to be with him.

At the end of the week, I flew to Iowa to be in Ellen's wedding. I had a "buddy pass" from Colleen's sister who worked for an airline. It was the early 70s and you didn't have to show an ID to get on a plane, so I simply flew under her sister's name.

Ellen ordered pink-flowered bridesmaid dresses for me and her two sisters. Some of our teaching friends saw red flags about her marriage from the beginning, and her fiancee did nothing to endear himself to us. He was a self-described "spoiled Air Force brat." He had traveled the world with his parents, his dad being a Colonel in the Air Force. When we met his dad before the wedding, he informed us that we must address him as "Colonel Castralie." However, the wedding was beautiful, and we wished the happy couple the best as they left for a week-long honeymoon.

I visited with my Mom after the wedding. I mentioned that I had moved to a small apartment until the end of the school year, but I did not tell her that my roommate was a guy; I knew she would be very upset about that.

When I returned from Iowa, Luke seemed happy to see me. We got groceries, and I started to clean his apartment. It was a very sweet six weeks, and I said "thank you" to God everyday for helping me find this special person. I loved talking to him; we talked non-stop whenever we were together. He had found temporary work at a place called Berlinski's, picking up discarded metal pieces to bring to a junk yard. He did whatever he could to earn money while he waited for a more lucrative position in state government. After only two weeks in the apartment, the landlord, who lived downstairs, asked if I was living there. Luke explained that I needed a place to stay for only six weeks. He immediately ordered Luke to move out. They were a strict Catholic family and didn't approve of unmarried couples living together. We were truly just getting to know each other, but they felt their children would get the wrong message.

So we began the search for another place to live. It was just four weeks before I planned to move to Chicago, and Luke would be moving as well. He had accepted a position with the State of Illinois as a Spanish-speaking interpreter. A few blocks away from our old apartment, we found a tiny, cheap, seedy-looking place attached to a main house that we could rent by the month. It was furnished, which we needed badly since neither of us had furniture. We had been there one week when I got a call from my Mom, "I want to come for a visit! I haven't seen you in a long time." She had not visited me once since I left the convent. She might have felt bad that I was living alone in a dinky apartment and needed company. That was the farthest thing from what I needed at the time!

Her impending visit necessitated lots of confessions to Luke. I had to tell him all about my family, the struggles I had with my Mom, and how I grew up in poverty. He confessed that he was estranged from his family and hadn't spoken to his parents for a year. This came as a shock to me because he had previously shared pictures of his nine siblings and his parents. I was horrified! His parents must be very worried about him. We both agreed that our parents would surely disown us if they found us living together. I knew my Mom was fragile and had gone through so much, with me entering then leaving the convent and my sister's divorce. What should we do? Luke suggested that he move to the YMCA for the weekend while she visited.

He loaded his belongings into his car and left for the weekend at the YMCA. I missed him and, during my Mom's visit, found myself watching every word I said so I wouldn't reveal that I was living with Luke or that I had fallen in love with him. Being away from him for the weekend made me realize how much I loved being with him; I wondered what would happen when we went our separate ways in a couple of weeks.

I talked to Luke about reconnecting with his parents. He decided to visit them over Memorial Day weekend, before he started his new job. When he asked if I wanted to go with him, I was shocked. I felt I didn't know him well enough to visit his parents, but I agreed. He did warn me that he had a big Catholic family and there would be lots of little kids; I worried about keeping the names of his nine siblings straight.

His father picked us up at the airport; he was a handsome man with a lot of personality. He was an executive for General Motors, in charge of East Coast fleet sales. Luke's parents lived in a large, beautiful new home facing Valley Forge State Park, with five newer cars out front. All of his older brothers inherited a car each time their father finished driving it for the required six months. The first time I was alone with Luke, I whispered to him angrily, "Why didn't you tell me about your family's wealth?" We both were living on the edge of poverty, so it shocked me to find his family so wealthy. He didn't answer me. He wasn't focused on their wealth, only the pain he felt being with his parents. I believed he had a great life growing up: two parents, his mother at home taking care of the children, and an abundant income to care for ten children! That was my dream life!

Luke had left the Christian Brothers after graduation, and he returned to live with his parents in Philadelphia. His parents were busy raising the other eight children; the last thing they needed was for their twenty-three year-old son to leave his religious vocation, and "lie on the couch drinking beer." He was processing the past five years, which he believed he wasted as a Christian Brother, but this was not the place to do that. They wanted him to get a job NOW and get on with his life. They were strict Catholics and felt sad that their son left religious life. Their first-born son had gone to a seminary but had left the year before, a double blow to his parents who loved having a religious vocation in their family. One night

Luke's parents said something hurtful, so he left, angrily, in the middle of the night, driving his '57 Chevy, with no working windshield wipers, through a driving rain storm, back to the Chicago area. His parents, busy with raising their younger children, were not able to help Luke with his difficult transition. He seemed as alone as I was in my life.

His parents were happy to see him during our visit and to learn that he had a wonderful new girlfriend—me! They did not like the woman he was engaged to previously. They credited me with Luke reestablishing contact with them, and that first night his mom put a rose on the night stand by my bed and asked me if I planned to marry her son. I told her that I didn't know him well enough to even think about that; I liked him a lot, but we had just started dating. Encouragingly, she said, "If my son is bringing you home, he is serious about you."

I had been nervous about meeting his family, but it was fun watching his siblings and hanging out in their beautiful home. His mom was a great cook; she liked to be in the kitchen alone, so we were free to spend time in the park and then sit down together in the evenings to her wonderfully cooked meals. She believed you could have a beautiful, orderly "Good Housekeeping" home even if you had ten children.

My sister Colleen was visiting her boyfriend's family in the Washington, DC area at the same time we were in Philly, so they drove up to meet us. I was happy to have my sister meet Luke and his family. They stayed only a couple of hours, but I loved that they came.

Luke and I talked all the way back to O'Hare Airport. I couldn't understand how he could have become so upset with his parents. I loved and envied his family and believed he had the perfect family.

We arrived home on Sunday night, and the very next day I packed my things, said goodbye to Luke and drove to Oak Park to live with my friend, Marian. The next day I began working as a cashier at a Volkswagen dealership. Luke was starting his new job as an interpreter for the state employment office. We had made no plans for the future, so I just said, "Goodbye. I hope you like your new place and your job." He needed to get settled into his new job and his new apartment, and I needed to get settled in Oak Park with my friends. The month of June went by slowly for me. I spoke with Luke only a few times over the phone. At work everyday, I wondered what would happen to us. I was trying to be patient as the psychic had counseled me to do.

The long-time secretary at the dealership often talked to me while we worked. I told her about Luke. She was older and wiser, and her words of wisdom to me were to trust that things would work out. The biggest impact she had on me, however, was her great philosophy of life. She was proud of how she had raised her children; she believed she did her best and was NOT going to blame herself for the choices her children made. That was refreshing. My mother always worried and fretted about every decision I made.

On July 1, 1972, Luke called to invite me to go camping with him over the Fourth of July holiday. We planned to drive to Madison, Wisconsin. I was excited to hear from him, and camping sounded fun. Neither of us had any camping equipment, but that didn't matter. He spread a couple of old blankets in a pasture halfway between Chicago and Madison, and we enjoyed the hot, muggy midwestern night with a full moon. We were happy to be together for the weekend. When the sun came up, we got back in my car and continued on to Madison. We enjoyed exploring the city and shopping. Luke bought me a new outfit; it looked great on me—a blue and green Irish-plaid short skirt, a white blouse and a cute matching plaid vest. No one had ever bought me a brand new outfit. I was thrilled. That night I wore it to dinner at a fancy Italian restaurant. During dinner Luke and I talked about what we were going to do with our lives. I said I wanted to be together. He said he did too. We agreed: Our only choice was to get married! (We knew that neither of our families would tolerate us living together.) So we decided to get married in two weeks. Why wait? We called my Mom first. I knew she would not be happy with my decision, and she wasn't. I figured we should just do what we wanted because she would never be happy. She had not been happy with any of my decisions—to enter the convent, to leave or now to marry the man I loved.

Luke's parents sounded excited, but a bit hesitant, because they still had seven children at home, but they did promise to drive to Chicago for our wedding. My Mom called me every night for the two weeks before the wedding, begging me not to go through with marrying Luke. She argued, "You used to be so sensible. What has happened to you? Why are you doing this?" With every call she asked me if I had changed my mind. I kept telling her that I was NOT going to change my mind.

She did agree to make my wedding dress, so I flew to Iowa to pick out a pattern and fabric. Luke took me to the airport but told me that he wanted to be with me, so he bought a ticket and got on the plane too. I thought it was the sweetest thing. When Mom picked us up at the airport, she was upset to see Luke. I am sure she wanted to have me alone so she could "talk some sense into me!"

That weekend Luke unwittingly sealed his fate with my Mom. He confessed he had only $79.00 in his checking account and had spent his last money flying to Iowa. That revelation was the last straw. Mom wanted me to marry a man with money. She often said, "It's just as easy to marry a rich man as a poor one." It was clear that Luke had no money. She even asked me, "Do you know that he has no money?" I told her that we didn't need money; I was marrying Luke because I loved him, not because of how much money he did or didn't have.

That night we invited Mom to dinner to celebrate our brief engagement. She finally agreed to go with us, but first, from her bedroom closet, she amazingly unearthed a bottle of Mogen David wine. I had never seen her drink a glass of wine or any other alcoholic beverage. She carefully washed three wine glasses hidden on the top shelf of the kitchen cabinets. She poured the wine, and then Luke made a toast. Luke and I were celebrating the beginning of our lives together, but my Mom was drinking this glass of wine to drown her sorrow. Her body and her face told us that she couldn't be more distressed if she had heard that one of her children was dead. When Luke made the toast, she murmured something like, "I guess so."

We went shopping the next morning for fabric for my wedding dress. I had no idea what I wanted; I had never imagined what a wedding dress might look like because I never thought I would get married. At first, it was like old times, the two of us together in the fabric store, my mother getting upset at me because I didn't know what I wanted. I finally said I wanted an empire waist dress. Then she exclaimed: "YOU MUST BE PREGNANT!" I assured her that I wasn't; I just liked that style. She scowled at me and said she would have my dress ready in two weeks. At that moment I wished I could go to the attic and choose a dress from a rack, like I did when I was in the convent, becoming a bride of Christ.

During those two weeks we called our families and friends to invite them to our ceremony. We said, "No gifts, just bring a dish to share." Luke arranged for a priest from Joliet who served the migrant-worker community to marry us. He knew the priest from his volunteer work at the Joliet Spanish Center. We decided to compose our own wedding vows and chose the Catholic chapel near the school where we had both taught as the ceremony's location.

Needless to say, everyone we called was surprised about our marriage plans. My high school friend, Marian, with whom I lived with in Oak Park, seemed the most distressed. She was convinced I was bribed. She believed it was out of character for me to run off and marry anyone! (It was 1972 and we were strong women's liberation sisters.) I told her I was making this decision freely and was truly in love with Luke. She asked, "How do you know if you are in love?"

I wasn't sure how to answer that question, but I told her I had to follow my heart, even though it was hard for everyone around me to understand. Somewhere inside me, I found the wisdom to know that true love is proven over a lifetime, and I trusted Luke enough to believe we could and would stay together for a lifetime. During those two weeks, we rented an apartment on the third floor of an old house halfway between our places of employment. I would go back to teaching, and he would continue to work as a Bilingual Employment Interviewer at the Illinois State Employment Service.

We were both committed to creating wedding rings that would last our entire lifetime together. Luke found J.J. Silversmith on State Street in downtown Chicago; the silversmith said he could make our rings in two weeks if we knew what we wanted. Luke found a Bible quote he loved: "Let us not love in words, but in truth and in deed." 1 John 3:18. He asked a rabbi at the University of Chicago to translate that quote into Hebrew and we took the translation to the silversmith. We were able to pick up the rings the day before the wedding. They fit perfectly. The silversmith said he would never make a wedding ring for someone who planned to get divorced. We assured him that we were committed to staying married for our whole lives.

I didn't know who to ask to be my maid of honor. I wasn't close to my sisters, and although there were a number of friends I could have asked,

I didn't know how to choose just one person. I finally decided on Sis because I felt indebted to her for making my European dream come true. She accepted and said she had a dress she could wear. I had no color scheme or flowers, so that worked perfectly. I planned to ask my brother to take pictures at the wedding, but he didn't remember me asking him and I am not sure I did. This detail had fallen through the cracks in our two-week rush to the altar. There was no official photographer at our wedding.

The morning of the wedding, we arrived late at the church. The guests had already gone into the chapel. I did not have an opportunity to introduce my Mom to Luke's parents before the wedding. I got scared when I walked up the steps of the church, and I started to shake when I realized that everyone was already waiting inside for us. Luke had to literally pull me into the building. I kept saying to him, "I can't go in there now." Luke kept encouraging me, but finally he said, "Okay, I am going down the aisle by myself." I immediately grabbed his arm and walked with him. We walked down the aisle together and stood on the first step of the altar right in front of my Mom. The priest began the Mass. Luke's younger brother, Jeff, played the guitar and sang a couple of songs during the service.

We thought a Catholic wedding ceremony would somehow please my Mom and Luke's parents, but at one point during the ceremony, my Mom poked me and said, "I thought you were getting married in the Catholic Church." This was a small chapel, unlike the large church my Mom attended. I ignored her, but I heard her all during the ceremony, clicking her tongue to the roof of her mouth and making a "ttsss" sound. During the homily, Father Martin stated that there was no such thing as a one-time commitment. "To make a marriage work for a lifetime, you must make a daily commitment to each other and be willing to stay together when things get tough, which will certainly happen." I loved that he said that; but when we walked out of the chapel after the service, my Mom followed us out, and the first thing she said (in a very harsh voice, slowly enunciating each word) was: "Where is that priest?" She did not congratulate us, just told us she was angry about what the priest said. She asked us, "Why would he say there is no such thing as a one-time commitment?" I hoped that she would not find him, but I knew he would be at the reception.

We had not ordered a wedding cake because one of Luke's friends had a bakery in Chicago and had offered to make a cake. That was a great idea, except that the cake he made was an ICE CREAM wedding cake! An ice cream cake in the first week of August in hot, humid Illinois was NOT a great idea. Right after the ceremony, his panicked friend asked Luke to show him where we were going to have the reception. Luke jumped in the car with his friend and took him to the reception site. After I spoke to everyone, I realized that all the guests had already left for the reception, even Luke. I asked Sis for a ride.

When I arrived at the reception, I realized a lot was already happening. I started to welcome everyone and thank them for coming. Soon I was told that my Mom was crying in the bathroom. I went into the bathroom, but she did not even speak to me, so I left immediately. She was upset for a number of reasons. I believed that the main reason was she had no time to get to know Luke or get used to the fact that I was getting married. She still needed me, and now I was truly leaving her. She was distraught and needed her sister, Agnes, to talk to, but her sister was not there to comfort her. Agnes was in the middle of her own pain. She and her husband had just driven in from Iowa, after being up all night with their daughter who had given birth to her baby girl. Their daughter had already decided to give her up for adoption because the father had left her. My favorite aunt and uncle were distraught. I tried to comfort them. What could I say to console them in face of the fact that they would never get to know their first grandchild? Their hearts were heavy.

Right after I talked to my aunt and uncle, I saw my former roommate, Ellen, who had married during spring break. She was dealing with her recalcitrant husband. They had brought a stereo to play music during the reception; he got mad at one point and decided to leave the reception, so he dismantled his stereo system halfway through the reception and they disappeared. Suddenly, we had no music.

I found out later that the biggest event impacting our wedding day actually happened the day before. My older sister had stopped in Iowa on the way to our wedding and announced that she was divorcing her husband. The thought of it: How could my marriage ever work if my sister, who had a proper courtship and marriage to a wonderful man with a bright future, couldn't make it work? It turned out to be just one of the reasons my Mom spent most of the reception in the bathroom, crying.

The wedding reception finally ended, and my Mom was getting ready to drive back to Iowa with a couple of my siblings. She looked at the mess that needed to be cleaned up after the reception and said, "This is what you deserve....You haven't done anything else the right way, so you might as well clean up after your own reception." Then she walked out of the reception hall with my siblings.

Right after that, I found Luke's mom, who was equally upset. She declared, "Your mom made me so upset." Luke's parents and family walked out too. Before they left, we made a quick plan to see them in the morning for breakfast, before they made their long journey back to the East Coast with their children.

Luke and I stood there in disbelief! Luke hugged me tight and assured me, "This is just one day in our lives; we have the rest of our lives to create together." I vowed that I would never speak to my Mom again. My new husband said, "You don't have to."

I was in shock for a couple of days after the wedding whenever I thought about all that happened. I could not make my mother happy about the man I chose to marry, but I was still invested in trying. After the wedding, Luke reminded me many times of this truth. Luke was so patient with me. He assured me that I didn't have to see my Mom if I didn't want to, that we should focus on our lives now that we were married.

We did not go on a honeymoon. This made me sad, but I knew that Luke could get only two days off work. We used those two days to clean the hall, return plates and trays, and open the few wedding presents we received.

We found a rental apartment, the former servants' quarters on the third floor of a majestic old house in Plainfield, Illinois. This quaint little town was located halfway between the two cities where Luke and I worked. Luke's friends from the Spanish Center, where he had worked before I met him, gave us a used bed before our wedding. We bought a sectional couch and card table at an auction house that Luke passed every day on his way to work. A sectional couch was all we could get up the narrow and winding stairs to the third floor. (I think the auction house would have actually given us the green brocaded couch, but my husband offered them $15.00.) It was worn and dirty and we planned to get a blanket to tuck around the cushions. We bought a used dresser for our bedroom. The bedroom had a small closet, more than adequate because neither of us had many clothes. We had more books than anything else, so we built a traditional "poor student's" bookcase out of wooden boards and cinder blocks to set next to the dirty couch in the living room.

The nights were wonderfully fun as we settled into our third-floor apartment. We didn't know anyone in town, but we lived one block from the main street so we could walk everywhere. We had each other and that was all we needed. During that first year, we both worked hard at our jobs all day and then crashed at night. Luke found an old bike, took it completely apart, cleaned it and put it back together so it looked brand new. On the weekends we went for drives in the country around Plainfield. We talked about everything; we spent that first year getting to know each other.

There was so much I didn't know about this man, but what I did know, I loved. I learned quickly that he had mechanical talent. He was confident, calm and patient. Very little upset him. He believed he could do or fix anything. I was convinced that I was the luckiest woman in the world. Had life ever been this good to me? Never. I believed I would be happy for the rest of my life. We acted like two young kids in love and we were.

Months went by with no word from my Mom. I refused to call her. Then one day in the middle of November, I got a call, asking if I had found the money she gave me for our wedding. I said that we had used it to pay the priest and other wedding expenses. We talked for a while. Her bad behavior at our wedding was never discussed.

At some point in our conversation, I asked my Mom what she was going to do for Thanksgiving. She said nobody was coming home, so I invited her to spend it with us. She accepted. Luke suggested she catch the train into Chicago where we would pick her up at the closest station. I was nervous about this visit because I still felt angry with her about the wedding, and I knew she didn't like Luke. Luke said that I could either continue to hold a grudge or forgive her; she was doing the best she could. He was very good at humoring her and protecting me from her unhappiness. She was not cruel to me when he was around.

My Mom arrived the Wednesday before Thanksgiving. She looked tense and unhappy. I knew she was still upset that I had married Luke, but I hoped she would get over it once she saw how happy we were together.

In preparation for the holiday meal, my first as a new bride, I placed the frozen turkey in the attic to thaw. The attic was next to the kitchen and much cooler than the rest of the apartment. When my Mom found out how I thawed the turkey, she was appalled. She accused us of trying to poison her, certain we would all get sick and die from tainted turkey. She refused to eat it, and the three of us sat there in silence for the entire meal.

Luke broke the silence by pretending to be sick. He fell off his chair onto the floor, grabbing his stomach, and yelled, "Help me. I am sick! I've been poisoned! Help me! Get me to a hospital. Quick!"

All this silliness did not prompt my Mom to crack a smile. I tried to reason with her. We were both angry. The spoiled turkey was just an excuse. I was devastated by her negativity, and by the time we took her to the train station to return to Iowa, I was sure I would never speak to her again. I swore I would not go to Iowa at Christmas.

I would like to report that indeed we did not go to Iowa for Christmas—but that would be a lie. We did go to Iowa for Christmas. Most of my siblings were there with their partners, so I was able to blend in with the holiday events, and there were no major altercations with my Mom.

We returned to Illinois for New Year's Eve, 1974. My husband and I spent a wonderful New Year's Eve alone. It was a freezing cold, snowy night. He kept insisting that we run outside naked at the stroke of midnight. (He was teasing; I had yet to realize how much he liked to tease me and that I shouldn't believe everything he said.) Looking out the frosted window at the falling snow, I tried to imagine myself out there—without any clothes on. Finally, he admitted that he was just kidding. We climbed into our warm bed, and I believe our darling first daughter was conceived that night.

Our first year together flew by as we got to know each other. I was in heaven, living with this man that I loved so much. When I wasn't busy, I found myself writing his name over and over.

We enjoyed reading together. One of the books I read was the *Autobiography of a Yogi* by Paramahansa Yoganandya. We discussed the ideas in the book and decided to attend a Sunday morning Meditation Group of the Self Realization Fellowship, started by Yoganandya's followers in downtown Chicago. The group was composed of members of the Self-Realization Fellowship founded by Yoganandya. His followers wanted to learn to love everyone unconditionally and to live in harmony with all people. One Sunday morning, I heard this statement: "Everything else can wait, but your search for God cannot wait." I knew I wanted to begin a new search for God. We loved these treks to downtown Chicago on Sunday mornings. We wanted a new way to think about God, and this path gave us a new perspective. It was not about sin and hell, but love.

At that same time, Luke started reading the works of Aerobindo and studying ideas promoted by the Theosophical Society, based in Wheaton, Illinois. This society focused on the realization of the oneness of all life. Followers were encouraged to do an independent spiritual search. Luke shared what he learned with me, and we used those ideas to make sense of our strict Catholic upbringings and our five years in religious life. We were searching for another way of thinking about and understanding God.

We celebrated our first anniversary. I felt happy and relieved to celebrate our first year together. I had taken vows to marry Christ, but I had broken them when things got difficult. I worried I might do the same with Luke. We went out to dinner and Luke gave me a sewing machine in a beautiful oak cabinet. It was such a great gift. So much was unsettled in our lives, but we were together and believed we could figure things out as we went along.

Janice's parents during their ten-year engagement.

Official wedding portrait of Janice's parents.

Janice with her father and older sister Shirley.

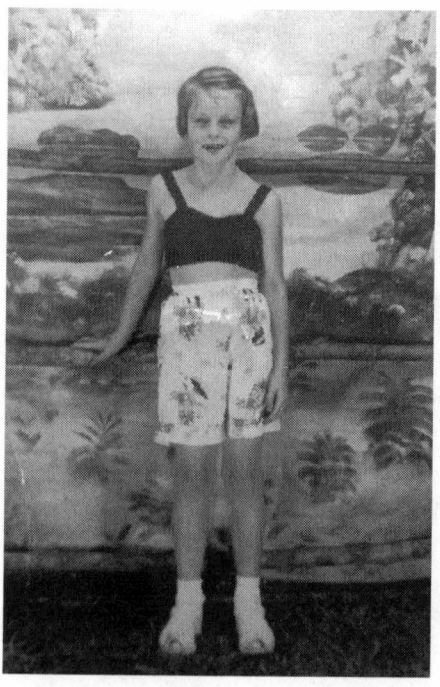

Janice, age 7, immediately after her father's death.

Janice, age 8, wearing her first "store-bought" dress.

St. Mary's Orphanage: Janice (in front) holds the tray for May crowning. Her sister, Colleen (second row far left), prepares to make her First Communion.

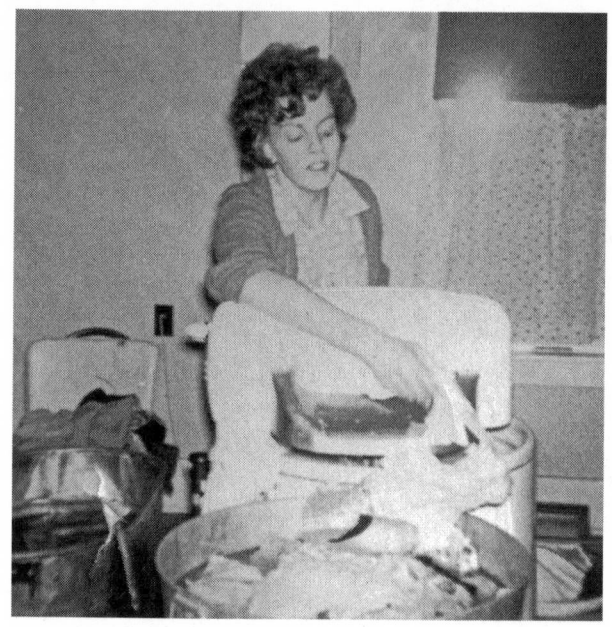

Janice does Saturday laundry in the kitchen of the family home.

Janice and her friend, Marian, at their Convent Farewell Party.

Janice's first visiting day with her family.

Janice dressed in a wedding gown as a bride of Christ,
preparing to receive her habit.

Christmas in Denver: Janice and her mom with Janice's new wig.

Janice and Luke on their wedding day.

Janice and her family celebrate the
purchase of their home in Colorado.

Janice poses with her diplomas at the
Huntington Learning Center.

Luke and Janice celebrate her departure from
CDE to start her coaching business.

Janice's family in 2018.

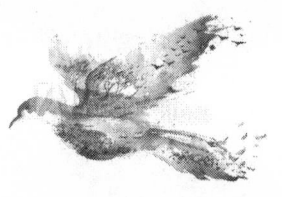

CHAPTER ELEVEN

BECOMING A FAMILY

It became clear that the stressful job of teaching was not something I could continue to do if I wanted to get pregnant. During our first year of marriage, Luke decided he was not happy working at the Illinois State Employment Agency. Looking at his co-workers, who seemed so unhappy and disengaged, he decided he didn't want that life for himself. His co-workers seemed to lack patience, compassion and empathy, and they felt no urgency to help the desperate people in line on the other side of the counter. He concluded, "If I stay there, I will end up like these guys. I want to quit." I didn't argue with him. He had already made up his mind and knew what he was doing. At the same time, I decided I couldn't go back to my teaching job, so I resigned too. With no reason to stay in Plainfield, we decided to move to Aurora at the end of the school year. The plan was for Luke to look for work (not sure what), and I would quit teaching and use my sociology degree to work as a social worker.

Neither of our families said anything about our decision to quit our jobs. Luke's parents were busy raising his younger siblings. My Mom's problems consumed her. Perhaps it was too painful for our parents to pay attention to our lives. Even if they were paying attention, we probably wouldn't have listened to their advice. With neither family nor friends to support us or question our decisions, we were on our own. We were young, foolish and not mature enough to think through the consequences of both quitting our jobs at the same time.

We talked about having a baby, but this frightened me terribly. Before I met Luke, I was sure I never wanted children. I believed the five of us had created so much misery for our Mom that I knew I did not want to repeat that pattern in my own life. However, I also realized that I married a man who LOVED children, so it was a given that we would have children sooner rather than later. Although it terrified me, I believed this was something I could not put off, or I would never want to do it. We gave no consideration to the fact that we had no way to support a baby or ourselves.

I quit my teaching job at the end of May, and Luke quit his well-paying state job within weeks. In Aurora we rented a small, one-bedroom apartment. As soon as we moved our meager belongings into the apartment, we both started looking for work. Luke found a job selling chemicals to hospitals and other big institutions in the Chicago area. He traveled a lot and made very little money. His paycheck varied depending on how successful he was at persuading the buyers to purchase his products. It was frustrating because he often thought he had a sale, but then it fell through. He was not good at sales, something he was to figure out much later.

I found a job as a case manager at a private agency called "The Association for Individual Development." One of the services the agency offered was to deliver sub-contract factory work to disabled people in two nearby counties. I traveled these counties, delivering work to the people on my caseload. A few weeks later, I would return to pick up their completed work. The clients were always anxious for me to pick up their work as they got paid only after I brought their work back to the agency. One of the contracts was with a company that made plastic alphabet letters. My clients glued thousands of small magnets into the slots on the back of the letters. They always wanted more work because they were living on their Social Security Disability checks. The part of the job I loved the most was driving to and from each client's home. It was the first time that I actually had time alone! It gave me time to think and wonder about the new life growing inside me. Yes, I found out I was pregnant a few months after we moved to Aurora. I needed a lot of time to think about how to deal with my irrational fears about having a baby.

I secretly believed I would not get pregnant—because we were too young and unsettled. But that was not to be the case. When I went to my first doctor appointment, the nurses looked at me strangely; it was obvious that they were concerned about something. One of the nurses finally said something to me about not being married. I informed them that I was married to the father of my baby. They had assumed there was no father because I was using my maiden name, unusual at that time. One nurse even remarked, "If you are married, then you should have taken your husband's name." I felt that this was none of her business.

I was extremely nervous about being pregnant but, with all the stress of my teaching job gone, I was able to spend hours thinking of our unborn baby. I was irrational about hospitals and doctors, and had no idea how I would overcome these fears. I spent most of my driving time lost in a dream about the baby growing inside me. Every evening, I read everything I could get my hands on about being pregnant. My favorite book was *Let's Have Healthy Children* by Adele Davis. It was my "bible." It didn't matter to me what the doctor said; in fact, I didn't even ask him questions. I took all the vitamins Adele suggested, even when the doctor cautioned that I should be very careful about taking "all those pills." The doctor asked me directly, "Which vitamins are you using?" He warned me, "You could overdose on those vitamins." I believed he didn't know what he was talking about because nutrition was not part of a doctor's medical school training. In her book, Adele cited copious amounts of research that convinced me that I was doing the right thing for my baby.

We called my Mom and Luke's parents to announce that we were expecting our first baby. The reaction of our parents was tentative. Only my sister Shirley sent me a note congratulating us, and expressing how happy she was that we were going to make her an aunt. It didn't matter to us that our families thought this was a bad decision. We were thrilled and scared at the same time.

My main goal in raising my first-born child was to not repeat the mistakes I believed my Mom made while raising us. I wanted to breast-feed my baby and to make sure we bonded as soon as he/she was born, so we insisted we not be separated from our baby at birth. We had read *Touching* by Ashley Montague, which emphasized how important such early contact was to bonding. I insisted on natural childbirth with no drugs during labor or delivery and no fetal monitor, and that Luke be with me in the delivery room. This was 1972, and my doctor thought I was crazy. He consented to everything only after first arguing with me. I gained fifty pounds during my pregnancy, although the doctor told me he wanted me to gain only twenty pounds. He finally gave up on arguing with me about my weight but warned, "By the time this baby comes, you are going to be one fat woman!" I believed I would never be fat, that I would lose the weight after the baby arrived. Adele Davis cautioned that it was never good to diet during pregnancy. She believed that eating more aided the baby's development, so that is what I did.

I continued to work during my pregnancy so time flew by. The biggest problem during my pregnancy was that my senses of smell and taste were adversely affected. The smell of the car made me nauseous, a problem because I spent so much time in my car. I constantly had a bad taste in my mouth; I tried to get rid of it by eating, which was part of the reason I gained so much weight. I was frightened, and I felt out of control and uncomfortable about what was happening to my body.

Luke and I attended prenatal classes; we toured the hospital where our baby would be born; we signed up for Lamaze classes. I quit work two weeks before the baby was due and attended breathing classes every day. After we had practiced breathing, the instructor answered our questions. I was learning to breathe, but what I really needed to do was learn to relax. Someone in my class suggested that we purchase a stop watch to use during labor to time my contractions. This turned out to be the best suggestion because I used it to distract myself during contractions.

We were still attending Sunday Meditations at the Yoganandya's Self Realization Fellowship Center when we learned about a retreat center in eastern Michigan, along Lake Michigan. When I was nine months pregnant, Luke and I decided to attend a weekend retreat there. We needed silence and reflection to prepare for our first child, and we hoped the swami would bless our baby. As the swami blessed my very pregnant belly, he pronounced, "You will have a girl and she will be the light of your lives." Even though I suspected I had started my labor early by climbing down the very steep banks of Lake Michigan, it was a wonderful weekend. We returned home ready for this new step in our lives, but, like all first-time parents, we knew very little of what was in store for us.

The night before my due date, Luke and I went to dinner at a Greek restaurant near our apartment. We decided to go out for dinner because I was panicking; I couldn't take being pregnant one more day! I was huge, and my ongoing fear of not knowing how I would handle the birth was driving me crazy. Could I have my baby without drugs? How bad was the pain going to be? Could I handle it? What if I had complications? What would Luke do and would I let him support me? I had heard scary stories about how some women turned on their husbands when they were in labor. I did not want to do that.

I ate a Greek salad at the restaurant and immediately began to feel sick. Luke took me home and suggested I lay down. I fell asleep almost immediately. A couple of hours later I woke up feeling worse. I woke Luke and we decided that I was probably in labor and that we should go to the hospital. My bag had been packed for weeks, so we got in the car and drove to the hospital.

The hospital was nearby, but Luke pretended that he was lost and not able to find his way to the hospital. He kept saying, "Is this the way?" Then he would turn on the wrong street. I finally said, "Stop it." Between contractions, I begged him, "Just get me to the hospital." He always had a good sense of humor, which I needed, but he finally saw that this was not the time for joking, so he said, "Okay. Okay."

When we arrived, the attendant asked me to sit in a wheelchair. I didn't want to get in a wheelchair, but I did. He pushed me into the emergency room. Luke helped me check in and then went to move the car. I was wheeled to the fifth floor and was examined immediately. The nurses determined I was in labor. I got a room immediately because I needed to throw up and run to the bathroom at the same time. Finally I heard Luke's voice. The nurses insisted he get dressed in full medical garb. They were not used to having husbands in the delivery room and were unsettled by his presence. He was not happy with this delay. When he finally arrived in my room, I hardly recognized him in his scrub outfit. He looked cute but as frightened as me. His presence comforted me, and I was glad he was finally there. He helped me to stay focused on my breathing, getting through the contractions and monitoring the stop watch.

During the summer of my pregnancy, I had signed up for a Philosophy class at the University of Illinois. I wasn't sure how my labor would go, so I packed my Philosophy textbook and notes. I needed to study for my final exam, scheduled for the week after my due date. As my labor progressed, I put away my textbook; studying would have to wait. There was no way I could concentrate on the fundamental questions of reality, existence, reason and knowledge or the theories of Plato, Aristotle or Pythagoras. There was something much more pressing at the moment!

I was handling my contractions well when we heard a young woman screaming in the corridor. The screams came closer. Before we knew it, a young teen mom in labor was delivered to the other bed in my room! I had never thought of this complication. She was young, alone and scared. With every contraction she screamed louder. I tried to talk to her, but she kept screaming. I was proud of how I was dealing with labor; I had read so much and attended so many Lamaze classes.

Finally, the nurse decided I was dilated enough, and I was put on a gurney and wheeled to the delivery room. I was relieved and happy to leave the screamer behind. Moving to another room was not easy because my contractions were close. This was a hospital operating room. Normally I would have been totally freaked out, but I felt amazingly calm. I just wanted our baby to be born. The nurse kept reminding me not to push; I wasn't even thinking about pushing. When I did get on the table, I was told to "PUSH." It was much harder than I had imagined. Pushing wore me out, but finally I was able to push out our tiny baby girl. She weighed 7 lbs and 12 oz; she was beautiful and Luke and I stared in wonder at our beautiful, healthy baby. We got to see her briefly before the nurses took her to "get cleaned up." There was no need protesting this "hospital procedure." We were put into a room where we waited for our daughter.

Luke and I had a number of discussions about what to name our baby. If it was a girl, I had my heart set on naming her "Sarah" after a cousin's cute little girl who had red hair and freckles. I didn't know her well, but I loved the name. I told Luke that we had better name this first girl "Sarah" because, if not, I would have to keep having girls until I had a "Sarah." He wasn't fond of the name but agreed to name her Sarah Anne (after Luke's mom) which means "princess." My name in the convent was Sister Sara Marie, and I liked the connection her name provided to my religious life.

Sarah remained with us instead of being placed in the nursery. The nurses had their opinions about this request. They said, "In a few days you will have full responsibility for a newborn; you need your rest." I heard that the nurses gave sugar water to newborns who cried in the night, so I requested they bring her to me as soon as she woke. This was a battle that I only partially won. I was allowed to keep her until 10 pm. The nurses agreed to bring her one time in the middle of each night. She spent the rest of the night in the nursery with the other newborns.

I stayed in the hospital for three nights. One night I was awakened by a nurse who said she had a little baby girl who was very hungry. She gave me the impression that she had been holding her and rocking her for hours. She seemed to know more about my baby than I did!

Three days in the hospital did help me to relax; the nurses showed me how to bathe Sarah and to make sure she was nursing correctly. Luke and I stared at Sarah and talked to her non-stop. It was truly a special time for the three of us. We couldn't have been happier with our beautiful baby.

The first night at home, neither of us knew how to calm Sarah, who seemed inconsolable. I begged Luke to call the hospital to find out what they did in the middle of the night to calm her. Luke said we needed to figure that out for ourselves. With ten siblings, he had a lot of experience with babies.

I was determined to breast feed and had taken classes at the La Leche League. I called them for advice. They recommended that I wait at least three hours between feedings. Sarah started fussing after only an hour and a half, but we tried to keep her happy until it was close to three hours. This involved lots of walking and bouncing. I felt inadequate as a mom because she seemed hungry all the time. The worst part of those first days of breastfeeding were when I ate something that affected my milk, Sarah "projectile vomitted." It always scared me, and I worried that my body couldn't make enough milk.

We fluctuated between being totally amazed with our beautiful baby and struggling to figure out what she needed. I was thrilled that Luke had so much experience with babies. Initially I thought that I wasn't needed because he was so good with babies, but I soon realized I was desperately needed to feed her, change her and bond with her. For our first week at home, Luke put a note on the front door: "Mom and baby are resting. Do not disturb." I was grateful for the rest, but I quickly started to feel isolated. I hadn't gotten to know anyone well enough to call them when I was feeling alone. We had lived in this city for almost a year, but I hadn't made any close friends, mostly because I spent most of my days in my car.

My Mom came to visit on the same train that had brought her to our ill-fated first Thanksgiving. She seemed to enjoy holding Sarah, wrapped in the green blanket she had crocheted for her. It was her first grandchild so we took pictures of them together. I wanted her to be thrilled with our beautiful baby. She might have been thrilled, but she was convinced we were "spoiling" her. She kept saying, "Put her down. You will spoil her."

The second day of her visit, we decided to venture out to a restaurant for lunch. Soon after arriving, Sarah started fussing. She needed to nurse. My Mom protested, "Why do you have to do THAT here?" I replied that I had to nurse her because it was time for her feeding; surely it was better to nurse her than to have her cry in the restaurant. My Mom, who had bottle-fed all of us, wasn't comfortable with nursing. I was well versed in the benefits of nursing and knew it had to be my choice. I wanted her to be proud of me for making this informed choice, but she wasn't. She was embarrassed. I was still too young and vulnerable to sort out why my Mom's negativity affected me. She had a powerful impact on me. Her disapproval always sent me into a "tailspin." I was clear that I would always choose what was best for my daughter.

The weeks passed quickly, and, when Sarah was six weeks old, Luke and I drove to Iowa for my "Irish Twin" brother's wedding (we were both born in the same calendar year). We were excited because it would be the first time my family would meet Sarah. She cried a lot during the four-hour trip, so we stopped many times to comfort her. When we finally arrived, she slept through the night. I felt self-conscious about the weight I had gained during my pregnancy. I searched for a dress that would hide my weight and be big enough on top for me to nurse Sarah. The wedding was beautiful, and Sarah slept through most of the reception. Many people looked at our sleeping baby and said she was beautiful. We were so proud of her.

Late in the afternoon, she woke, and I nursed her in the bathroom downstairs. When I returned, most of the guests had left the reception. The wedding was over and we had survived our first real outing with our newborn. I was so different from my sisters. My younger sister was fine with her very obedient dog. She proudly stated: "My dog does not wake me up in the middle of the night and always poops outside!" She had been with her husband for a number of years, but was still years away from having a baby. She said she would have a baby when and if her husband got his PhD. My older sister, Shirley, was already divorced and adamant that she never wanted children.

By December, we had saved enough money to fly to Philadelphia to introduce Sarah to her other set of grandparents. We called Luke's parents to say we wanted to come for Christmas; they asked if Sarah had been baptized. We said, "No," realizing that this was a mortal sin in such a very devout Catholic family. His mom offered to arrange a baptism for us. We agreed reluctantly.

Luke's parents asked their parish priest to schedule the baptism for the day after we arrived in Philly. Anne bought a beautiful baptismal gown for her granddaughter. She wanted to make sure at least one of her grandchildren was baptized. She already had three grandchildren who were not! We arrived at the cold, dark church in the middle of a snowy, cold and dark wintery Philadelphia afternoon. Any heat from the Sunday services was gone. I felt a pit in my stomach because Sarah had already been fussy about putting on the frilly, uncomfortable baptismal gown. Now we would take off her blankets and pour cold water over her head. I knew she would be very unhappy, and she was. She started screaming as soon as she felt the cold water—and only stopped when we got inside her grandfather's new blue, warm Cadillac to return to their beautiful Valley Forge home.

After our trip east, we settled into our apartment, but it became apparent almost immediately that Sarah needed her own room. Four months later, with her dad gone most of the time trying to sell chemicals, we decided to move to a two-bedroom apartment only a couple of blocks away. We did the move by ourselves. I was working part time at the same agency I worked at when I got pregnant. I now planned recreational activities for mentally impaired adults. Sometimes I brought Sarah along so I could nurse her. We were struggling financially; Luke was working hard to improve his sales. It was clear we needed to make different decisions about our life. I felt lost as to what to do.

One night, when I was particularly worried about what we were going to do, Luke and I stood together in our bedroom holding Sarah. He asked me what I would do if I didn't have Sarah. I said, "I would move to Milwaukee to take the Montessori Training." I needed to escape the low wages/no benefits in the Catholic schools. I wanted to get into the public schools. However, there was a bigger reason for me to take the training. I wanted to learn to become a loving mother so I could raise my child differently than I was raised. Luke said, "Then, let's do it." It was only four words, but his willingness to fulfill my dream completely changed our lives!

I got the idea to become a Montessori teacher from Luke's close friend who had visited us while I was pregnant. He had completed the Montessori training and was teaching in a Montessori school in Toronto. He described the training and suggested I look into the Milwaukee training center because it was an international Montessori training center, which he thought was superior. The Milwaukee center had a great reputation because the trainer grew up in Germany and had worked with Maria Montessori's son, Mario.

I called the next day and set up an interview at the Midwest Montessori Institute with Hildegard Solzbacker, the Directress. After the interview, Hildegard assured me I was accepted for the fall semester. Luke and I were happy to have some direction to our lives. Luke wanted to quit his sales job. He had already switched from selling chemicals to selling International Harvester semi-trailer trucks, which he was no better or happier at, so he gave notice and we notified our landlord that we were moving. We were so excited about this new adventure that we didn't think about all the issues we would face once we moved. We were young, adventurous and just beginning to navigate life as a couple with a young child. Neither of us had much experience living life; we were making it up as we went along. I was comfortable knowing that we were guided and protected during this whole process. It all felt right.

Luke went to Milwaukee alone to find a place for us to live. He rented an inexpensive second-story apartment in the inner city on 39th and Vliet, close enough to the Montessori training center on 54th that it wouldn't take me long to drive to school.

Our first task was to get our belongings to Milwaukee. We asked the two lesbian women living upstairs if we could borrow their pick-up truck; they agreed, if we filled their truck with gas when we returned it. In our two years of marriage we had accumulated only a meager amount of possessions—the living room furniture from an auction house, a used crib from a neighbor, a folding card table for a kitchen table, chairs, and clothes for the three of us. We realized that any items that didn't fit in the pickup truck would be left by the curb.

As we drove away, we did leave a pile of things. It looked like some-one had been evicted, but we were too frazzled to deal with the stuff that wouldn't fit in the pickup. When we arrived in Milwaukee, we discov-ered the landlord had given Luke the wrong move-in date; it was a week later, so there we sat in the middle of the alley with all our possessions—and nowhere to put them! I prayed hard in that moment. I saw a man working in his garage behind our rental apartment. I impulsively got out of the truck and boldly asked if we could store our things in his garage for one week. He reluctantly said, "I guess so." We felt just as hesitant to leave everything we owned in the garage of a complete stranger. We agreed to return in a week to move our belongings into the apartment right across the alley.

This was definitely a stressful time that tested our resiliency, but we wanted to stay strong by looking at the opportunities, rather than the challenges we faced. We hoped to rebound stronger and more resourceful. Even though I was still mad at God, there was nothing to do but trust that God would help us. I reverted back to the deep faith I had learned as a child. My faith was being tested, and I was learning to trust that, somehow, everything would work out. I prayed often, "Please help us, God. Please calm our fears, keep us safe and show us the way to a better life in Milwaukee."

CHAPTER TWELVE

THE MIDDLE YEARS
IN MILWAUKEE

When we returned to Milwaukee the following week, all of our things were still in the garage across the alley from our newly-rented upstairs rear apartment. I didn't see the apartment until the day we moved in. The first thing I noticed was that there was no front door at the entrance to the stairs leading to our second floor apartment. This was Milwaukee—much too cold in the winter to not have a front door! There was also no furnace, only an oil-burning stove. The carpet was worn, with holes in spots; the apartment was dirty. There was no grass in front of our building, only concrete, separating our apartment from the large home directly in front of us.

The owners of our apartment lived on the first floor. They did not clean up after their dog that pooped on the concrete everyday. My heart sank as we moved in. Sarah was crawling and ready to walk, and she needed grass and a place to play outside. However, our first priority was to find a babysitter; the second, for my husband to find work.

After our very first night in the apartment, we woke to find parking tickets plastered on both of our cars. We were distraught. "Welcome to Milwaukee!" How could we get tickets for parking in front of our apartment? We went to the police station, only a few blocks from our house, to plead our case. We learned that parking on any Milwaukee street required a monthly permit—for which you had to apply in person on the first of each month. The police refused to forgive our tickets: "There were signs posted." It seemed like a perfect ploy to keep track of everyone coming and going in their city. Since we lived close to the police station, they checked the cars on our street the first day of each month, so we must not forget to buy a permit on the first day of the month.

We had only a week to get settled and locate a babysitter for Sarah. We walked around the neighborhood to see if there were young families who might recommend a babysitter. This was the scariest part of our move because we had never left Sarah with anyone. I had breastfed her until we moved, when I realized I would be in school and needed to wean her. We searched the newspaper for a babysitter and interviewed a number of possible sitters. Nobody seemed right and we began to feel desperate. Luke needed to find work, and I would be in school all day. We finally decided on a woman who had a baby herself and seemed responsible. However, she also had a dog, a doberman; she assured us that Sarah would be fine with her dog. I, however, was not fine with her dog. In fact, I was scared to death each time I entered her house to get Sarah. After only a week, we decided to find another sitter, one without a dog. The next sitter was not any better. She did not have a dog, but I had an unsettled feeling the first morning I left Sarah. I couldn't put my finger on it, but something didn't feel right. In class, the director asked me why I looked worried. I told her I had left my daughter with a new babysitter that I didn't feel good about. She said that I must leave immediately to pick up Sarah—and take a classmate with me. I followed her advice.

I took my friend Dana. The babysitter met us at the door and immediately became angry when I asked for Sarah. I truly feared she might not give me my child. She reminded me I had promised her a full week of work. Dana, in a very stern voice said, "Give her child to her." Dana agreed that I had good reasons to be freaked out about this babysitter. I couldn't stop hugging Sarah when we returned to the car. I believed the babysitter was not a bad person, but was taking in children only because she needed the money, never a good reason to be caring for children. I was so grateful that I had followed my intuition, confided in Hildegard, and brought along Dana for support.

Now Luke and I were even more freaked about finding another babysitter. We heard about a divorced woman on the next block who had foster children. We interviewed her and she seemed genuinely loving; she assured us she would be thrilled to have Sarah. We felt good about her and she seemed to love Sarah. She told us stories about all the things she did during the day. We were concerned about one of her foster children, an older boy who seemed unsettled. However, we liked the mom and felt Sarah was safe. Her rates were reasonable, which we needed because I was paying tuition for my year-long Montessori program and Luke still hadn't found work. We had so little money that we were eligible for food stamps. We were living on the meager savings I had accumulated from my teaching job.

The Montessori training was intense. All morning we attended lectures where we were required to take precise notes on how each piece of material was presented. Every afternoon we either observed in a Montessori classroom or practiced our own precise presentations of the Montessori materials.

Every night Luke and I fixed dinner together, played with Sarah, gave her a bath and put her to bed. Once she was asleep, I typed the exact words I would use to teach each lesson in the classroom. Our class was required to write sixty-seven theory papers and create four albums with free-hand illustrations of the materials and step-by-step directions for each lesson.

Luke finally found a job with a temp agency, but it lasted only a couple of weeks. Then he found a position at an alternative school, but the director was mismanaging the funds, and the school closed after only a few weeks. By this time, Luke was desperate to find work and finally was hired by a residential treatment center for emotionally disturbed teenage girls. Not an easy job, but the position came with insurance and a guaranteed paycheck. He had "fireman's hours": 24 hours on and then two days off. It was hard when he was gone, but his schedule made it possible for him to care for Sarah on his days off.

Our living situation, however, was not good. We had frequent disagreements with the landlord about issues such as putting a front door on the apartment. He was happy to receive our rent money but refused to fix anything. It was after one such argument that I had a problem with my car. I had started parking it in a private lot at the end of our street so it wasn't within view. The day after a disagreement with the landlord, my car was vandalized. The driver-side window was smashed, and someone had taken a hammer to the dashboard. I was devastated. Why would someone do this to my car? I suspected the landlord but had no proof. We had no money for repairs, but I had to get it fixed because I needed it to get to school. It felt like our lives were completely out of control. I had no time to feel anything, and I was dead tired every night; I slept well but I made it through each day by sheer will power. Luke was just hanging on too.

We didn't have money for a phone, but one day I walked to the 7-Eleven on Vliet Street to call my Mom at the public phone booth. I told her everything that was happening to us. I am sure she was upset but she said, "You made this bed, now lay in it." I hung up feeling more discouraged than ever and so alone. What was happening to my life? How had we gotten ourselves into this difficult situation?

Despite our bleak circumstances, our first year in Milwaukee went by quickly due to my intense Montessori training schedule. I got to know a few people in my class, but I was the only one with a child, and I did not go out at night or on the weekends. The program was exhausting and time consuming; we had a great trainer who was a strict taskmaster. She grew up in Germany and was friends with Mario Montessori, the son of Maria Montessori, founder of the Montessori Method. She set high standards and did not let anyone pass her course until they adopted the same high standards. Completion of the course included a five-hour written exam, an oral exam and four Montessori albums that were hand-typed, hand-illustrated and approved by our trainer. Our sixty-seven theory papers were due by the end of May. I began to see that there was a light at the end of the tunnel. Even though this program was rigorous, I began to recognize how I was changing. I became calmer and more patient with Sarah. I began to understand her stages of growth and to sense what she needed. I held her close at night and enjoyed talking to her. I was fascinated by what I was learning and how she was passing through the same milestones I was learning.

In early April I was walking down the block with Sarah when I saw a little girl playing in her fenced-in yard, equipped with a large sand box and swings. I spoke to her mom, telling her that I needed a yard like that for our daughter. She mentioned that they were putting in new carpeting and painting their upstairs apartment so they could rent it out. I said that I wanted to rent it but would need to wait until I graduated in late spring. I assured her that I would be employed by the Milwaukee Public Schools (MPS) in the fall because the district was opening their first public Montessori school. (I had already put in an application at the district offices. The district required an elementary teaching certificate as well as a Montessori diploma to teach in the new Montessori school. I had both.)

The landlord said we could move in right away, and even offered to accept a lower rent until I started my teaching job in MPS. This was an answer to many months of praying, yes, praying. We needed to get out of the place where we were living for so many reasons. I was distraught about God when I left the convent, but I always resorted to praying when I felt lost and alone. I prayed, "Please help us, God. Please help us."

I was uncharacteristically certain about getting hired by the Milwaukee Public Schools. I had gone to the central office at the end of March, spoken to the Human Resources Director and handed him my resume and application. He invited me to sit down as he looked over my paperwork. I was not expecting to see him, but he looked at me and asked, "Why should I hire you?" I confidently and nervously responded that I had finally learned how to teach reading. He sat up straight, with a look both curious and incredulous, and said, "I see you have an elementary education degree from a private Catholic college. Are you telling me that you didn't learn how to teach reading in college?" "Yes, that is exactly what I am saying." He sat up even straighter: "How can that be true?" We had a great conversation.

I explained that Maria Montessori was the first woman physician in Italy and had spent years observing poor children in the slums of Italy. From those observations, she discovered young children learn best by starting with concrete ideas and then moving to the abstract. I said I had spent the past year learning how to set up an environment where all children could work at their own pace and skill level, and the classroom materials were all self-correcting, so students could see for themselves if they made a mistake. The teacher was called a Directress, not a teacher, because they were trained to direct their students' learning by observing them and offering them new lessons when they were ready. When I left his office, I felt sure I would be offered a job working in the first public Montessori school in Milwaukee.

I graduated from the Midwest Montessori Institute in late May. As soon as I graduated, I returned to the central office to submit a copy of my Montessori certificate. I spoke to the same HR person. He said he was intending to call me because he wanted to process my paperwork for a Montessori teaching position at McDowell, an inner-city school not far from our apartment. They planned to open only a couple of Montessori classrooms the first year but, eventually, the whole school would be a Montessori School. I left that office with the happiest feeling in my heart and a giant smile on my face. I had set a clear goal to teach in a public school; I didn't know how I was going to do it, but setting that goal, and trusting, allowed the Universe to make it happen. All my work the past year would pay off. I had a teaching position in the public schools with a decent salary and good benefits. I was elated and proud of myself. I thanked God for this blessing and felt that I was finally on the right track.

That weekend Luke, Sarah and I drove to Iowa to tell my Mom about my new job. I was never willing to give up the hope that *this* time she would be impressed with me. She was not impressed. I wanted to reward myself by shopping for a new outfit, but I ended up not buying anything. Why? I didn't have any money yet and was still not sure what I liked or wanted. Every item of clothing I owned was made by my Mom, but she really didn't like sewing for me. She did talk me into buying a pattern and material so she could make me an outfit. I had worn black for those five years and, before that, I wore the same uniform for all twelve grades of school. It seemed, in Montessori terms, that I had "missed the sensitive period" for learning what I loved.

Everything did settle down in our lives now that we both had jobs and a stable babysitting situation. I loved teaching Montessori—and being with our two-year old who taught me more about teaching than I could ever learn in the classroom. When I started at the Montessori Institute, I had registered Sarah for a community Montessori school not far from our house. When she was two-and-a-half she began attending that school.

I called my Mom every Saturday. She always blamed Luke for all our problems. If Sarah was misbehaving, it was his fault. If I was unhappy, it was his fault. She spoke badly about him and his family, even though she met his family only once, at our wedding. Despite all this, once a month we packed our car and drove the four hours to eastern Iowa to visit her. These weekend visits were meant to cheer her up; she was lonely because most of my siblings had moved away. I always ended up crying on the way back to Milwaukee, as I told Luke all the things she had said to me. Although I knew intellectually there was no way to make my Mom happy, I slipped into my old familiar role of trying. I was deeply entrenched in this role and didn't know how to change it. My relationship with my Mom was addictive. I couldn't stay away. I was so compelled to visit her to try to make her happy, but nothing worked. I was like an alcoholic. .... I always wanted another drink (going to Iowa) to help, but never succeeding (coming home feeling emotionally exhausted because the drink didn't help). Luke's wise counsel was always the same: "Happiness is a choice and you can't make that choice for your Mom; she could only choose that for herself. You need to choose your own happiness, in spite of what your Mom is choosing." I heard Luke's words but could not figure out how to change old patterns. How could I live without a relationship with my Mom? I laughed when I asked myself that question.

I worked as a Montessori Directress for five years at McDowell. During this time, we looked for a home in the inner city, within the boundaries of the community Montessori school that Sarah was attending. We found a "fixer-upper" only four blocks from where we were renting. We paid $25,000 for the house. This seemed like an unbelievable amount of money, but our house payments were the same as our rent so we knew we could afford it. This three-bedroom house without a garage was on a one-way street. It had beautiful wood cabinets and doors. It was perfect for us, and we were thrilled to be first-time home owners.

Sarah had her own room in the middle part of the house, and Luke and I had a small bedroom at the back. It was our home and we loved it. We needed to do major cleaning, painting and yard work. I had the summers off, so I painted the outside of the house that summer. Luke didn't mind cooking and loved playing with Sarah, so this worked out to a good division of labor. Sarah got to know the neighborhood kids, and we got to know Bev and Les and their children next door. Even though we finally had our own home, I knew it was not my dream home and certainly not one where we could put up a white picket fence and our name on the house. It was still the inner city and it never felt completely safe.

We started talking about having a second child; we wanted Sarah to have a sibling. Luke said he wanted a second child, but only if I was ready. Even though we were just getting by on our salaries, we decided to get pregnant. Sarah was four years old. It was time. Somehow, I deceived myself into believing that I could take time off when I had a second baby. I needed a break and a baby would give me that break.

I got pregnant right away with our second baby, due the last day of the school year. A June baby seemed lucky timing because I would be home all summer. We would see what would happen when it was time to go back to school in the fall. I felt exhausted during this pregnancy; I was working full time and had morning sickness for the first six weeks. This time I was calmer about my body and enjoyed being pregnant a bit more, but I gained sixty pounds and had the same terrible taste and smell issues. As before, my doctor was upset with my weight gain. He felt sure I would have a boy. At one of my routine visits, he wrote the word "boy" with a magic marker on my very pregnant belly. I thought I might have a boy too, but I wanted another girl after my years of working with very energetic boys in my classroom.

I was feeling more and more distant from my Mom so, when my husband's mom volunteered to come help after the birth, I agreed. I wasn't particularly close to Luke's mom, but it seemed better to have her help than my Mom's.

Our beautiful second baby girl was born on her due date by natural childbirth without drugs. We were thrilled! She was as beautiful as her big sister, and we were elated for Sarah to have a little sister. Both Luke and I were more confident as second-time parents. I made a promise to myself, however, which later proved just how inexperienced we really were. I said, "This second time around I'm committed to not being pampered. I will get up and get busy right away." I wanted to prove that I didn't need to be coddled or need bedrest like I did with Sarah. We named our precious second child "Rachael." I had chosen Sarah's name, so Luke got to select our second daughter's name. Toward the end of my pregnancy Luke and I sat at a small restaurant close to my school reviewing a list of boys' and girls' names he liked. He loved the biblical name Rachael, and it seemed to fit with Sarah's biblical name. I loved the name too, so we made our decision. If we had a boy we planned to name him David.

The first weekend home from the hospital, Luke's parents and his sister visited for a full week. The second weekend my Mom, Paul and Colette and their baby, Paula, came to see our precious new baby. We decided to go to Summerfest, a yearly music festival held on 75 acres in a park along Lake Michigan. Even though Rachael was only two weeks old, I carried her in the Snugglie, all over the Summerfest grounds for the entire afternoon, and even took her on a gondola ride the length of the Summerfest grounds. I was breastfeeding, so I didn't have to worry about preparing bottles. I didn't realize how exhausting it would be to walk the grounds all day. The fourth weekend after Rachael's birth, we attended Luke's company picnic. It was there that I started not feeling well. It was hot and humid and I felt I had a fever. I finally told Luke that we needed to leave. He looked at me, surprised. Neither of us realized that we were "burning the candle at both ends." We thought we were experienced parents.

In addition to not feeling well, I started to show signs of having a breast infection. I wish I could report that I went home and rested. I did not. I was frustrated with Luke because he had decided to quit his residential treatment center job right before Rachael was born. He wanted to make more money, so he took a job selling insurance. But, since his paychecks were based on commission, he was now making a lot less money. I started to realize that I would have to go back to teaching, as I watched his adventure with selling insurance unfold.

I was frustrated and angry. Then I did something even more irrational than Luke quitting his job. I decided to take both girls and fly to Denver so my family could meet Rachael. My family planned to be in Denver for a week. So, with my six-week-old and my five-year-old-daughters, I flew to Denver. My body hadn't time to heal from giving birth, but my emotional state was more unstable. When I looked out the plane window during take off, I saw Luke standing on the hood of his car, waving wildly to us. It touched my heart. I was taking our two children away without him; he looked sad and lost, standing there on the car. I was unable to deal with all the emotions I was feeling. I was sad, scared, angry and frustrated—and now I was running away to Denver to be with my family.

By the time I arrived in Denver, my breast infection was in full bloom. It was incredibly painful to breastfeed; I was in constant pain and didn't know what to do. My sister-in-law suggested I switch to bottles; she was bottle feeding her baby, Paula. My Mom agreed. Neither of my sisters had a baby so they couldn't help. After two days of excruciating pain, my Mom said, "I can't stand to see you suffering. I am going to walk to the Safeway to buy you bottles and formula." I gave up breastfeeding. I was heartbroken and felt my "super-mom" status was ending miserably.

I remember sitting by the pool, watching my older daughter play in the water, and telling my sister, Shirley, that I was thinking about leaving Luke because he had quit yet another job. She had divorced five years before, so I thought she would have some advice. My heart ached every time I thought about leaving Luke. Telling my sister about our problems, I flashed back to the image of Luke standing on the hood of his car, waving goodbye. I felt stuck in a situation I couldn't control, and I had no idea how to solve any of our problems......... our finances, how to be a good wife and mother, leaving my newborn with a sitter, and finding work I loved. Somehow during the trip to Denver, I realized it wasn't just about Luke. Both Luke and I were simply being forced to grow up and both of us resisted it.

While in Denver it became clear to me that I had to return to my teaching position in the fall. When I came home and talked with Luke about my conversation with Shirley, he told me that he loved me and we had two children together, and that he would NEVER leave me. He said that I might leave him, but he didn't want me to leave and would always be there for me and our girls. This shocked me. I had experienced so much loss in my life that I thought he would leave me like everyone else had. We talked about how we both knew that, if we left this marriage, we would bring our problems to another marriage, so we might as well stay and try to figure it out together. Luke loved us so much, and I never wanted to hurt him; he was so good to us. I had been raised without a father and knew I didn't want that for our children. I would not run away. Growing up was not easy, but we committed ourselves to learn how to make our marriage work.

As Luke and I got used to having a second child, the summer flew by. Rachael was a happy baby; she slept through the night after only a couple of weeks. She woke up happy, cooing and playing in her crib every morning. We went for long walks, especially to the park, where her big sister played on the playground. Rachael and Sarah both just loved being outside.

It was a very happy summer for us. As it came to a close, I started to dread having to leave Rachael because she was still so small. It was one of the hardest things I would ever have to do. I was sure I would cry all day on my first day back at school, but when the day came, I was so busy with my fifty new students that it flew by and was over before I knew it. Sarah was in school full days, and Rachael seemed fine when I picked her up from our babysitter who lived two houses away. I was so happy to find this child care situation so close to home.

Our neighbors were teachers and had a baby the same month as us. The mom had decided to stay home with her newborn. They needed money, so she consented to care for Rachael too. However, this situation lasted only two weeks. When I came to get Rachael on Friday of the second week, my neighbor said it was too difficult to care for two babies. I remembered the hard time we had finding a day care for Sarah, so I felt panicked immediately. I asked God for help to find a great babysitter.

The next day I mentioned my babysitting crisis to a group of parents who were dropping off their children in my classroom. Jenny's mom told me she had a day care in her home and that she could take an infant. She offered to give me a reduced rate because I was teaching her daughter. They lived nearby. Maureen, a friend and a teacher at my school, picked us up and dropped off Rachael and then drove both of us to school. This was a great blessing. Maureen did not have children but she was a good listener and she was positive. I was able to confess how overwhelmed I felt about everything. She supported me by listening and driving me to work and day care.

It was during this time that I started writing in a journal. In high school I owned a five-year diary where I recorded events, but the diary had no room for reflection or introspection. Starting to write in my journal allowed me to express how I was feeling and to see on paper what I was thinking. I noticed I felt more peaceful when I wrote. It was the beginning of falling in love with writing.

I taught at McDowell for six years. The teachers were a fabulous professional learning community; we ate lunch together daily and had time to talk, laugh and ask lots of questions of the experienced Montessori teachers. We planned our group lessons together. Every year we added more Montessori classrooms and eventually took over the entire building, but still maintained our core group of primary teachers.

The dual roles of being the major breadwinner in our family and having so much responsibility for so many students every day continued to be stressful for me. I wondered if life had to be this difficult. I believed I was making a huge difference in the lives of my students, but something was missing. I was not happy and I couldn't put my finger on why. I wondered if I had taken the wrong path in becoming a teacher; even though I consciously remember the exact moment, sitting in Mrs. Casper's fourth grade class, when I decided I wanted to be a teacher. I wondered if I might be conflicted about this work because my Mom had been a teacher in a one-room school house. She had repeatedly told us, "Whatever you do, DON"T become a teacher."

One day I made a call to a counseling office that started me on a journey of self discovery. I took Sarah with me to my first session. I told the counselor I was depressed and didn't know why. She said she thought I might be overwhelmed with being a new mom and not having enough support. She suggested I come to group therapy sessions. There, I learned a lot. It forced me to look at my life and to put it in perspective, as I listened to group members who were addicted to drugs, had suffered sexual abuse, and had other serious mental health issues. My problems paled in comparison. I was a sensitive child who had grown up in a negative home environment. I wanted to learn to think more positively, but I wasn't sure that was possible. At one point, I had a serious talk with God. I basically said, "I don't know how to change. Please help me. I surrender my life to You. I let go and let You run my life." Gradually, little by little, I worked on giving up the idea that someone else was going to rescue me. I had hoped for all of my adult life that someone would rescue us, that someone would give us money to create a better life. I had already lived forty-plus years, and no one had come to help. If my life was going to change for the better, I was the only one who could make that happen. It was the start of a new way of thinking and acting for me.

After six years at McDowell Montessori School, I applied for a sabbatical. This seemed like the best choice at the time. I was exhausted and

I felt I needed to rest. Luke and I talked about me stopping teaching and beginning to work on a Masters degree in Social Work (MSW). I thought I might be happier doing social work because my undergraduate degree was in Sociology. I remembered the social workers who had come to our house to take us away each time my Mom went to the TB sanitarium. I was sure I would be more compassionate and could become the kind of social worker that we had needed when we were swept away from our Mom.

I applied and was accepted into a Master's degree program in Social Work at the University of Wisconsin (UWM). I wanted to hold a REAL Master's degree, not just a Montessori diploma. Even though I had worked hard to earn my Montessori Master's diploma, and was on the pay scale for a Master's degree with the district, it didn't feel real to me because the Montessori Institute was not a university.

When Luke and I talked about taking a sabbatical, I said, "Luke, this is what I know: I can't keep teaching." Luke was skeptical but supportive of my dreams, so I began taking classes. We had no real source of income at the time, other than Luke's insurance sales, which were proving to be fruitless.

It didn't take long before I realized this was a financially foolish move. I needed to go back to teaching. We couldn't make it financially more than six months, so I contacted the district to say I would return at the semester. I was assigned to Greenfield, a second Montessori school that was scheduled to open. That semester off was long enough to help me feel like I had a new lease on life and could go back to the classroom. I convinced myself of this because I had no other choice. A new school, a new classroom with new teachers, students and families would surely help me to get resettled.

Meanwhile, our two girls were growing and thriving. Sarah was still at the Highland Community Montessori, and Rachael was three and could attend Greenfield Montessori with me. We enrolled the girls in piano lessons and dance classes. They were the joy that kept us going as we continued to figure out how to grow up. Both of us were used to making it on our own. I was grateful for the life we had created with our children whom I loved more than I could ever have imagined. The Montessori training had worked; it taught me how to become a different kind of mom from my own mom. Luke was always incredibly supportive, encouraging and calm, no matter what was happening. He was an amazing father to the girls. We both knew we loved each other, but we still felt unsettled.

It was not long after I started at Greenfield that I began to have the same feelings of not knowing what I was doing with my life. I kept asking myself, Luke and God, "Where am I going? Is this all there is? Why do I feel so unsettled about my career?" Why was I so unhappy? My teaching took so much energy; nothing about it came easily to me. Why? Why? Why?

Then something happened at UWM that completely changed my plan to earn a degree in Social Work and leave education for good. I was informed I had to take a year off to do an unpaid internship, a requirement for a Master's in Social Work. I knew this when I started taking classes, but I thought my life would be different by the time I had to do the internship. I realized right away that I couldn't possibly do that; I was the major breadwinner in our family. What could I do?

I had already taken a lot of social work classes. One day, in a flash of brilliant insight, I made an appointment with a professor who was head of the UWM Education Department. I told him I believed all my social work classes would help me to be a better teacher and asked if they could be applied to a Master's degree in Curriculum and Instruction. To my great surprise, he agreed; I needed just three more classes and a thesis to complete the degree. I was thrilled. There was a light at the end of the tunnel. I would now have a second Master's in education. I questioned getting yet another degree in Education when I was so unsettled with teaching, but I told myself I could use it to move into school administration. It made perfect sense at the time: getting this second degree with plans to escape teaching forever.

I completed the three additional classes, wrote my thesis on an old typewriter, asked a neighbor to proofread it and submitted it to the Education Department chairperson. This was not an easy task. I taught every day, and one night a week Luke picked up the girls while I drove across town for classes. I was always hungry during class but I had to wait until I got home to eat. At the first break, I bought a package of peanut M & M's and ate a few during class and more on the way home. The sugar held me over until I could get home to eat.

The girls were always in bed by the time I arrived, so Luke and I had time together. We talked about the girls, which led to discussion of what we could do to create a happier life for our family. Luke knew I wasn't happy in the classroom. I couldn't quite explain the cause of my unhappiness; I was loving and attentive to my students and believed Montessori was the best way to help them become independent, self-confident, peaceful and loving adults. My teaching assistants helped me to be a better teacher. Their strong faith instilled a miraculous quality in each grace-filled day. With the help of my assistants, everything flowed in our classroom and the children were well loved and cared for. With all these blessings I still felt unsettled. What was missing?

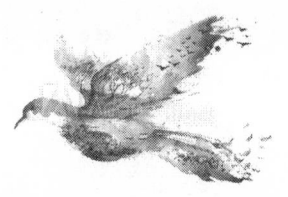

CHAPTER THIRTEEN

A New Life;
A New Career

I thought God was what was missing in my life, so I decided to start attending St. Ann's, an independent church with no religious affiliation. Finding this church was a gift from God and from Rosie. Rosie was one of the McDowell teachers that I had gotten to know. She told me about St. Ann's. Luke had no interest in attending any church, but I believed we should give the girls a spiritual foundation so I took them there.

The minister, Rev. Tom, had left the priesthood after fifteen years, and his wife, Rosie (my teacher friend), had spent many years in the convent. They left their religious communities, found each other and started this church to focus on teaching a guilt-free, happy life based on new thought principles. Even though I didn't know anything about "New Thought," the positive, upbeat philosophy of this church felt right. The girls got a healthy introduction to meditation, prosperity thinking and yoga; I listened intently for new ways of thinking and acting to help me create a more prosperous life. I learned about the Law of Attraction, that God was truly present within each of us, that we needed only to take time daily to pray and meditate, that I could use my mind to visualize a better life. I learned that my thoughts created my reality and that I needed to change my thinking in order to change my life. All these concepts were foreign to me, but they made sense and gave me hope. Little by little, I worked to incorporate this new philosophy into my life. It was a long, slow learning process.

I created a "vision board" with guidance from the Catherine Ponder book, *Open Your Mind to Prosperity*. She suggested using a large piece of poster board with a circle on it which you divide into the various departments of your life: finances, work, family, health, etc. In each section you place pictures of the good you wish to have in that section of your life. The work area of my vision board showed a professional woman dressed in a navy blue business suit with a crisp white blouse. I had no idea why this picture called to me but the answer came in the form of a small ad in the *Milwaukee Journal*. The ad announced that a Learning Center was opening in a Milwaukee suburb, and a director was sought to run the start-up franchise. Hundreds of people responded to the ad. I was called for an interview in a downtown Milwaukee hotel, along with twenty other hopeful applicants. I had recently completed my Master's degree and was scheduled to defend my thesis. I was thrilled to get a call from the young, smart Chicago-area entrepreneur, saying that he, and his two brothers, had chosen me to become the Director of the Huntington Learning Center. Saying "yes" to this opportunity scared me to the core of my being, but I was ready for a new challenge and eager to leave the classroom for the LAST time! The vision board was working.

I loved the concept of the Huntington Learning Center, started by two New Jersey teachers. They used their own teaching experiences to create the first center. They knew that working individually with students to teach them the skills they were missing would catch them up quickly. Using a battery of assessments to determine which skills were missing, they designed an individualized learning plan for each student enrolled in the center. I deeply believed in individualized instruction after all my years of teaching Montessori. The day I got the call from Michael, my new boss, I hung up and screamed with elation. I quickly wrote a resignation letter to the Milwaukee Public Schools and delivered it to the Administration Building. I was thrilled and prayed, "Thank you, God."

My first assignment, as Director of the Center, was to attend a two-week training at the home office in Oradell, New Jersey. This was exciting and scary. Our training included how to market, hire, conference students and their parents, and administer assessments and how to set up an individualized learning plan. Michael asked if he could send all of the materials for the new center to my house because they had not yet made a decision about where to locate the center. I said, "Sure." Our dining room quickly filled with books and office supplies.

During my two-week training in New Jersey, I got to know a couple of my colleagues. Two bright, articulate, fun women asked me to join them for a weekend in New York City. The train ride into the city was easy and we planned to share a hotel room. This sounded wonderful, but I did not have the confidence to spend the weekend in the "Big Apple" with such fun, loving, confident women. I told them I already had plans. I had talked to one very quiet, boring person about renting a car and driving to Cape Cod. That would be the safe choice. I chose the less exciting option because I was scared. I based many of my decisions on my fears. All weekend I told myself that the training program was stressful and I needed downtime, but the truth was that I had a lot of time to worry about passing the exam. In the end, I did fine. I received my Huntington Director training certificate and was ready to open the center. This is an example of a time when I was NOT resilient. I caved into worrying about everything, instead of trusting myself to go to New York with the fun, happy and loving women.

When I returned from the training, my boss, Michael, told me the staff at the franchise center "did not like the sound of me." For one thing, I had younger children who needed me in the evenings and my work hours were from eleven in the morning until eight in the evening. It was true that late afternoon and early evening hours were the times the girls needed me most, but I convinced Michael that Luke was totally capable of caring for the girls. I wanted to get out of teaching so badly that I was willing to do anything to make this schedule work. Only later did I realize the toll this took on my family.

I defended my thesis and completed my Master's degree. Michael suggested I hang my diplomas on the wall—a BA and now two graduate degrees. I was proud of my accomplishments, pretty spectacular for a young girl who finished high school in the lowest track, with little hope of attending college.

In early August, with construction of the center complete, I moved into my new office. The girls were back in school, and I was thrilled to be part of a new business. I had always carried our family's health insurance through my teaching job, so now we had no insurance. This was so upsetting for Luke that he decided to apply for a special education teaching position in the Milwaukee Public Schools in order to have insurance. He was offered a position immediately. The district offered Luke a beginning teacher salary and my starting salary at the center wasn't great, but Michael promised a salary increase "as soon as I enrolled enough students." We were still in a precarious financial position, but Luke loved his teaching job and I was loving the new challenge at the center.

I worked hard and was successful at getting the center running and attracting students. On the way to work every day I affirmed Catherine Ponder affirmations: "Everything I touch is a success" and "I am successful in everything I do." One of the reasons for my success at making the center profitable was that I was masterful at marketing. I visited all the elementary schools in the area, asking to meet with each principal for only five minutes. Most administrative assistants would say "yes" to five minutes. I made a short presentation about how the new center offered individualized instruction for struggling students. After leaving business cards and brochures, I went to the next school. I loved visiting the schools.

The first year at the center was fun. I was able to convince parents that we could help their student. The center started to thrive and soon we hired more teachers and an Assistant Director. I was good at hiring too. I knew the success of the center depended on having excellent teachers and I was good at finding them. One of the teachers was so talented that she was promoted to Assistant Director soon after we hired her. We made a great team because she had many of the skills I lacked. We worked together for two years and I was grateful for her help; we both felt proud of what we accomplished.

I was just getting settled into my new work and feeling more balanced at home when my Mom came for a visit. She was seventy-five but still able to drive from eastern Iowa to Milwaukee. I asked her to visit me at the center on her way into the city. I wanted her to see my office. When she arrived, I gave her a tour; she looked around and sat in my office where all my framed diplomas and my Huntington Learning Center certificate were hanging. I said to her, "Well, what do you think?"

She replied dismissively, "It's a nice office." It would be years before I realized it was my ego that wanted her to recognize me and even longer to realize that my Mom could not give me what I wanted most: her love, support and approval. She did not love or approve of herself, so she could not give me that gift. She was not able to tell me she was proud of my work. I felt sad about her lack of enthusiasm; I longed for her to say something positive.

It was during this visit that I invited my Mom to lunch at the Burger King near our house. I told her then that I had never heard her say one positive thing about me. I asked her, "Could you say just one positive thing about me?" It took her a long time to respond. The silence was painful. Finally, she said, "You are good with people." It was so little so late, but it was something. The idea to ask this question came from the Forum training by Warner Erhard, the man who invented the Erhard Seminars Training (EST).

Earlier in the year I had signed up for the Forum. (The EST training had received a lot of negative press, so Erhard changed the name to the Forum.) I had talked to Luke about taking the training. He encouraged me because we both wanted me to be happier and more peaceful. I believed I could heal if I dealt with my painful past. A teacher next door had taken the training and told me about it. I admired her confidence and how she interacted with her students. The Forum guaranteed that the "training would make a profound and lasting difference in your life, and make a positive, permanent shift in the quality of your life." I felt a deep desire to let go of the heavy baggage I was carrying.

The three-day workshop was held in a hotel in downtown Milwaukee. The all-day, all-evening sessions were grueling, but I was engaged and fascinated by the exercises that taught us new ways of thinking and acting. Through the training, I gained insight into my life and how I could change the trajectory of my life by speaking and acting differently. The investment paid off in many small ways.

It was shortly after my Mom's visit that a number of significant events happened. I was required to go to Florida for the Huntington Learning Center's annual conference, so I was not able to go to Iowa with Luke and the girls for my niece's First Communion. When Luke returned, he reported that my Mom wasn't feeling well. I spoke with my Mom every Saturday, so I knew she wasn't well. She kept saying, "Something isn't right." I asked her what was wrong; all she could say was that she didn't feel well.

A few weekends later, we went back to Iowa so I could accompany my Mom to her doctor appointment. The doctor gave her a clean bill of health. That was confusing because she continued to not feel well. My older sister heard about Mom's health concerns, so she came back to Iowa six weeks later to take Mom back to the doctor because she continued to insist she was ill.

This time the doctor recommended exploratory surgery because he found some suspicious cells on her pap smear. The doctor scheduled her surgery Friday morning of that week. I took the day off work and drove alone to Iowa to be with Mom when she came out of surgery. Shirley was with her when she awakened, drowsy from the anesthetic. The doctor was there to tell her that her uterus was filled with cancer and that he was not able to remove the tumors. She didn't seem to register this news. A little later I arrived; she was more alert so she asked us what the doctor found. We told her the news again. She asked, "Did he mean that he didn't take out the cancer?" We both said, "Yes." The doctor told us that she had three to six months to live, but we didn't tell her that news.

She simply said, "I am not doing this." We knew what she meant. She always said that she would NEVER go to a nursing home; she would NEVER be a burden to anyone. Chemo treatments were not an option because of the advanced stage of the cancer. We asked the doctor how this could happen. She had regular checkups, and her most recent pap smear was "normal." The doctor told us she had a fast-growing cancer.

Shirley called our siblings to tell them the bad news. They decided to come immediately. I stayed all day Saturday and Sunday with Mom. Late Sunday afternoon I decided to return to Milwaukee for work Monday morning. During the weekend, I prayed that Mom would have the courage to let go if it was her time. Her body was filled with cancer; her spirit had to be willing too. I silently told her it was safe for her to let go, that we would be fine.

Saturday afternoon Colleen arrived. She painted Mom's nails, fixed her hair, played cards and worked crossword puzzles with her. On Sunday morning, a Catholic priest visited Mom to give her the Sacrament of Extreme Unction, the last rites of the Catholic Church. When he came into the room, my sister and I were telling Mom that she had done a good job raising five children by herself. She kept closing her eyes and saying, "NO." The priest finally called us into the hallway and said, "It's too late to change your Mom's mind. You need to let her be in peace. Please don't keep arguing with her." I knew the priest was right. It was sad that my Mom chose to think her life had been a failure and even sadder that an unfamiliar priest had to tell us to stop arguing with her.

After the priest left, we went back into her room. I didn't know what to do or say, so I started doing some exercises. My Mom asked me to please stop moving around. I told her I should drive back to Milwaukee before it got dark. She asked if I could stay a little longer. I said, "Sure." As the sun set, I said goodbye and told her that I would be back at the end of the week.

My heart was beating rapidly as I walked out of her room and drove out of the hospital parking lot. I was scared; I felt weak and tried to cry, but tears would not come. Crying was not how we dealt with a crisis.

I took some deep breaths and admitted to myself that I was too scared to stay with my Mom. I did not want to know what was coming next. I wanted to get back to my life. I did not want to see my Mom suffer or to face her death.

I prayed all the way back to Milwaukee and when I got home, I wrote this prayer in my journal: "This situation does not dismay me. God is with me to sustain and uphold me and to make all things right. I trust everything to the tender care of the Father. Your Will Be Done. Grant my Mom a peaceful death if it is her time. I am willing to forgive her for all the ways she hurt me, and I ask her forgiveness for the ways I have hurt her." Even though I wrote those words, I wasn't able to face the fact that my Mom was dying. I had learned about the stages of grief from the work of Elizabeth Kubler Ross. The first stage is denial; I was in denial. The doctors said she had at least three to six months, so I believed I had time to say goodbye. In a way I had said goodbye to her. I had thanked her for giving me life; I told her I loved her. I thanked God for how she loved me in her own way. I knew that trying to make her happy made me crazy. I admitted it had been a difficult relationship, but I forgave her and myself for our difficulties.

The next morning, I got ready for work. I was at the center only a short time when the phone rang. It was my sister saying that my mom's lungs filled up with fluid during the night and she had only a couple of hours to live. She told me not to hurry because I could not get there in time; I was four hours away. I called Luke at school. He said he would finish the school day and wait for the girls to come home before we could leave for Iowa. I said, "Okay" even though I felt my mom might still be alive if we hurried. In the car we told the girls that their grandmother was dying. They asked if she was still alive and we said we didn't know.

We drove as fast as we could, but the kids were hungry so we detoured through a McDonald's Drive-Thru. I wanted to get there, just in case Mom was still alive. When we finally arrived at the hospital, the nurse told me that she had died only ten minutes before. Luke waited in the lobby with the girls, and I went into her room by myself.

My siblings were standing silently around Mom's bed, having said their last goodbyes. Her body was still warm, so I just laid my head on her bed and cried. I didn't give her a kiss or try to talk to her. Ours had been a difficult relationship; now it was over. (That is what I believed at the time.) What would I have said to my Mom if I had been there when she was still alive? Today I would say I was sorry for being a difficult daughter, but back then, I would not have known what to say.

A nurse came in shortly to say it was time to leave; the mortician was there to retrieve her body. We made a very quick trip to the lockbox to retrieve the cash she had saved to cover her burial expenses. We then went to the funeral home to choose a casket and plan her wake and funeral. None of us had extra money, so we bought the best casket we could afford with the money she had saved.

We were all in shock. Mom died so suddenly. She used to say to us, "You act like I will live forever." Our response was, "When you get sick, we will prepare for your death." If we had been paying attention, we would have seen she gave us plenty of hints that she was ready to die. Her own mother had died at seventy-six and she had just turned seventy-six. True to my mom's personality, she made a quick exit—she had the surgery on Friday, found out she was filled with cancer on Saturday and died on Monday.

We decided to honor her life by ordering lots of flowers. We carefully planned her funeral mass. Her five grandchildren carried up the gifts at the offering. The gifts offered included her pin cushion filled with needles from her sewing box, a box of cards and the prayer book that she used for her nightly prayers. The organist played her favorite song, *Somewhere Out There.* The parish priest's homily described the many challenges my Mom experienced and how "she was a brave soldier of Christ who never gave up but remained steadfast in her faith through everything she endured."

We all filed out of church, watched the pallbearers load the casket into the hearse and then, orderly and systematically, climbed into cars to go to the cemetery. Her casket was placed on a frame that sat above a large hole next to my father's grave. The priest blessed the casket and said the customary graveside prayers. My older sister read a very moving Emily Dickinson poem, "Because I could not stop for Death." It was the same Catholic rituals we had experienced thirty-two years before when our father died. Now we were all grown, with families of our own. Mom was laid to rest next to my father, right in front of her name plate on the grave stone. We had visited this grave many times as children and always noticed that her birth date was there, followed by only a dash that represented the expanse of her life. Now they could fill in the date after the dash. My Mom had gotten her wish—she lived long enough to see her children raised.

We went back to the house; it felt so empty. Our family's life had been structured around our Mom, we didn't know how our lives would look now that she was gone. We wondered how we would stay close. A chapter of our lives was over and lots of family secrets were buried that day. Shirley destroyed all my Mom's journals right after the funeral; Mom had made that request. She wanted to ensure there was no chance anyone would learn of her dashed hopes and dreams, the ones she had refused to speak about when she was alive.

Shirley brought up the idea of buying Mom's house and living there in between her overseas teaching jobs. After the service she decided to lay out things that were special to mom so we could take turns choosing things we wanted. We found handmade quilts for each of her grandchildren. It was hard to look at the precious items she had never used, but kept for "good," storing them in the cedar chest with her initials that our father had given her when they got engaged. There were handmade doilies, embroidered pillowcases, dresser runners and tablecloths. There was a yellow, blue and red striped woolen blanket she had bought at the Amana Colonies when our 4-H club toured a woolen mill. Mom loved that blanket, but she never used it. I promised myself I would use it.

We said goodbye at the end of the week and headed back to our own lives. I returned to work the next Monday, but was physically and mentally exhausted and unable to concentrate. I had no idea of the emotional toll Mom's death took on me. I tried to focus while doing conferences with the parents of my students. One of my student's moms said, "I heard you just lost your mom. It was the most traumatic thing that ever happened to me; we can meet for coffee if you want to talk about it."

That was a great blessing; we met for coffee the next day. She gave me the gift of listening; she listened to everything I said about my fractured relationship with my Mom. She said she had a similar relationship with her mom, but it had been ten years, and she still missed her mom. She believed that you never heal from losing your mom, that the pain subsides but will never completely go away.

At some point I realized life must go on. In processing my mother's death, I made a list of the things I knew about her: she loved me in her own way, she sewed for me and my children. She was willing to help me with anything I asked her to do. She taught us great values—compassion, humility, goodness and honesty—and to never repeat a negative story and to always tell the truth. She believed in God and prayed constantly. She taught us to grow our own food, to eat good food and to trust our bodies to heal themselves. She gave us everything she had to give.

Everything changed after my Mom's death. I stopped trying to prove that I was successful. My job title didn't matter anymore. I was unsettled before her death about working as the Center Director, but now it was clear I was doing this job to impress my Mom. I was making so little money and working too hard. I missed Sarah and Rachael more than ever now. Sarah seemed deeply distressed and unsettled as she navigated her way through middle school. Luke never complained, but my schedule was not easy for him.

I started to look at other options. Should I get my real estate license or go back to school? I talked to Joan, the Assistant Director, about feeling lost. She did not want me to leave the center, but she listened and helped me work on my resume. I waited patiently to see where I was guided.

During this time I read Louise Hay's *You Can Heal Your Life*. The idea that I could heal my life was just the message I needed. Louise had healed her life by changing her thinking. She believed in the power of taking action and repeating affirmations. Some of the affirmations I learned from her, and repeated over and over, were: "Divine Intelligence, I release this situation to You. I now know where to go and what to do. I lighten up. I forgive myself. I go with the flow. I am willing to let Divine Intelligence work through me. I know. I remember. I understand. I express myself clearly. I am safe. All is well. Nothing but good can come into my life because God is in charge." Louise Hay was a Religious Science minister, and by reading her book, I deepened my faith in God.

The biggest change for Luke and me was that we felt free. We could move if we wanted. We stayed in Milwaukee for twelve years, even though we had planned to stay only one year. We stayed to be close to my Mom.

Luke and I had long conversations about where we wanted to live. We discussed moving closer to his family on the East Coast; he said he didn't like living on the crowded East Coast. The other option we discussed was to move to the Denver area, close to my two sisters and brother. Luke said he would love to move to Colorado. We decided to move and it felt so right. My biggest concern about moving was that Luke would have to leave his teaching job. He had discovered his buried passion for teaching and was finally settled and enjoying teaching. Now we were planning to give up our jobs and move across the country.

We talked to the girls about moving to Colorado at the end of the next school year. Sarah objected the most; she was finishing eighth grade and she didn't want to leave her friends. She boldly announced, "You might be going to Colorado but I'm not!" She repeated this every time we talked about moving. Rachael was finishing third grade and not as attached to her friends or to Wisconsin.

That summer we took a trip to Colorado to talk to our family about our relocation plans. Luke applied for a Colorado teaching license. (That would turn out to be the best thing he did to secure our future.) We explored the Denver metro area. We stayed with friends in Boulder but realized that buying a house in Boulder would not work. We visited the Longmont School District; that didn't feel right. We stayed in south Denver with David and Jenny. We didn't want to live in the mountains; we wanted the girls to experience a different life from inner-city Milwaukee. We had a whole year to decide.

Upon returning to Milwaukee, we listed our house and started to get rid of things. I packed nights and weekends and notified my boss that I would be leaving at the end of the school year. Our house was on the market for the whole year, but not a single person came to look at our inner-city home with no garage, in a drug-infested part of the city.

Milwaukee was in the midst of a recession; we had bought the house for $25,000 and were asking the same price. We scheduled open houses; no one came. We listed it with a different real estate agent, still no luck. At the end of the year, we still hadn't sold the house and neither of us had a job; we decided to move to Denver anyway. I ordered the moving van.

I had spent the year of 1988 dreaming/visioning how to create a new life in Denver. I made a vision board. I cut out pictures of how I imagined our Denver life would look. On my board I had placed a picture of a brick, ranch-style home with a two-car garage located in the suburbs. I wanted wood floors, three bedrooms and two bathrooms, and for our girls to attend the Cherry Creek School District. (I had learned about this district while working on my undergraduate teaching degree.) I wanted to make $24,000. (My dreams were low.) I stared at this board daily and repeated the affirmations whenever I glanced at it.

In late July, Shirley and I drove Colleen's old white van back to Colorado. (She and Robert had left the van in Iowa earlier in the summer.) I planned to look for a place to live, and Shirley wanted to sell her Denver house. We briefly considered buying her house, but we were set on living in the suburbs so that Sarah and Rachael could walk to school, ride their bikes around the block, feel safe and have their friends nearby.

Shirley had a friend who sold real estate, so we called her as soon as we got to Denver. I didn't want to move twice, so we looked for "rent with an option to buy." At the end of the second day, after looking nonstop, Marlene took us to a house in Aurora on Joliet Street, located between Iowa Street and Florida Street. I joked with her that this MUST be our house because my husband and I met in Joliet, Illinois, then moved to Aurora, Illinois, and our parents lived in Iowa and Florida. Sure enough, when we drove up to the house, we saw that it was a brick house with a two-car garage. It had four bedrooms. The owner was willing to rent with the commitment to buy the property within six months. It was perfect! I called Luke, and he agreed that I should put down a deposit.

At the same time, a friend from Milwaukee was living in Denver. She was the principal of the first Denver Public Schools Montessori School. She knew we planned to move to Denver, so she called to say the district was looking for Special Education teachers. We faxed Luke's resume; she hand-delivered it to the district office. Luke got a call the next day from the HR Director, asking him to come to Denver for an interview. Luke drove straight to Denver, had his interview and got hired the same day, with plans to start the following Monday. He flew home, helped pack as much of the house as he could, and then flew back to Denver to start work on Monday.

I prayed "Thank you God" at least a million times. I got to see how God responds if you set a clear intention and trust. Our biggest concern was what to do with our Milwaukee house; we did not want to leave it empty. I felt Divinely protected and guided to make this move to Colorado. What happened on our moving day was indeed a miracle.

The moving van arrived early on August 3, 1988. It was 101 degrees and 100% humidity, a typical hot, humid, summer Milwaukee day. The men loading the van had sweat dripping off their bodies the whole day. I kept bringing them water. I was both scared and excited. I stood in front of our house, praying about what to do with it. A man pulled up and asked me for directions to a house on the next street. I asked him if he was looking for a house to rent. He said, "Yes." I told him that he didn't need to find the house on the next street; he was actually looking for our house. He got out of the car and went inside. He said he needed a place right away and would rent our home! This was a miracle. He wrote a check for the August rent, and I gave him the keys and our contact information in Colorado.

As soon as the moving van left, we started cleaning the house. Sarah and I cleared out the refrigerator, vacuumed, dusted and loaded the vacuum into the car. We spent the night on our sleeping bags and began the journey to Colorado the next morning. It was a hot, sweaty, restless last night, but I was thrilled to be leaving Milwaukee. The next morning we left without saying goodbye to anyone. We were ready to start a new chapter of our lives.

Once we were in the car, both girls got excited and settled in for the long ride to Colorado. My plan was to drive to Lincoln, Nebraska, where my husband's brother lived, sleep over there, and then drive the next day to Denver. I wanted to arrive at our new house on August 5, just in time to celebrate our 16th wedding anniversary.

There was a miscommunication with Luke's brother. He was not home when we arrived, and I didn't have his phone number. We sat in front of his house for a long time, waiting for him to come; it started getting dark so I decided to look for a motel. We stopped at three motels; all three were full. Finally, the clerk at the third motel told us that we probably wouldn't be able to find a motel anywhere close to Lincoln because the state fair was in town. At that point, I made the decision to get on I-80 and just drive straight to Denver. The kids could sleep, and I would stop if I got too tired. I was operating on pure adrenaline, so excited to see Luke and celebrate our move and our anniversary.

I drove through the night and stopped only once at a rest stop because I was having trouble staying awake. I was nervous about being at a rest stop on the interstate by myself with the girls. It didn't feel safe. I couldn't sleep, so I decided to keep driving. I wasn't sure how long the drive was, but when the sun came up, we were close to Denver.

As we approached Denver, I stopped to consult a map about how to get to our new house. When we drove up in front of the house, we saw

Luke sweeping the garage. He had vacuumed, mopped the kitchen floor and scrubbed the bathrooms so we would arrive to a clean house. He gave us huge hugs and said he was worried all night. I told him about stopping at his brother's house, that no one was home, and then trying to find a motel. He wished me a happy 16th wedding anniversary; we kept hugging each other and saying how happy we were in Colorado. We took pictures in front of our new house.

I no longer had to worry about my Mom. We were free to create our own lives in Colorado. We would have lots of challenges before we got settled, but we didn't know it then. We were so happy to have this new lease on life. What a great anniversary it was!

This move is a great example of how resilient we were! We were faced with many adverse conditions as we made this move. We coped with each challenge. We did not become victims by blaming others. We did feel fear, anger, anxiety and distress, but we just kept going by coping with whatever was in front of us and, somehow, being propelled forward with the joy of the journey. That is what resiliency looks like.

CHAPTER FOURTEEN

COLORADO AND DENVER PUBLIC SCHOOLS

We arrived in Denver—but our furniture did not. The moving company had ten days to deliver our belongings without a penalty; they were finally delivered in the late afternoon of the ninth day. We immediately went to work unpacking and getting settled.

Luke had already begun his new job, so I registered the girls for school and explored Denver with them. We were thrilled to be living in this beautiful city so close to the mountains. We couldn't actually see the mountains, but they were off in the distance, at the end of our street. (I was now confident enough to venture to the end of the block to see them clearly!) Even though we had so little money, Luke and I were happy and very proud of ourselves for making our dream a reality.

The house was very dirty because it had been empty for months. The woman who had lived in the house (nicknamed "Corky") had "mental health issues," so she did not cook or clean." The neighbors said she had not done anything in the house for years. The oven was covered with plastic wrap, never used. The whole house desperately needed updating. There was red shag carpet everywhere, even behind the window shutters in the basement. Green, red and gold flocked wallpaper covered the walls. I decided to take time, before looking for work, to make the house more livable.

When I pulled up the old, worn carpet with no pad, I found beautiful hardwood floors. The tack lines on the edge of each room were the hardest to pull up; Luke used a crow bar to remove them. I was concerned about finding work but enjoyed losing myself in the house projects. Each project was therapeutic and a great escape.

We did not own the house, but since we had promised to purchase it within six months, I got permission to pull off the old wallpaper. Some of the rooms were easy, but a couple required spraying water on the wallpaper, then waiting until the water soaked in and then scraping it off. This was a long, slow, messy process. The basement had a family room, a large room with a pool table, a bathroom and an extra bedroom. The bedroom was claimed by Sarah, who was going to be a freshman and wanted more privacy. She had her own bathroom too. There were three bedrooms upstairs. We took the largest room, Rachael chose the middle-sized room next to us, and the smallest bedroom became our office/exercise/yoga room. This house was perfect for us.

Our living and dining/kitchen area needed a lot of attention. The dirty gold-flocked drapes went out the sliding glass patio door into the backyard. My time cleaning the house was a joyous time. I kept smiling because it seemed a miracle that we were in Denver. The only things left for me were to find work I loved and to sell our house in Milwaukee.

Luke was settling into his middle-school bilingual special education teaching position. While he did not have a Master's degree in Special Education, he had signed a contract committing him to acquire it within five years, so he registered for classes immediately and started pursuing his degree at the University of Colorado in Denver. We were grateful he was employed, even though he was on the beginning teacher salary schedule. Life was good, very good.

Our first Christmas in Denver, an old friend from Milwaukee asked us to attend the candlelight service at Mile Hi Church of Religious Science. It was a beautiful service and I loved the philosophy of this church. I discovered the Cherry Creek Church of Religious Science was less than two miles from our house. I attended regularly. It reminded me of St. Ann's in Milwaukee. I loved the teachings of this church: that there is One living Spirit that manifests Itself in and through all creation, that heaven is within us, that there is a unity to all life and that our thoughts create our life moment to moment. The Universe is *for* me, not against me.

I needed to find work quickly so we could buy the house. I searched the employment section of the newspaper and eventually registered with an employment agency. The employment counselor reviewed my resume and said, "You should apply at a school district." I said immediately, "I don't want to teach." With a very puzzled look, he asked, "What do you want to do then?" I had two Master's degrees in Education and an undergraduate minor in Education. I didn't know what I wanted.

I decided to substitute in the same district where Sarah and Rachael were attending. I was nervous every morning and after only a few times, decided I couldn't sub. My Milwaukee principal friend asked me to sub in her Montessori school. I said "yes" but I didn't want to end up teaching Montessori again. I had left all my materials and books in Milwaukee with friends, to make sure I wouldn't go back to teaching Montessori. Even though teaching Montessori was a great work of heart, I felt pulled to look for a new challenge.

My principal friend told me about a job posting for an alternative high school that planned to open a Montessori infant and toddler center. In Milwaukee, I remembered saying that I needed to work with babies because the three-year-olds were already at-risk. Some of them had never been read-to and were seriously lacking pre-literacy skills. I was learning that the type of thoughts and intentions that I "put out into the universe" came right back to me, so I started to watch what I was saying and thinking.

I applied at the alternative high school and got a call immediately. The principal gave me a tour of the school, and several teachers took part in my interview. I felt scared but I knew I would be offered the position. I cried the whole way home. I had to take this job because we needed to buy our house within six months, and five months had already passed. I had to have work to qualify for our mortgage. The position did not pay a teacher's salary but a day-care center director's salary. However, it would enable us to buy our house, so I accepted the job.

I opened and licensed the center within the high school. I did need a few classes to be director-qualified, so I took them at a community college. I realized almost immediately why I had cried when I left the interview; working with teen moms and their babies was heartbreaking. They were caught in a cycle of poverty; their own mothers had been teen moms. They looked for love and found it in a very small baby who was dependent on them. All of them agreed that they did NOT know what they were signing up for when they got pregnant. Often their boyfriends disappeared when they got pregnant. Only two of the ten girls had a father present.

I loved taking care of the babies and showing the moms a better way to care for them. (No Kool Aid in bottles, no screaming at their babies, watch/observe their babies for what they needed, etc.) Often I felt overwhelmed, even though I had an assistant, with the responsibility of caring for ten babies. A lovely, kind nurse at the high school named Bev came to check on us often. When she found me alone, she helped by holding one or two babies and rocking them to sleep. After all was quiet, we talked and got to know each other. This help was invaluable; we have stayed close friends to this day.

I worked at the school for a couple of years until it became apparent that I had a philosophical difference with the principal. Many of my teen moms were getting pregnant with their second child, even the thirteen-year-old mom. I asked that the teen moms be required to attend their high school classes. (They often dropped their babies at the center and then walked out the front door, to hang out with their boyfriends.) I didn't want the center to be a free babysitting service so the girls could get pregnant again. I wanted to support them by making sure they were in class, so they could graduate. When I asked the principal to require the teen moms to sign in for their classes, he said that didn't fit the philosophy of the program. I knew at that point I had to resign. The philosophical disparity was too great. My boss told me I would never be allowed to work for that district again. I also needed a higher salary. Sarah was applying to colleges and we were still living on a "shoe string."

Again, I was determined not to go back to teaching, so I took a somewhat unusual job, driving cars at the Denver Auto Auction. I could drive a stick shift, so I was often chosen first from all the guys who showed up to work the auction. Our job was to drive the cars through the bay to be sold. The cars often smelled badly. Sometimes I got to drive brand new cars through the bay. One time we got to drive a hundred brand new Subarus, from the location where they were taken off the train, to a lot closer to the auction house. The manager in charge was gruff. He said, "Drive and don't ask questions. Just do what you are told." Moving all those new cars was fun. Each time we moved a car, the van was there for us; we jumped in and returned to the field to get another car.

During this same time, I also got took a job at Veldkamps, a local flower shop, delivering flowers to hospitals, nursing homes and individuals. I loved the smell of the flowers in the back of the van. I thought it would be fun to deliver so much joy to people, but often people were receiving flowers because of a death or because they were ill. One young woman who received flowers from her ex-boyfriend complained to me, "Why is he still sending me flowers? I don't want his flowers." The hardest part of this job was finding the correct addresses. I did not know Denver; it was years before GPS. One day, my very grumpy boss, who sported a goatee and had a five-year growth on his pinkie nails, asked me where I had been, because it had taken me so long to deliver the flowers. I told him I had trouble finding some addresses. He replied, "You are slower than molasses in January! I have never met anyone as slow as you." I explained that I had recently moved to Denver and didn't know the city, and I was cautious because I was learning to drive a large van filled with flowers. He yelled, "SLOW. Get out of here."

When I had enough of that boss and his pinkie fingers, I quit and took a job with a small company planting flowers in business parks around Aurora. Despite these feeble attempts to make money, I wasn't making enough for our family to survive, but I felt carefree and happy. Subconsciously, I wanted to experience the life I had missed because I went to the convent so young. However, this was not the time to be exploring different jobs. I needed money to help support our family, and to make sure Sarah could go to college. Luke was teaching and slowly making more money each year, but we needed both of our salaries.

Finally, at midsummer, in desperation I called the Denver Public Schools Human Resource Department. The director set up an interview. When I entered his office, I was nervous but gathered my confidence and asked about teaching jobs. He looked at me and asked, "Why did you leave your previous position at the alternative high school?"

He seemed to understand completely. He told me the district closed the school as soon as the federal funds dried up. Almost in the same breath, he told me that the district had just received a huge federal innovation grant for working with at-risk kindergarteners. They needed six teachers to work with ten at-risk kindergarteners for part of the day. The only opening they had left was in Montbello. He said I could sign a contract that day. Elated, I said, "I will take the position." It was a teaching position, but it no longer mattered because I needed to get serious about making money.

I had prayed all summer for guidance about work. My prayers were answered with this job. I was going back to teaching, but the position sounded wonderful. If I had to teach again, this was the best situation I could imagine. I taught ten at-risk students in the morning and then they attended their regular kindergarten class in the afternoon. Another group of ten at-risk students attended their regular kindergarten class in the morning and then came to my classroom in the afternoon. It was a dream job. I taught in Montbello for six years and loved every minute. The students got lots of individual attention, and I was making a difference in their lives.

Many of my students from Montbello spoke Spanish, so I decided to go to Mexico for a summer to be immersed in the language. Luke worked with a young woman whose family lived in Xalapa, Vera Cruz. They owned a home in the family compound that was empty. She said

I could live there for the summer, immerse myself in the language and the culture. I loved the idea. I signed up for classes at the Universidad of Veracruzano in Xalapa. What a courageous and resilient thing to do! I had taken some Spanish but I was going there on my own, with limited skills. Language is not my strong suit, and I had no idea how lonely I would be, not being able to communicate with anyone. My classes helped some, but either the teacher was not very good or I wasn't a very good student. I did accomplish my goal to become a better communicator with my students and their parents.

In the sixth year the grant money ran out, so the Director placed all twenty at-risk students for the full-day in my classroom. That changed everything. Teaching twenty troubled kids in one room was an overwhelming challenge. They had no models of what good behavior or good student work looked like. I took a medical leave toward the end of the school year. Now what should I do? Sarah was in college, and Rachael was applying to colleges.

Again I looked for work outside of education. I applied many times to United Airlines; being a flight attendant had been a childhood dream. My resolve to not go back to education was even stronger. I felt called to do something different, but I didn't know what. I was stuck in an endless repeating cycle: I was a good teacher; I could earn a good salary teaching, but I was unsettled. Every time I left teaching, another teaching job presented itself almost immediately. I was confused. I knew my heart was calling me somewhere else but I didn't know where. Again, I prayed for direction. I felt helpless, and angry about this cycle; but I couldn't think of anything else to do other than pray, so that is what I did.

The summer quickly passed as I searched for work. I considered going back to school for another Master's degree but this was not an option with two daughters in college.

Through a friend, I heard about a teacher who had started the school year but was planning to go on maternity leave at the end of September. I called the principal to ask about the position, and she invited me to come for an interview. We had a great philosophical discussion. When I left, I thought she would hire me and she did. She called that night to offer me the job. I needed to start the next Monday. It was a Head Start classroom. I had one week to learn everything from the very pregnant teacher: Head Start rules and regulations, the students' names, their education issues and their family's challenges.

I was relieved to be working again, and the kids made a great transition as I turned the classroom into a Montessori-type environment. My assistant struggled with the changes. She commented, "This is not the way we do things." We barely made it through the year; she left as soon as the term was over. It was not an easy time for either of us. An even bigger challenge was that the other early childhood teacher in the adjoining classroom did not want to collaborate. She kept her door closed all the time. I was more isolated than I had ever been in my teaching career.

The principal who hired me left at the end of that year. I was sad because she was a good principal and we liked each other. The new principal lacked strong leadership skills; she was unpredictable, inconsistent and we "walked on eggshells." My new assistant became good friends with the new principal and hung out in her office during her breaks. The principal didn't speak to me directly; everything she knew about me she learned from my assistant. Early morning staff meetings were painful. Everyone was filled with fear and afraid to speak up. When the principal asked a question, only a few brave souls would speak.

Working in a Head Start program had a number of great benefits. The children attended class only four days a week. On Fridays, the teachers attended district Head Start meetings, held parent meetings, assessed eligible children or did lesson planning. At one of our Friday Head Start meetings, we were told that money was available for further teacher training. I knew my public speaking skills were poor, so I applied to take a Dale Carnegie course.

I attended the course every Tuesday evening for six months. The classes taught us how to speak in front of a group, how to manage stress in the work place and how to remember people's names. I could never have estimated at the time the impact this training would have on my life.

During the training I was irrationally nervous as I prepared an extemporaneous three-to-five minute speech every week. We were required to deliver this speech in front of the class. I was frustrated that I was terrified! I dreaded every class. The building was cold and I felt faint every week. At the breaks, I tried to compose myself in the bathroom. With forty students in the class, I sometimes had to wait three hours for my turn. Each week we had to create an even more dynamic, stimulating speech than the week before. The class voted on who was the most improved and who gave the best speech. I was actually awarded "best speech" one week. This helped to boost my confidence.

As part of the Head Start grant, I also had the opportunity to attend the National Head Start Convention in Minneapolis. I had lots of ideas, questions and concerns about Head Start. Every time I asked my boss a question, she told me I would understand once I attended the national convention. This was a large and powerful political organization, and at the convention I learned how difficult it was to make changes to Head Start; it was like turning around the Titanic.

I felt passionate about the plight of the Head Start mothers. Most were single mothers on welfare who had dropped out of school. Every morning they hung around after dropping off their children, talking to each other and to my assistant. They seemed lonely; they needed support. I could see the school needed to set up a GED class for them or teach them marketable skills so they could find work and escape the chains of the welfare system. I spoke with my supervisor about this idea. She said that there was a different department that would need to deal with that issue. The system was broken and I felt powerless to change it.

In my second year at this school, I got to know a new teacher in the building. Every day she came to my classroom during lunch so we could walk to clear our heads and get some exercise. I often made excuses to skip our walk, but she insisted I go; she believed walking would help us. We walked and talked nonstop. Our school was located one long block from a golf course, so it was easy to get there and walk our path. After much walking and talking, we decided that our situation was intolerable, and we resolved to find other jobs at the end of the year.

My friend found the perfect out. She got married and moved out of state at the end of the school year. I did not resign because I needed to find another job first. I applied for a number of central office positions in the district and believed that something would open up over the summer. During the summer, I called about the administrative positions I had applied for and was told the district had not decided who they would hire.

Even though I was scheduled to start my third year at the school, I believed that I couldn't go back. When August arrived and I had no other position, I was deeply depressed. I started the school year a mere shell of myself: no heart, no soul, no enthusiasm; I was just going through the motions. I was alone now that my friend was gone. I kept praying for an answer. Luke said, "When you come home from work and lay on the bed, you look like you are dead. You HAVE to find another job." I had packed all my personal belongings so that I could leave as soon as I had another job. I hoped the administrative job I had applied for would be funded and I would get hired.

That third year I had the most difficult student of my entire career—a four-year-old with severe anger-management issues who was constantly hurting other students. My assistant and I tried to always keep him separated from the other students, which was virtually impossible. Whenever he got near another student, he would kick, hit or scratch. The injured student would then cry, so the classroom was constantly being disrupted. My job was to keep the students safe; I could no longer do that.

I went through the proper channels to make a referral for this seriously disturbed student. I felt he needed either a day treatment program or a residential treatment program. I was informed I couldn't recommend alternative placement options because the district would have to pay for it. I completed the necessary paperwork for the referral. Lots of people spent time in my classroom observing and working with him. They all witnessed "incidents".

In the end, the professionals who had observed him recommended he remain in my classroom. If I did not agree to this plan, they would look for another teacher who would be "more understanding and compassionate to him." I told them to look for another teacher. This was the most professionally insulting accusation of my teaching career. I had always been good with my students. This was the first student that I had ever referred for more intensive services. I believed this was a clear sign from the Universe that I needed, once and for all, to leave teaching.

By late October, I could barely get out of bed in the morning, but I was doing a lot of praying and reading. I read Louise Hay's books, *Heart Thoughts* and *The Power Is Within You*. I saw that I had played the victim role most of my life. Louise said that the moment you say affirmations, you step out of the victim role into your own power. I had filled another entire notebook of affirmations, writing each one five times, sometimes ten times. I learned to stop saying, "I don't know" because it caused me to shut down access to my inner wisdom. I went to Louise's *I Can Do*

It conference in Las Vegas with a good friend. We had front row seats and even talked to Louise at a book signing in a local mall. We got to see Louise Hay, Jerry and Esther Hicks, Debbie Ford, Wayne Dyer, Dr. Christianne Northrup, Gary Renard and many more "new thought leaders." I was feeling impatient.

Then one Friday, in late October, everything changed. I attended a Head Start meeting and happened to ask my supervisor if the position I had applied for in April was still open. She said yes, the position was going to be filled, but they wouldn't take anyone from the classroom to fill it.

At that moment something snapped in me. I asked God to guide me and show me a way out of my "stuck" life. After the meeting I sat in my car, thinking, "What should I do? Where should I go? I must do something." I prayed for guidance in a way that I never had before. I asked God to help me; I could not figure it out myself. As I was sitting in the car praying, I asked myself, "If I can't have the administrative job, then what did I always want to do?"

Somehow I remembered thinking I wanted to work at the state Department of Education rather than in a school district. It was like a lightning bolt went off in my head. For the first time in a long while, I had a clear vision of what I wanted and the feeling was electrifying. I had wanted to work at the department, but I had been talked out of it eleven years ago when I first started subbing in Denver. I didn't go to lunch that day but instead went straight to the state education department office building.

The building was located across the street from the Capitol on a very busy street. I found an open parking space next to the building. I asked the security guard in the lobby where the Human Resources Department was located. He told me to take the elevator to the fifth floor. I asked if there were any openings. They said there were no openings, but gave me an application and told me to check the website regularly.

The inside of the building was beautiful, decorated with white marble from Marble, Colorado. The inner atrium opened to all five floors. I took the stairs from the fifth floor to the fourth. I was so excited I was barely able to breath. When I opened the door on the fourth floor, I saw a name on the office door that I recognized. I recognized this man's name for two reasons. First, he had the same name as my younger brother's best friend and, second, this man had just visited my classroom the week before with the mayor of Denver. The mayor had come to my classroom to read a book to my students for National Literacy Day.

I knocked on the door and he opened it immediately. I shook his hand and asked if he remembered me. He nodded, allowing me to explain that I always wanted to work for the Colorado Department of Education. He said there were no openings at the moment, but there could be tomorrow because everyone there was an "at-will" employee. He explained, "They could be here today and gone tomorrow." He asked me to send my resume and he promised not to file it. I was elated as I left the building.

Only one day later, Luke and I attended his middle school staff party. The wife of the vice-principal at Luke's school worked at the Department of Education. We spoke briefly and she said there was no reason why I couldn't work there; in fact, she knew of one opening in the Regional Services Unit. She thought I was qualified for the Regional Service Coordinator position, and she would help me apply. She would talk to the Assistant Commissioner about me. A couple of days later, Luke handed me an envelope that contained a job description for the position. I was thrilled.

The job description scared me, but I would apply anyway. I got a call in my classroom two days later from the Assistant Commissioner, asking me to come for an interview. I could not stop praying, "Your Will Be Done. I let go and let God be in charge of my life." I set the interview for four o'clock on the last Monday in October. I had one week to prepare for the interview.

To say I was psyched about the interview would be an understatement. That day, I taught class, but as soon as the students were dismissed, I drove downtown. I didn't want to risk anyone knowing about the interview, so I changed into my navy blue suit and crisp white blouse as I was driving. I threw my school clothes in the back seat and grabbed my leather briefcase—the one my boss had given me when I was the Director of the Huntington Learning Center. I had read *How to Dress for Success* and had attended a workshop on dressing professionally in the work place, so I felt confident.

I went to the second floor as instructed. I assumed the interview would be with the Assistant Commissioner. When I arrived, his assistant asked me to wait next door in a large conference room with one huge table and many chairs. She said it would take a few minutes to gather all the managers for the interview. My heart beat so fast as I waited for the eight Regional Managers—who all happened to be men. I had only one thought as I sat there. I MUST give this my best shot; this was my dream for many years. I took deep breaths, smiled and shook hands with each of the men as they came in, dressed in their black or navy blue business suits. It was an imposing group.

The Assistant Commissioner spoke first. He asked me to tell them about myself. I spoke about my passion for education, deeply rooted in my commitment to give my students a fighting chance at a better life. I described my twenty-nine years of teaching in the inner-city schools near Chicago, then in Milwaukee, and now in Denver, and about how difficult it was to help my students catch up. Even though they came into my classroom as three-year-olds, they were already at risk. I explained how poverty impacted each of my students' confidence and their ability to show up and enjoy the learning process. I had worked in so many different settings and programs, all in my quest to figure out why we were working so hard, yet making little progress. I told them that I thought the gift of working in the Regional Services Unit would be that I might find the answer to so many questions that plagued me. I confidently shared that I had a great track record of success in all my jobs; they were hiring me because I was a hard worker and was willing to do whatever it took to do the job successfully. Each of the managers asked me questions, and at the end of the interview, the Assistant Commissioner told me to call him if I had additional questions. I walked out of the building in a daze and was able to take some deep breaths only when I got to my car. This time, I smiled. I loved the interview and was sure this was where I wanted to work.

The next day I called the Assistant Commissioner to ask a few questions. He told me one of the managers was interested in me and would call for a second interview. He called the next day to set up the interview and told me the Deputy Commissioner wanted to be present for the interview. I was thrilled.

I was calmer for the second interview. The Pikes Peak Regional Manager asked me more questions, the first of which was about my Dale Carnegie Training...... he asked me why I didn't mention the training during my group interview? I told him, "I simply forgot, but the training had a huge impact on my life." This was a stroke of luck because he was a Dale Carnegie Trainer and was getting certified to teach the highest-level course.

He asked me if I really wanted the position, when I could start and what reservations, concerns or questions I had. After we talked for an hour, we went to the office of the Deputy Commissioner, who asked me more questions. I could tell he liked me, perhaps because I had worked in early childhood education and that was his passion. He had told the manager (before the interview) to hire me if he believed I was the right person for the job. He gave him a nod as we finished our interview.

Back in his office we agreed on a starting salary and a start date. I thanked him and told him I was looking forward to working together. I planned to submit a resignation letter to the school district, which I did the next day. I informed my principal, my students and their parents that I would be leaving in one month. This time I KNEW that this would be the LAST time I would leave teaching.

That last month of teaching flew by. The district hired an early childhood teacher who was familiar with Head Start and would work well with my assistant. I could not stop smiling. I felt excited but scared whenever I thought about my new job. Could I learn the job? How would I get downtown every day? What would I wear? I called my younger brother to tell him I got a job working right across the street from him. He worked in the State Controller's office; we could go to lunch together.

On the last day in my classroom, two fun things happened. The teachers gave me a farewell luncheon and a cute little "Bon Voyage" bear. I hadn't had this much attention since I got there. One teacher said it was her dream to work at the department; she hoped to join me there someday. Everyone wished me well.

At two o'clock on my last day at school, I got a call from the principal, asking me to come to her office because she wanted to conduct an exit interview. (I had asked her if it would be possible to have an exit interview before I left the district.) I was thrilled to have this opportunity. When I entered her office she was busy with paperwork. She said to wait in her office; she needed a few minutes to finish up some things. Finally she looked up. I thought she was ready to listen to my concerns about Head Start, the school, and the district. I started to speak but we were interrupted by two phone calls and then her administrative assistant. It gradually became clear to me that she was too busy to talk to me. After her third phone call, she said I was free to return to my classroom. So much for an "exit interview."

I returned to my classroom to find the room filled with parents. I had been called to the principal's office so my assistant and the parents could set up a farewell party. It was a huge surprise, and I was happy for the chance to say goodbye to my parents and their children. It was a grand send off, and I was thrilled.

During these years, I searched for ways to heal my childhood pain by going to therapy. One therapist said I had such a damaged childhood that I could never recover. I stopped seeing her. Another therapist, dressed in an angel costume, who believed that angels spoke through her, gave me a scary prediction about the outcome of my daughter's marriage. That was the end of that relationship. One psychiatrist was so concerned with my review of his services that he called my home to say his job depended on my good review and requested I give him an excellent rating. A female minister at my church told me so much about her own problems that I ended up counseling her. Through it all, I floundered many times but, somehow, I found the ability to take the steps necessary to follow through with the guidance I was being given. I had confidence in my strengths and abilities. I was unflappable in reaching for the goals I wanted to achieve.

My mom was right that I was "good with people." She could have also told me that she believed in me, that I was a good person, that she cherished me, that she saw so much good in me, that she saw me growing stronger each day, that she was here for me. She was not able to tell me those things. I was learning to tell myself things I needed and wanted to hear.

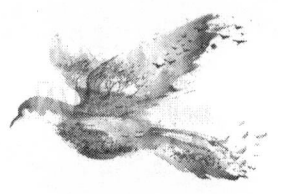

CHAPTER FIFTEEN

STATE DEPARTMENT
OF EDUCATION

It was November, 1999. My new position was an answer to years of praying, hoping and wishing for work I loved. It took more than praying, hoping and wishing to create a new life; it took action. Religious Scientists say, "Pray and move your feet." I had prayed incessantly, but it took years to actually "move my feet."

I began this new adventure—as a Department of Education Regional Coordinator working with school districts in the Pikes Peak Region. The first day on the job, everyone in my department was out of the office, even the administrative assistant, who was always there. I sat in my cubicle most of the day, wondering what I had gotten myself into. I was nervous and couldn't concentrate. A few people passed by and I asked them a couple of questions. They suggested I read the *Colorado Law Book*; I needed to know how Colorado laws affected education. These unfriendly colleagues gave me the message that I was disturbing them.

From the very first day, they seemed not to like me. It would take me a full year to discover why they resented me. Around midday, I got a call from the Human Resources office, asking me to complete the paperwork for my position.

I took the application home, and that evening when I pulled out my job-search file, I found the initial application I had started to fill out thirteen years before. One of my first days in Denver, I went to CDE to get an application because I knew I wanted to work there. I started filling it out but put it away when I heard so many negative comments about the department from teachers at the DPS school where I was subbing. They said, "Oh, you DON'T want to work there. It is not a good place to work because all they do is enforce federal government rules. You probably aren't qualified, and it is really hard to get a job there." But now I completed that unfinished application and delivered it and my resume to Human Resources the next day. I realized how easily I had been talked into giving up my dream many years earlier. That was not being resilient.

After my first day of feeling unsettled, I decided to give myself time to learn my new position. Every day was a little better because my boss explained things and shared the politics of this job. Everything was new and exciting. I loved attending meetings and savored every opportunity to learn and grow. I was happier than I had been in a long time.

The department had divided Colorado school districts into eight regions. My boss and I were responsible for twenty-four school districts in the Pikes Peak Region. We provided leadership and service to these districts "to promote high quality learning environments, high performance standards, and equitable learning opportunities for the students in their districts." I loved providing service to our districts. We also had a team of other CDE staff assigned to our region. They provided specialized expertise and technical assistance.

After a few weeks in my new job, our family drove to Nebraska to visit Luke's brother and his family for Thanksgiving. His parents were visiting from Florida. I was standing at the front door when my mother-in-law said, "Wow! Look at how great Janice looks!" I replied, "Yes, I have a great new job." I had gone shopping, bought a couple of new outfits and was wearing one of them—leather boots and a beautiful purple winter coat. I had a whole new lease on life.

I was thrilled to go to work every day. I had the amazing experience of smiling all the way to work, all day at work and then smiling all the way home. It was the first time in my life that I had a boss who believed in me. Every day was exciting and challenging, yet different.

Some days I traveled to districts to do accreditation reviews or to make presentations or meet with superintendents. Upon returning to the department, I consulted my boss about the appropriate responses to their issues. After a couple of months of attending superintendent meetings with my boss, he sent me alone to the meetings. I always did a presentation, so the Dale Carnegie training proved helpful. I prepared by calling a few superintendents to find out their concerns and questions.

My boss was the best. I quickly learned to love him; he believed in me and thought I could do anything. Shortly after I started, he was promoted to Assistant Commissioner, which came with many more responsibilities. In turn, he gave me more responsibility for our region. I loved it and I thrived. My work life had been almost exclusively with young children and women; now I worked with men. The guys were members of the "good old boys club" but they were fun. There was no jealousy, back-biting or gossip. Their "club" was exclusive and I was not part of it, but they sometimes asked me to join them for lunch. I loved walking alone at lunch; most days I walked "my circuit," which was ten blocks down Lincoln Avenue to Watson's Drugstore. There, I sat on a cement ledge to eat my lunch and then quickly walked back in time for afternoon meetings. In time, I made several friends who joined me on the Capitol grounds for lunch. These were happy days; I was learning and growing and loving my life.

The "superior" performance evaluations I received thrilled me and felt well deserved. I reviewed grant applications, did presentations at conferences and in districts on the new federal legislation (No Child Left Behind), did workshops and site visits to school districts, and made presentations in the department Board Room for groups of foreign visitors. I attended presentations and conferences to learn as much as I could about every issue confronting districts. I attended all the state science curriculum meetings and facilitated writing of the Science grade-level expectations.

I used nights, weekends and long drives to listen to and read self-help books. One of my close friends invited me to attend Louise Hay's I CAN DO IT conference and got us VIP seating close to the stage. We met Louise at a bookstore before the conference, where I purchased her latest book, *Meditations to Heal Your Life*. When she autographed it, I asked her a question about my life: "Louise, I feel confused about the next steps in my life. I like my work, but I would like to write a book. Is that a good idea?" She promised she would answer my question by email. A week later I received Louise's answer, and a personal affirmation: "I relax and appreciate the perfect unfolding of my highest potential. As I stand in my power, I embody love, healing and compassion for myself and all my relationships."

I carried this affirmation with me every day and began to take my writing more seriously. Rachael helped me turn our guest bedroom into my office. She gave me her heavy wooden desk with file drawers and a glass top, with room for my small stereo, a candle, printer and computer.

We placed it in front of the double windows so I could glance at the mountains while I wrote. In another corner of the office, I set up a small altar on top of my convent trunk. She also gave me a round, purple cushion called a zafu and a zabuton, the rectangular cushion placed under the zafu when meditating. For Christmas Rachael gave me a gorgeous cherrywood traveling Buddha, which took its place on my altar with a lotus flower candle. I lit a candle every morning and spent time sitting quietly as I read the Course in Miracles cards and wrote in my journal. I said a Buddhist affirmation every morning: "May we all be peaceful and at ease. May we all be filled with loving kindness. May we all be free from fear and danger. May we all be happy." Rachael was getting her Master's degree at Naropa, a Buddhist University in Boulder, so I read everything I could on Buddhism.

After working at the department for four years, I was presented with an incredible opportunity. Denver had a sister city, Yamagata Prefecture, in Japan. Two men from Yamagata had an office in downtown Denver, and one day they visited the department, looking for students to perform in their National Cultural Festival. They were offering an all-expense-paid trip for nine days for twenty-four students and six adult chaperones.

I volunteered to find a high school student choir to take advantage of this amazing opportunity. I researched online all the schools that had performed at past music teacher conferences in Denver and contacted every high school that had performed for the past few years. I left messages for the music teachers, but most didn't return my call. A music teacher from Rocky Mountain High School in Fort Collins called immediately. She had taken her students to Europe the previous year and said she would LOVE to take her students to Japan. She promised to send me a CD of her students' performances. When the CD arrived, our administrative assistant and I delivered it to the Yamagata representative's office. They called the next day to say they wanted this group to perform in their cultural festival. I called the music teacher to give her the good news and to tell her that our administrative assistant and I wanted to be included in the group of adult chaperones. The music teacher had already decided to bring her own friends and colleagues. They had traveled to Europe as a team the year before. If we went as chaperones, it meant two of her friends couldn't go.

We submitted our names with the list of students. We were elated about this opportunity. The music teacher invited us to hear the students perform two weeks later at the Capitol. They were talented and were comfortable performing. The music teacher invited us to a meeting to talk about the Japan trip with her students. She introduced us as the two people who had made this trip possible. We enjoyed meeting the students and made plans to meet them at the airport the morning of our departure.

We landed at Narita International Airport outside of Tokyo. After clearing customs, we were transported by bus to the Tsubasa Super Express train that brought us northwest to the Yamagata Prefecture. We had reservations at the best hotels, restaurants and hot springs in Japan and received two hundred dollars in spending money. I loved being in Tokyo. I had never seen so many people on the streets anywhere else in the world. There were thirteen million inhabitants of Tokyo, compared with eight million in New York City. The extra five million people made a huge difference. Exploring the city, we found a one-yen store (like our 99-cent stores), where we had much fun shopping for gifts for family and friends.

Afterwards, I felt grateful for the Japan trip and continued to work happily at the department. I stayed out of the limelight, secure in knowing that my boss believed in me and protected me. As new people were hired, a number of my female colleagues confided that they thought I was "being used" by my boss. I was doing his job because he had been promoted to Assistant Commissioner. However, I was not eager to take on this issue because I knew women didn't have a good track record dealing with this male-dominated power structure. I was grateful to have a supervisor who believed in me, helped me and protected me.

At one point during my first six years, I got permission for and applied to the Fulbright Exchange Program for a six-week administrative leave to go to Thailand. I would learn about the education at the "Harvard of Bangkok," and one of the administrators from that university would come to the department. I got glowing reference letters from my boss and the deputy commissioner. When I was chosen for the program, they told me that I could not go unless I used my personal vacation time, for which I had an insufficient amount of time, so I was told I couldn't go. This is one time that I wish I had been resilient enough to say I was going anyway. Maybe the administrators thought I wouldn't be chosen. Whatever the reason, I was not strong enough to stand up for an incredible opportunity.

Then, something terrible happened in my sixth year. My boss started to complain about not feeling well. I didn't take these complaints seriously because he routinely rode his bike fifty miles on the weekends. Once a week he biked to work from his home, a twenty-five mile trek. He was an incredible athlete, played basketball in high school and then attended college on a basketball scholarship. When he complained about his aching muscles, I thought, "I would be tired, too, if I pushed my body the way he does." But his symptoms continued to get worse, and he finally revealed that he was having tests to confirm that he had either Muscular Dystrophy or Lou Gehrig's Disease (ALS). He preferred the first diagnosis because he would be dead in two to five years with ALS. I didn't know anyone with ALS, so I had no idea of the severity of such a diagnosis.

His diagnosis was ALS. It is a progressive neurodegenerative disease that affects nerve cells in the brain and the spinal cord. It would eventually render him completely paralyzed. He was given two to five years to live. The day he received the diagnosis, he was scheduled to give a presentation at the Colorado Association of School Executives (CASE) Winter Conference. Our administrative assistant called me, requesting that I help him because his fingers were already too weak to use his computer. It was one of the most powerful presentations he ever gave. He looked like he might cry during the entire presentation. Afterwards, we all gave him a huge hug, when he told us the doctor had given him the bad news that morning. This was unusual because we didn't normally hug each other. I knew this disease had terrible implications for him but, also for me. He would no longer be there to protect me.

My boss was dying and my first instinct was to bolt, a pattern I had established early in my life. I was working long hours, traveling every week to the Southeast part of the state. (Yes, he promoted me when the Southeast Regional Manager position became available.) Then the perfect opportunity to "bolt" presented itself. I belonged to my next door neighbor's book club. Three of the book club members were going to China with a couple who had taught in Shanghai for three years. My neighbor needed a roommate to qualify for the double occupancy discount, so she invited me to go. I was distressed about my boss and this sounded like a grand adventure—and a great escape. Luke was teaching full time so he couldn't go, but he encouraged me to go.

The trip to China began with some big drama. I was traveling for work the week before, so I packed late the night before we were leaving for China. After I had gone to bed, I realized that I had forgotten to pack my passport, so I got up and grabbed it out of my top dresser drawer and threw it in my backpack. I felt frazzled and unprepared for the trip, but I consoled myself with the idea I was getting away and would return home refreshed.

I got a ride to the airport with my neighbor. When the airline attendant asked for my passport, I pulled it out of my backpack. My face turned white when she informed me that my passport had expired. I had renewed it months before but, in the haste of my last-minute packing, I grabbed the expired one. My heart started racing. Was I going to miss the trip to China? How could I get my passport in time? We lived forty-five minutes from the airport. There was one saving factor......Rachael and her boyfriend had visited the night before and were still at the house. If they answered the phone, they could run my passport to the airport before I had to board my flight. They answered the phone, located my new passport and brought it to me before the flight left. That was a miracle in itself. I tried to calm my jangled nerves as I boarded the flight. I looked for my seat and saw that it was far from my neighbor and the book club members. We landed in San Francisco and had only an hour to get to our connecting flight to Shanghai. This trip would last eighteen days and would give me a chance to fulfill deeply-held dreams about China. We would visit Shanghai, Xi'an, Lijianing and Guilin, take a cruise on the Yangtze River, visit the Three Gorges Dam, and end up in Beijing with a visit to the Great Wall of China, The Forbidden City, and Tiananmen Square.

We landed in Shanghai late in the day. When we got off the plane and gathered outside, I realized, for the first time, that there were thirty-five people in our group. I had never traveled with a large group, and I immediately felt overwhelmed. (I had not yet learned that I didn't do well in large groups.) Large groups of people drain my energy, and I need time alone to recharge. At the orientation, I asked if we were required to attend every scheduled event. The organizers said we could opt out of any event; this turned out not to be true.

I was in China, and I needed to figure out how to cope with our large group. A bus took us to a Chinese restaurant located next to our hotel; our luggage was delivered to the lobby to claim after our meal. I was not hungry. I sat at a table next to a man who looked about my age. His name was Jim, a retired attorney. After dinner he said he wanted to send an email to his wife, to tell her that he had arrived safely. I wanted to email Luke, so went together to find a computer. It was during this search that I noticed a huge sore on his head. I asked him, "What happened to your head?" He said he had fallen that morning. I said, "That is a bummer!" and he said, "It sure is...." He told me his wife was worried about him taking this trip; she believed he wasn't well enough. He came because his daughter was teaching English in Beijing, and he wanted to see her. I wondered why he didn't just go to Beijing to visit her. Little did I know that this chance meeting with Jim would impact my trip at such a deep level.

We spent two days in Shanghai and then flew to Guilin, China's most scenic city. The next day, we rented bikes and had a treacherous ride through the city, navigating the traffic through all the roundabouts. Out of the city, we rode along quiet fields, seeing traditional residences, stone bridges, winding canals and the beautiful countryside. We stopped at a peasant's home to see how simply Chinese peasants lived. The poverty I saw there was indelibly etched into my memory. Nothing in our country comes close to that level of poverty.

I sat next to Jim at a number of meals and noticed that he wasn't eating. One of our tour members had given me a can of tuna and crackers, and I offered it to Jim in hopes it would make him feel better. The next morning we took a flight to Lijiang. Later, I noticed Jim sitting near the bus. He said he wasn't strong enough to walk down the pathway to see the Leaping Tiger Gorge. He appeared to be getting weaker. I asked if he had eaten the tuna and he said, "No." When I asked him why, he said, "I'm not hungry."

That evening we took a flight to Xi'an. After resting, we toured the incredible Terracotta Warriors. I was seriously worried about Jim because he seemed even more lethargic and weak. That night I didn't sleep well, so the next day I rested on the bus instead of touring a silk factory. Jim was resting, too. I heard other people on the trip commenting on how anti-social he was, how he refused to talk to people and just sat there staring blankly during meals. I believed he was getting sicker every day of the trip.

At the airport in Xi'an, I asked Jim if he wanted to fly straight to Beijing to see his daughter. He looked puzzled. I shared my concerns about his deteriorating health with our guides. I said, "I believe he is too ill to continue and too sick to make the decision to fly to Beiing to be with his daughter." Miraculously, they agreed and quickly made arrangements for a direct flight to Beijing. I helped with his bags and said goodbye to him.

While Jim was on his way to Beijing, our group flew to Chongqing, a large city with twenty-nine million inhabitants, located in southwestern China. This was one of my favorite cities. We saw little children with slits in their pants peeing in the street, men carrying numerous boxes of shoes balanced on a pole on their backs, and many Chinese people staring at us. It might have been the first time they had seen Westerners. We took their pictures and they took ours.

The next morning, we boarded a ship for a Yangtze River cruise on China's longest river. As an early childhood Montessori teacher, I read The Story of Ping, about a little duck named Ping who has adventures on the Yangtze River. When I read that story, I thought I would love to see the Yangtze River someday. Now "someday" was happening. Our cruise lasted three days. I realized, once again, that if you have a strong desire and do not worry about how it will happen, the Universe provides the circumstances to make your dreams come true.

After the Yangtze River cruise, we visited the site of the Three Gorges Dam Project, the largest hydroelectric dam on earth. I had read about the controversy surrounding the dam—millions of people had to be displaced to build the dam. They had lost their land and their livelihoods and were relocated to high-rise apartments in small cities along the banks of the river. We saw these high-rise buildings on the cruise. Many Chinese people believe that once you start interfering with the course of the mighty Yangtze River, there will be huge consequences to pay. Time will tell whether this is true.

The last leg of our trip was a flight to Beijing, where we visited Tiananmen Square, the largest city square in the world. During the protest of 1989, a solitary Chinese protester stood in front of a line of oncoming military tanks, in a brave attempt to prevent the tanks from entering the square. My boss had a poster of this encounter hanging in his office; I had often studied it and dreamed of seeing the Square and summoning that kind of courage for my own life.

Across from Tiananmen Square, the huge painting of Mao hung in front of the magnificent Forbidden City, a palace filled with imperial treasures from many centuries of Chinese history. The next day we walked along the Great Wall of China. Built over two thousand years ago, it stretched four thousand miles through mountains and deserts across northern China. It was thrilling to walk on the wall. One of the few things I purchased in China was a red shirt that said, "I HIKED THE GREAT WALL OF CHINA." I wore that shirt for years, until it was too faded to wear. On our last day in China, I joined a large group of women doing Tai Chi in the park. These elderly Chinese women had

RESILIENT

maintained their courage and strength by working with the Chi energy during the tumultuous times in their history, especially during the Cultural Revolution.

Toward the end of the trip we heard that Jim's daughter had picked him up at the airport in Beijing, but Jim had immediately lapsed into a coma from which he never woke up. He was eventually airlifted back to Denver, where he died in a local hospital. I had taken the trip to escape thinking about my boss's death but found myself confronted with another man equally ill who was also dying.

My trip to China was finally over and I was thrilled to be going home. I learned so much about myself. I knew I would never again take a trip without Luke or with a large group. I called him to tell him to tell him that. He asked, "Are you having a good time?" I said, "I have seen so many great things, but I wish you were here."

Back at work things got worse. My wonderful boss retired and I had a new boss. I was more unsettled than ever. If I had been truly resilient, I would have had the courage to leave my job at that point. Three distinct times my intuition, or the still small voice of Spirit, told me to leave. The first time was while I was riding the 16th St. mall shuttle to catch my bus home after a long week on the road. The assistant commissioner was riding the bus as well, and I was talking to him about the dismal state of the department. (I was feeling particularly despondent that day, after a long week of travel.) Suddenly, the bus driver slammed on the brakes. I was thrown into the horizontal bar that connected the large double doors that let passengers on and off the bus. After I hit the bar, I was thrown back onto the floor. My bag and shoes flew off in different directions. The assistant commissioner helped me up. The driver stopped the bus and came back to check to see if everyone was okay. She apologized for

285

the quick stop, saying she had to brake quickly or she would have killed a pedestrian. The assistant commissioner asked, "Are you okay?" I replied, "I think so."

He got off at the next stop; I felt dizzy and struggled to breathe. When I got off the bus four blocks later, I knew that I needed help. I saw an RTD employee standing by the bus stop and told her I was injured while riding the bus. She took me into the RTD offices located in the same building as the station. She asked if I needed medical attention and I said, "Yes". They called an ambulance which took me to the nearest hospital.

I called Luke from the hospital to tell him what happened. I insisted that my injuries were not serious. He said he would come right away. I was sure I would get checked out and released. I had pain in my rib area and had trouble breathing, but I knew there was no treatment for cracked or bruised ribs. I thought my shortness of breath and lightheaedness were due to shock. I was so sure the doctor would let me go home that I put my clothes on under my hospital gown. But when the doctor returned, he said I would be moved to another hospital covered by my insurance. I had a number of cracked ribs and a punctured, partially collapsed lung. I heard the still small voice saying, "Now, will you leave this difficult situation?" I had full resolve to do that and prayed for guidance.

When I arrived at the second hospital, I had more tests. The emergency room doctor said, "The first twenty-four hours are critical for a partially collapsed lung, so the staff will monitor you every hour throughout the night. If you do well for the next twenty-four hours, you can be released." Luke and I settled into my hospital room, with pain medications for me, and we prepared for the twenty-four hour wait. Finally, morning came and I was released.

I called my new boss at the department; he asked to meet with me as soon as I was well enough. We agreed to meet in a week. I knew he wanted me to quit; in fact, he had already told everyone I was leaving. However, in the intervening week, I lost my resolve. At our meeting, I told him I would return as soon as the doctor released me.

The second time that I knew I should leave was when our daughter announced that she was pregnant with her second child. If I continued at the department, I would miss my second grandchild's birth and first years. I had already missed our first grandson's first year because I was traveling so much.

The third time that I knew I should leave happened when I purchased tickets to see Sylvia Browne, a working psychic and *New York Times* #1 bestselling author, who was conducting a workshop at the Denver Convention Center. When we entered, we received a wristband with a number on it. Sylvia would be calling numbers of the winners for a free reading in front of the audience. I felt SURE she would call my number, so I started thinking about what I would ask her. She called my number; I climbed down what seemed like hundreds of steps to a microphone to ask her advice about my stressful job. She immediately responded, "This job is killing you, and a lot of other people too. Leave it as soon as possible, and do the creative project you have been dreaming about for so long. Don't wait." In front of thousands of people, I was told to leave my job immediately. That should have been enough to move me to action.

Where was my resiliency during this period of my life? It was not there. If I had been strong, I would have walked into the department at that point and resigned. However, I had grown up with suffering as the norm. I still believed that suffering was a natural part of showing up in my life.

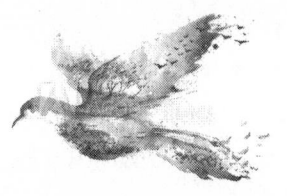

Chapter Sixteen

Leadership and Life Coaching

So I continued to suffer at the department. I was sad because I knew that my days were numbered. I no longer loved my work. I spoke to my friend, Karen, telling her that my daughter was pregnant and that I felt unsettled at work. Karen suggested I talk to her friend, Steve. She said he might be able to help me sort things out. She gave me his number and said I should contact him only if it felt right. I called immediately. He answered on the first ring and we set up a time to meet at a Starbucks halfway between both of our homes. I was excited, nervous and desperate about my life. I had begun my eighth year at the department; it felt like it was time to leave, but I was not sure about what to do next.

I met Steve two days later. He had balding white hair, dark rimmed glasses and a wonderfully welcoming smile with an air of confidence that scared and enticed me. I wanted his confidence. He shared his journey of working as a dentist for years, with a six-figure income, then choosing a new career when he no longer found himself loving his work. He hired a life coach who helped him realize that he had coaching skills himself, so he studied to be a life coach. Now he was coaching others. I believed that he might be able to help me, so I committed to meeting with him twice a month for the next three months. During those three months, he listened intently as I explored all that I was tolerating in my life, what was my passion, what options were open to me at this juncture in my life, and how to address the issues I was facing at work.

Steve gave me the courage to take actions I couldn't take on my own. I watched myself get stronger with each session. At one point, we talked about the possibility of me becoming a life coach. I was astonished when he said he thought I would make a great life coach. I was incredulous: "You have to be kidding me!" He said, "No. I think you have the skills to be a great coach." I found myself hyperventilating at the mere suggestion that I was strong enough to guide others. It was both terrifying and exhilarating. (The feeling was much like when I gave myself permission to leave the convent or to go to work at the department.) He said he would hire me if I got the coaching certification because he planned to start a "leadership coaching" company.

I loved the idea of becoming a coach and immediately registered for coaching classes at Coach University. I told Luke about Steve's suggestion and, as always, Luke was supportive. He said, "Do it." I chose the online coaching program that Steve had used. The school was founded by Thomas Leonard, the "founding father of modern-day coaching." I continued working at the department, taking classes and exams online and all my practice sessions by phone. Even though I had a clear goal to leave the department after I finished my classes, I doubted my plan. I forgot that every clear thought/intention creates our reality from moment to moment. Buddha said, "What you think you become." I pushed aside my doubts in order to move forward with my next steps.

My course work at Coach University was easy. Each student had a coaching partner so we could practice coaching. I told people at work that I needed "volunteers" to practice my new coaching skills, and a number of colleagues volunteered. In order to graduate, students were required to have a certain number of hours of practice sessions and a certain number of paying clients. Some of those volunteers became my first paying clients; I charged a small fee. In class we created a coaching packet and a planning document which I used in my practice sessions. I loved my clients and quickly became their "success partner" as they gained the courage to take action on issues that drained their energy. I had my clients complete the "Clean Sweep Program," a checklist of 100 items grouped in four areas of life: Physical Environment, Well-being, Money and Relationships. The program helped me to clean up my life, as well as my clients.

During my year of coaching classes, I continued to struggle with my new boss. His screaming at me was abusive. Somehow this screaming was the last straw. I was no longer willing to accept anyone treating me that way. When I spoke to the commissioner about the situation, he said, "If you have pissed him off, you might as well give it up." So, I said, "Then I am giving it up." He didn't argue with me and advised that if I wrote a "politically correct letter" he would agree to accept my resignation. I went to my office over the weekend to clean out my desk and file cabinet. I felt scared, relieved and sad, but I knew it was the right thing to do. My life was about to take a dramatic turn. On Monday morning I submitted my resignation letter, then met with the HR Director to sign exit papers. I spent the rest of the day saying goodbye to all the people there that I loved. This life-changing event happened the same month that I finished my coaching course work. Again, I was learning the power of my word to create my life. When I first started working at the department, I felt that I shouldn't stay too long, because it would become too easy to lose touch with what was important in the school districts. I had watched many people leave over the years; now it was my time to go.

The first person I wanted to tell about leaving the department was my old boss, who was still alive. So I made the fifty-mile trek to his home. He had been so good to me; we still had a special bond. It had been months since I last saw him. It was frightening to see him in his motorized wheelchair. He had lost his ability to do almost everything for himself, but he had very little pain, and he was incredibly grateful for that. The ALS had deeply affected his body but not his mind. I was thrilled to tell him that I had resigned. He said he was happy for me. Even though he was happy, I could tell his mind had long ago abandoned any thoughts about the department. He died two weeks later.

I would love to tell you that life after I left the department became "all peaches and cream," but that would not be true. I was happy to have ended that chapter of my life, but I wasn't ready to quit working completely. Now what? Keeping busy doing mindless tasks became my best, short-term answer. I found the answer in the basement of our home.

Luke had collected so many boxes of files from his years of teaching middle school. They sat piled up in the long hallway of our basement. With a mind and heart that needed to heal, this was the perfect project. The boxes held files and student work that needed to be shredded. For hours, I sat, mindlessly shredding papers. I cried and let go of all the pain I had experienced at the department but also in my whole life. I was learning a new level of trust and surrender as I "let go and let God." I had prayed the "Our Father" so many times growing up and during my convent years, but now one part of the prayer began to make so much sense—"Your will be done on earth as it is in heaven." I also repeated the affirmation, "I am willing to let go and let God run my life." I remembered a thought from one of the many books I was reading during this time: "You must let go of the small life you have planned, so God's bigger plans can unfold."

When I left the department, I had a few clients who wanted to continue with their coaching. They gave me hope that I could use my gifts of insight, listening and wisdom to help heal myself and them. At the same time, another brilliant Divine intervention happened: two of the regional managers I worked with left the department shortly after I did to take the superintendency and assistant superintendency of a small school district south of Denver. They contacted me to ask if I would be willing to work with one of their principals who was struggling. I agreed to meet with them. Parked in the district parking lot, I prayed, "Spirit, I thought I was finished with education.... Please let me know if You want me to do this work. Thank you." The answer was "yes." It seemed like the right thing to do.

I loved empowering my client to make the best decisions for herself, as she responded to school and district pressures. At the end of the year, the superintendent said that he didn't know how much he had paid me, but it was "not enough" because the situation with the principal was resolved smoothly. In the fall he offered his whole leadership team district-paid leadership coaching sessions twice a month, and almost everyone on the team participated. This situation was a dream come true because I knew that administrators desperately needed more support than they were getting.

Life gradually started to feel great again; I had some income to supplement my pension, but most importantly, I had time to enjoy my life. I volunteered at Project Angel Heart every Monday. I had time to walk and hang out with friends I hadn't seen in years. My daughter won a full scholarship for her Master's at Denver University right after her second child was born. Luke and I helped with her new baby and her two-year-old. We got to spend time with our grandsons. Gradually, it became clear that leaving my job was the best thing that ever happened to me.

The next year the superintendent asked if I would work with his Leadership Team and any teachers in two elementary schools who wanted to take advantage of leadership coaching. Both schools were "Turnaround Schools," a designation that meant the district could receive funding under the Race to the Top and School Improvement Grants programs. The district planned to apply comprehensive interventions to their low-performing schools, with the goal of making significant gains in achievement. My work as a leadership/life coach to private clients continued, as well as my coaching work with administrators and teachers in the district.

I had the best of the coaching world, and an enviable problem that most coaches would love to have: too many clients. After three years, I began to feel burned out. I worked with four or five clients a day. I knew I wasn't practicing self-care; my schedule didn't allow time to replenish myself. One day I had a profound insight: "If I were to die today, would I be pleased with this life I created?" I honestly had to say, "No." I didn't have time to enjoy life. I longed for time alone—to relax, to write, to slow down, to enjoy each day. I had managed to turn my coaching practice into a full-time job! I was out of balance!

I was learning to honor my intuition and the still small voice of Spirit that said I needed more self-care. I was aware of my lack of balance. I realized that I could no longer work as a coach in the district that next year because I was depleted. However, I was not honest with the superintendent because I couldn't be honest with myself. My clients were not happy that I left, so I met with the superintendent and was able to reach a compromise. I agreed to coach a smaller group of committed district clients whom I loved. The school district generously supported their leaders with a "mental health stipend" which allowed us to continue to work together. Although I had fewer clients in my eighth year of coaching, I found great joy in my work and knew I was doing what I came here to do. Finally, I found profound peace in using my gifts to support my clients to live a happier, more peaceful and more productive life. With each coaching session, I pray, "My voice. Your words." I know there is Divine Order in the Universe and that chance plays no part in deciding who my clients are; they have been called by Spirit. I have the privilege of playing a small part in their healing. I pray St. Francis' prayer before each session and remind myself that I step back, way back, so that Spirit can work through me, as me. I pray, "I am the face of God. I am among the ministers of God." It is the greatest honor to serve in this way. Each morning I start my day by reading a quote from the *A Course in Miracles* which hangs in my office above my altar:

"I am here only to be truly helpful.
I am here to represent Him who sent me.
I do not have to worry about what to say or what to do
Because He who sent me will direct me.
I am content to be wherever
He wishes, knowing He goes there with me.
I will be healed as I let Him teach me to heal."
from *A Course in Miracles*

I have always had a coach since I studied to be a coach. Recently I hired a new coach to support and inspire me. I wanted to know: What is calling me forth now? Have I accomplished what I came here to do? Should I continue coaching? How can I continue to grow and challenge myself? Ralph Waldo Emerson said, "People wish to be settled. Only as far as they are unsettled is there any hope for them." I was unsettled and needed to go deeper. In the deepest recesses of my heart, I knew I needed a stronger voice, to have more self-compassion, to speak my truth, to play bigger. I wanted to find the courage to put myself out there, to publish my book and share my story. I am committed to listening to the still small voice of Spirit which continues to call me forth to be the magnificent person I came here to become. This book is calling me; I could ignore the voice, but it will only get louder. So my resiliency kicks in, and I persevere.

Marcel Proust said, "The real voyage of discovery consists not in seeking new landscapes, but in having new eyes." In seeking new eyes, I decided to go to Brazil to spend two weeks with *John of God*. When I heard my coach describe her spiritual journey to John of God, I knew I wanted to go. So, in October 2016, I contacted the woman who guides trips to the Casa in a small town in central Brazil to be with John of God. I read a book by Mytrae Meliana, John of God. It asked, "Are you ready to open to your personal miracle?" I was ready.

But first I needed to know more about John of God. He is a full-trance medium. He was clairvoyant as a boy and became a spiritual healer as a teenager. He grew up in poverty. John barely finished first grade. He couldn't read or write yet, through his strong will and intuition, he managed businesses that supported him, his family, and the Casa. He dedicated his life to his healing mission. He doesn't remember what he says while in a trance. Very few mediums are able to incorporate as many entities as he does, and his work has touched millions of people over the course of his life. John of God says frequently, *"I have never healed anyone. It is God who heals."*

I felt called to go to Brazil. I applied for a visa, paid for my trip and bought airline tickets. I purchased white clothes. (We were required to wear white to the Casa on the days we went before John of God, which was Wednesday, Thursday and Friday.) Our group leader encouraged us to disconnect from our daily life, to focus on the beauty in Brazil and to set clear intentions to heal the areas of our lives that needed healing.

I spent two weeks at the Casa. It was springtime in Brazil. The azaleas, orchids and birds of paradise flowers were in full bloom; the weather was wonderfully warm and sunny. Our hotel had rocking chairs on both the front and rear patios. An enclosed aviary with love birds from Australia kept us entertained. The entrance to the hotel was locked; one could enter only if you knew where the bell was to call for a worker to unlock the door. Fresh, organic homegrown food was served every day. Beautiful music played throughout the hotel, and we were encouraged to be silent on the days we met with John of God.

I went before John of God with three thousand other people from all over the world on All Saints' Day on November 1st. We waited a very long time, but finally it was my turn. We passed first through the "current room," which was filled with people sending us currents of love to aid our healing. When we entered the room where John of God was sitting, we saw that he was surrounded by many large, beautiful crystals. We all felt his energy and each person asked for their own healing.

I loved sitting in the current room, praying and listening to beautiful music as each person passed on their way to meet with John of God. The second week of our stay, I was sitting in the current room when a miracle happened. Sitting in this beautiful space, I was overcome with the sense that my parents were there. They said, "We love the work you are doing in the world. We love you. Keep going. Don't stop." It was a brief message, but one I desperately needed in order to heal. I was overcome with emotion. I felt a huge weight lifted as I released years of resentment. I always wondered why my mother treated me so badly and why my dad abandoned me. With the receipt of this loving message, I was able to forgive them and let go of the resentment I had carried for so long. This was the healing I couldn't have articulated, but as soon as it happened, I knew I was free in a way that would change my life forever. It became clear that I must continue working as a life coach and that I would find a clear path to publishing my book. I returned home with an affirmation: "I am resilient. I love and accept myself, and by persevering, I will succeed." In Brazil I learned that we are never alone. I have the Entities and my Higher Holy Spirit Self to guide and support me. "Ask and you shall receive; seek and you will find and knock and the door will be open."

What I have learned as I reflect on my life is that resiliency is about being strong—physically, mentally, emotionally and spiritually. It is a daily commitment to live a fully conscious life. It's a commitment to love myself through it all. I realize that anything that happens TO me is a gift and, even if painful things happen, I believe this is happening FOR my growth. I see the mistakes I have made and the many decisions that were not in the best interests of my family or me. The greatest lesson might not be loving myself, but forgiving myself. With a strong, open heart, my work continues to be to forgive everyone in my life, including myself, and to love and accept myself throughout this life journey. This journey is not over yet, but I feel immense gratitude to everyone who has played a part in helping me learn the lessons I came here to learn. My deepest yearning is that I stay out of judgment and keep my heart open to unconditionally loving everyone in my life. I continue to seek, ask and knock, so I can receive Grace that comes with an open heart and mind, and with the mindset that, whatever arises, I will love that. We are simply walking each other home.

And so I conclude this book with gratitude and a prayer from Louise Hay:

"In the infinity of life where I am
All is perfect, whole and complete.
The past has no power over me
Because I am willing to learn and change.
I see the past as necessary to bring me to where I am today.
I am willing to begin where I am right now.
I am willing to set myself free.
All is well in my world."

"Promise yourself to be so strong that nothing can disturb your peace of mind—to think only the best, to work only for the best, and to expect only the best, to forget the past and press on to the greater achievements of the future. To live in the faith that the whole world is on your side, so long as you are true to the best that is in you." (From "The Optimist Creed" published in 1912 in the book, *Your Forces and How to Use Them*, by Christian D. Larson.)

AFTERWORD

My writing of this book has been Divinely inspired. I would never have done it on my own. Many people have told me they want to write a book, but most do not know how much courage it takes to keep going. That is why I decided to call this book *Resilient*—because it takes a resilient mindset to keep going, even when your inner voice asks: "Who do you think you are to tell your story? Why waste all your time looking into the past and trying to figure it all out? What difference does it make that you write this story?" In spite of all the negative thoughts, I persist because I must. My inner Divine Holy Spirit self continues to insist that I persist.

Looking back at my life has proven so helpful because it allows me to see how every conscious choice I made along the way helped me to get where I am today. Where I am today is filled with joy, love and a willingness to let the Universe unfold exactly as it is. I have learned to completely trust that whatever is arising is what is supposed to be happening, and I love and accept it exactly as it is. For much of my life, I felt lost and confused, that I was completely "messing up" my life. It is only in hindsight that I now see that everything was happening in Divine right order, and that Spirit had my back all along.

Leaving the convent at a time when I was so angry with God certainly seemed like a great detour on my soul's journey, but it was exactly what I needed to do in order to see how important Spirit was in my life. My conversion to a life lived in complete faith happened gradually over time. I started to make changes when I noticed the negative responses to my negative thoughts. One conscious choice at a time helped me awaken my spiritual nature. As I look back, I can see Spirit working through me every step of the way. In time, I gradually started to pay more attention to Spirit and then, to hear positive messages such as: "YOU CAN DO IT. YOU HAVE EVERYTHING YOU NEED TO SUCCEED. JUST LET GO, SURRENDER, RELEASE, TRUST AND DO WHAT I TELL YOU." It became clear to me that I wanted to let go of every one of my negative ego thoughts. This became my life's work because I do believe there is never a time when I don't have to be aware of the thoughts I am choosing to think. I saw that the ego thoughts were wrapped around the negative beliefs that I had allowed to run my life for so many years.

My call to coaching has been the greatest gift to me because, as I listen to myself working with my clients, I hear the counsel I so desperately need to hear for myself. (The teacher is always the student.) I remind myself that I want to live with integrity, that I myself must do exactly what I am advising for each of my clients. Coaching has taught me to say YES to me, to say YES to what feels right for me—and YES to my own self-compassion, self-forgiveness, self-love and joy. I have learned, and am still learning, to make self-care a priority. Taking care of myself enables me to offer loving kindness to everyone in my life. As I let myself off the hook for the mistakes I make, I am able to let everyone else off the hook as well. So I end this story with the deepest gratitude, and I know, without a doubt, that I have been blessed beyond any measure I could ever imagine.

AFFIRMATIONS

Affirmations are thoughts that are repeated many times. Affirmations are used to change our minds about our health, our relationships and our wealth. I have collected these affirmations from my journals. They have come from many books, articles and emails written by Louise Hay, Wayne Dyer, Deepak Chopra and others. I spent years writing these affirmations in my journal. I still write them in my calendar every week, and I teach them to my clients. I will start off with two affirmations regarding affirmations: "I have complete faith that all my affirmations are fulfilled" and "Never again will I doubt my ability to demonstrate my affirmations."

Health Affirmations
- I love my body and rejoice in its uniqueness.
- I lovingly create perfect health for myself.

- I am grateful for my perfect health.
- I allow the love in my heart to wash over me and heal every part of my body.
- My body is flexible and peaceful.
- Every cell in my body is filled with light.
- I am open to healing at every level.
- I marvel at the miracle of my body.
- I choose healing thoughts that create and maintain my healthy body.
- I am filled with an unlimited energy and ideas.
- I give myself permission to be well.
- I choose to be peaceful, and my body reflects this peacefulness as perfect health.
- Great health is my greatest blessing.
- I am at peace with my body.
- I accept perfect health.
- I release everything that needs to be released in order to heal.
- I flow in rhythm with my mind and body.
- I trust the wisdom of my body.
- My mind and body are in perfect sync.
- I commit to living in perfect health.
- I am perfect. I am healthy. I am strong.
- My body is a magnificent vehicle that connects me to Spirit.
- I am flexible, powerful and balanced.
- I take steps every day toward perfect health.
- My little changes amount to big benefits.
- I create my perfect health.
- I take loving care of my body now.
- The same Power that created my body knows exactly how to restore it.

- My body is my best teacher.
- My body tells me when I am out of balance.
- Sleeping is the fastest way to heal my body.
- I give myself permission to be well and rejoice in my good health.
- I recognize my body as a wondrous machine. I feel privileged to live in it.
- I accept perfect health as a natural state of being.
- I choose nutritious foods to eat.
- I am my perfect size and weight.
- I eat only when I am truly hungry.
- I am drawn only to foods that nourish my body.
- I eat slowly and drink lots of water.
- Food flows through my body with ease.
- All the foods I eat energize me.
- I love to exercise and to walk briskly.
- My positive thoughts are keeping my body healthy.
- My hair is thick and luxurious.
- I love the way my body feels.
- Every breath brings perfection, wholeness and renewal to every cell.
- There is perfection in every part of my being.
- I am responsible for my health but am not to blame for my illness.

Loving Myself Affirmations

- I am confident in who I am.
- I allow myself to express myself in every situation.
- I am enough.

- I radiate joy and share it with everyone.
- I am filled with peace.
- I surrender all fear and doubt.
- I am special and wonderful.
- I love myself unconditionally.
- I am so glad to be alive.
- I give to life exactly what I want life to give to me.
- I am guided and protected throughout this day in making the right choices.
- I am good enough just as I am.
- I choose to see everything through the eyes of love.
- I now choose thoughts that make me feel good.
- I listen to my heart in all that I do.
- I speak up for myself.
- I am a decisive person.
- It is safe to be who I want to be.
- I claim my power now.
- I ask for what I want.
- I see myself as a magnificent, wise and beautiful person.
- I trust the process of life to bring me my highest good.
- My future is glorious. I am free and all is well.
- I let go of all fear, doubt and uncertainty.
- I am perfect exactly as I am.
- I am willing to change and grow.
- I love being me.
- I lovingly create my own reality.
- I am loving and lovable.
- I love and accept myself right now.
- I am powerful and capable.

- I love and appreciate everything about myself.
- I am open and receptive to my highest good.
- I now build my life on courage and love.
- I forgive my parents. They did the best they could.
- I realize that we are all moving toward the light.
- I am strong, wise and powerful.
- I am filled with wisdom.
- I listen and trust my inner voice.
- Whatever I ought to do I shall do.
- I now allow this love to flow freely into all areas of my life.
- I surround myself with love at all times.
- I love and approve of myself.
- I now stop all criticism of myself and others.
- I lovingly release others to their own lessons.
- I move with ease through my life.
- I deserve to have the life I have dreamed of.
- Today I consciously choose to be happy.
- I allow my uniqueness to be expressed in deeply fulfilling ways.
- I am responsible for everything in my life.
- I choose my thoughts carefully because they are creating my life.
- I look in the mirror and say: "I love you. I really love you."
- I now share the love in my heart with everyone.
- I now create the great life I dream about.
- I am filled with magnificent talents and gifts that I willingly share with the world.
- I am willing to release the old story that no longer works in my life.
- I am willing to release limiting thoughts and create new beliefs

that affirm my self worth.
- I am a successful creator of my world.
- Every experience is perfect for my growth process.
- I am already perfect, whole and complete.
- I have all the time in the world.
- I open my heart and give unconditional love to everyone.
- I share only good news.
- Forgiveness is a gift to myself.
- I am willing to forgive everyone in my life so I can set myself free.
- I look into my eyes and say: I FORGIVE YOU.
- I have everything I need to be successful.
- I lovingly support myself as I learn new skills.
- I praise myself for big and little things.
- I am on my way to consistently loving myself.
- I am the treasure I have been looking for.
- I love and appreciate the beautiful world I live in.
- I imagine a peaceful planet where everyone has enough.
- I am so grateful for my beautiful life.
- I am open to change.
- I find beauty all around me.
- I look into my eyes and love and forgive myself.
- I am at peace.
- It is safe to express all that is within me.
- I am loved and respected wherever I go.
- I am grateful for this moment.
- I now wait with quiet expectancy and calm confidence.
- I commit to being a loving presence in the world.
- I breathe deeply and know how blessed I am.

- I take time to see the beauty in the world around me.
- I am at peace with the process of life.
- I now give more love to my inner child.
- I am a loved and loving child in the Universe.
- I am blessed beyond my wildest dreams.
- I am grateful for all the opportunities to grow and change.
- I am loved, wonderful and wanted.
- I am worthy of a wonderful life.
- I look for the daily miracles in my life.
- I am successful in everything I do.
- I always tell the truth.
- I am renewed and refreshed with all of Nature and Her beauty.
- I am perfect, fabulous and wonderful.
- I now recognize my creativity and I honor it.
- I take time to rest and have quiet time every day.
- I am willing to take risks.
- I am surrounded by love.
- I now open my life to more good news.
- I now see with compassion and non-judgment.
- I open my heart, hands and mind to receive and rejoice in the good.
- I accept more beauty, love, peace, abundance and joy in my life now.
- I am open to all possibilities.
- I now release everything that no longer serves me.
- I now begin to allow my inner child to blossom.
- I am willing to go deeper.
- I know how to take loving care of myself.
- I am fully equipped to live my magnificent life.

- I now allow the tiny child within to blossom and know it is loved deeply.
- I stay present to fully enjoy each moment.
- I am free from the good opinion of others.
- I trust myself and my intuition.
- I am a lIght to the world.
- I am so grateful for all that is.
- I am the stillness at the center of my being.
- I have everything I need to do this work.
- I slow down to enjoy the richness of each moment.
- I choose to be a blessing in every area of my life.
- I love waking up each morning with a thankful heart.
- I open my heart to give unconditional love to everyone in my life.
- I am only here to be truly helpful.
- I am living in the field of all possibilities.
- I let go of old habits, beliefs and thoughts that no longer serve me.
- I am a blessing at home, at work and at play.
- My uniqueness is a gift to the world.
- I am at peace as I watch the perfect unfolding of my life.
- It is safe for me to grow up.
- I love my car and fill it with love wherever I go.
- I release the need to be perfect.
- I release old habits with love.
- I commit to loving all parts of me.
- My inner dialogue is kind and loving.
- I appreciate the miracle that is my body.
- I don't have to be perfect to love myself.

- I lovingly create my life each day.
- I am so close to that which I desire.
- I believe that life is great.
- I am the perfect age.
- I take the next step now.
- I am worth the energy it takes to stay positive.
- I drop the list of expectations for myself.
- I am gentle with myself as I learn my life lessons.
- I am my own best friend.
- I affirm the highest good for all people on the planet.
- I am perfect, whole and complete.
- I claim my power now.
- I choose only thoughts that make me happy.
- I have inside of me what it takes to do the work.
- I am the only gatekeeper in my life.
- I am now prepared for the best life has to offer.
- I forgive myself for not being perfect.
- I recommit to taking loving care of myself.
- Love expresses through me and radiates from me.
- This day is a wonderful, productive, happy new day.
- I spread only good news.
- I keep learning and growing and changing my consciousness.
- I have nothing to fear.
- I now step into the field of greater possibilities.
- I am never alone.
- I now release all limiting thoughts.
- Today I celebrate the miracles of my life.
- I let every thought of discord float away.
- I go beyond other people's fears and limitations.

- I now release all destructive fears and doubts.
- I am willing to release old, negative beliefs.
- I am the only thinker in my mind.
- I choose my thoughts with care.
- I know that fresh new experiences are now coming my way.
- I am making positive changes in my life.
- I am now becoming all that I am created to be.
- I listen to and trust my own inner guidance.
- I only give out that which I wish to return to me.
- I love and accept others and they do the same for me.
- I now leave behind all feelings of not being good enough and love myself just as I am.
- I am responsible for this.
- I am in touch with my own magnificence.
- I wish happiness and the root of all happiness for everyone on the planet.
- I wish suffering and the root of all suffering be removed from everyone on the planet.
- The world is waiting for my vision.
- I bless my closet with love and always choose the perfect outfit to wear.
- My closet is filled with beautiful clothes that reflect my remarkable life.
- I can look in the mirror and say to myself: "I love you. I really love you."
- I am at ease with the changes in my life.
- I make right decisions quickly because I trust my inner guidance.
- The entire universe is supporting me.

- I am so grateful for my life and for all that I have.
- I am the most important person in my life.
- I am perfect just as I am.
- I am a blessing to the world.
- I am now becoming all that I was created to be.
- I surround myself with positive people.
- I do not have to prove myself to anyone.
- I open my heart and let the love dissolve the fear.
- I am filled with positive energy.
- I let go of all fear.
- I lovingly support myself as I learn new skills.
- I praise myself for the big and little things I do.
- I am on my way to consistently loving myself.
- I am the treasure I have been looking for.
- I imagine a peaceful planet, with all people with an open heart.
- It is safe to love everyone on the planet.
- I am at peace with the perfect unfoldment of my life.
- I am so close to that which I desire.
- I choose only thoughts that make me feel good.
- My best is good enough.
- I choose to make this day the happiest day of my life.
- I am perfect, whole and complete.
- I am kind, gentle and patient with myself.
- I forgive everything and everyone, including myself.
- I live in the present moment and easily release all past pain.
- I take time every day to count my blessings.
- I am open and receptive to all the good available to me.
- I release all criticism and blame.
- I am now becoming all that I was created to be.

- I surround myself with positive people.
- I am neither too little nor too much. I do not have to prove myself to anyone.
- When I listen to my inner self, I hear the answers I need.
- I forgive all those needing forgiveness and I forgive myself.
- I slow down and take time to really enjoy my life.
- I praise myself for the big and little things I do.
- I am the treasure I have been looking for.
- I am always free to let go and observe my life.
- The more I listen, the more profound the silence becomes.
- I know my higher self is ready to lift me up beyond what I experience with my senses.

Prosperity Affirmations

- I am a money magnet.
- I always have more than enough money.
- There is plenty for all.
- It is okay for me and others to bring in money without working hard.
- It is perfectly okay for me to prosper.
- I can accomplish anything I desire.
- I can fulfill my heart's desire.
- I can trust myself to make good decisions.
- I am always in the right place at the right time.
- People love giving me gifts.
- I am ready, willing and committed to taking action to create financial well being.
- I am willing to let go of beliefs that create lack and limitation for me.

- I give myself permission to have large sums of money in my life.
- I love money and welcome it into my life.
- I am worthy and deserving of all the richness and goodness of life and I claim it now.
- I forgive myself and others for any perceived hurts of the past.
- My consciousness for wealth is expanding each day.
- I am taking action today to decrease my expenses and increase my income.
- I am a generous giver and a gracious receiver of all good things.
- I am a good steward of my financial resources.
- I am proactive and creative in increasing my income.
- I am becoming abundantly prosperous and wealthy.
- I am compelled to see every opportunity that presents itself.
- I now say YES to unlimited abundance.
- My income is constantly increasing.
- I open my heart to more good in my life.
- I accept my abundance.
- I open the door to more good in my life.
- I step aside and let abundance manifest itself.
- I expect everything I do to prosper.
- My good flows to me easily and effortlessly.
- All my needs and desires are met even before I ask.
- I expect to experience even more happiness and prosperity.
- I rejoice in others' success because I know there is plenty for all.
- My good comes from everywhere and everyone.
- I open my mind and heart to the abundance of the universe.
- Something new and wonderful is going to happen today.
- I prosper wherever I turn.
- I am open and receptive to my highest good.

- I am a magnet for miracles.
- I am a secure, confident person who constantly attracts good.
- I now accept all that I hoped for and believed in.
- I am open and receptive to all the good in the Universe.
- I now move into an entirely new level of financial security.
- I bless my income and watch it grow.
- I know that only good awaits me at every turn.
- I am deserving of this wonderful, abundant life.
- I look forward to even more good in my life.
- My good flows to me freely.
- I now accept all that I hoped for and believed in.
- Joyfully I accept greater abundance.
- My life is unfolding with great success.
- All I give comes back to me multiplied.
- Today I see the great blessings in my life.
- I say YES to even more abundance.
- I trust the process of life to bring me my highest good.
- Before I call, I am answered.
- I am awake to my good and gather to me endless opportunities.
- I give thanks for my whirlwind success.
- I see clearly just what to do.
- A rich, full and abundant life is open to me.
- I go way beyond my family's level of prosperity.
- I now do the things that I can do and no one else can do.
- I never wander from my heart's desire.
- I claim my good now.
- Money is my friend.
- It is okay and safe for me to make more money than my parents.

- I deserve to be prosperous and wealthy.
- It is okay for me to receive money from various people and places at once.
- My wealth contributes to my freedom and my aliveness.
- I have enough time, energy and wisdom and money to accomplish all my desires.
- I am a financially successful woman.
- It is fun for me to be wealthy.
- Past negative experiences no longer distract me from my financial success.
- I forgive my parents for their financial problems.
- My income now far exceeds my expenses.
- The more willing I am to prosper others, the more willing others are to prosper me.
- Every dollar I spend comes back to me multiplied.
- Every day my income increases, whether I am working, playing or sleeping.
- I now accept the lavish abundance of the Universe.
- I have the power within me to live an abundant life.
- My prosperous thoughts create good health, loving relationships and fulfilling work.
- All my investments are profitable.
- A part of everything I earn is mine to keep.
- The flood gates of my good now open.
- I am guided to spend money wisely.
- I am a channel for all good things.
- The Universe finds unique ways to increase my prosperity.
- In the infinity of life where I am, all is perfect, whole and complete.

- All I need to know is revealed to me at the perfect moment.
- It is okay for me to make a good income without working so hard.
- That which I seek is seeking me.
- I know I am truly blessed.
- I say YES to all the blessings in the Universe.
- I give myself permission to fulfill my full potential.
- Nothing is too good to be true.
- I am attracting greater abundance to my life.
- I know something wonderful is about to happen.
- I bless my income with love and watch it grow.
- I am ready and willing to accept more good than I have ever imagined or manifested.
- The more I share with the Universe, the more I receive.
- Miracles follow miracles for me.
- I prosper wherever I turn.
- I constantly receive incredible gifts.
- I expand my faith and accept even greater blessings.
- I am willing to take a leap of faith, knowing divine law fulfills my every desire.
- Today is a day of amazing good fortune.
- Whatever I need is available to me right now.
- Only good surrounds me and only good comes to me.
- I am free of all limitations and limiting beliefs.
- I accept my divine birthright and rejoice in the abundance of the Universe.
- I now experience good beyond my wildest dreams.
- I am mentally and emotionally equipped to enjoy a prosperous life.

- I claim my good now.
- There is no need to compare or to compete. We are all different and that is perfect.
- There is plenty for everyone, including me.
- My prayers are answered before I even ask.
- My good comes from everywhere, everyone and everything.
- I pay attention to my dreams and do what they say.
- Abundance surrounds me.
- Abundance flows easily and freely to me.
- I am a powerful creator.
- All my needs are met abundantly for me now and always.
- Only good comes from each experience.
- I accept all opportunities when they come.
- I feel confident about my future.
- Abundance is my birthright and I claim it today.
- I now experience a good beyond my wildest dreams.
- Life supports me and supplies me with more good than I can ever imagine.
- I am open and receptive to new avenues of income.
- I now receive my good from expected and unexpected sources.
- Everything I touch is a success.
- I know I am only as successful as I make up my mind to be.
- I train my mind to focus on my desires.
- I dedicate my life to my dreams.
- I receive even more abundantly than I ask for.
- I have everything I need to be successful.
- More good is always available to me.
- I always have everything I need.
- I am constantly creating more good in my life.

- I prosper in all I do.
- I deserve the best and accept the best into my life now.
- It does not matter how slowly you go, as long as you do not stop.

Relationship Affirmations

- I now expect something wonderful to happen.
- There is a time to receive and a time to give, and I know the difference.
- I release all hurt feelings, misunderstandings and injustices.
- I have the power and strength and knowledge to handle all of life's challenges.
- I allow the love in my life to wash through me and cleanse all my emotions.
- I attract everything I need to create the happiest life.
- I have the strength and courage to face my fears.
- I am perfect physically, mentally, spiritually, sexually.
- I accept and am happy with my sexuality.
- I forgive you for not being the way I wanted you to be, and I set you free.
- Everyone in my life is off the hook. I take full responsibility for my own happiness.
- I send healing, love and compassion to all my relationships.
- Happiness is a choice I make ahead of time.
- I release all fears and accept peace and love.
- I now stop all criticism of myself and my partner.
- Every day I choose to do something fun with my partner.
- Nobody can make me feel good except myself.
- I release all need to control, manipulate or judge.

- Love is stronger than any difference.
- I now welcome more love in my life.
- I see the beauty and light that shines within my family.
- My heart is open. I allow my love to flow freely.
- A person who loves me back is on his way to me.
- The right person for me will know who I am.
- I don't have to persuade anyone to love me. The right person will love me.
- I choose to see clearly with eyes of love.
- Love happens! I release the need for love, and allow it to find me in the perfect time.
- I accept all the love from the Universe now.
- I forgive everything and everyone, including myself.
- I live in the present moment and easily release all past pain.
- I release all criticism and blame.
- I now welcome even more love into my life.
- I let every thought of discord float away.
- I am filled with gratitude for what has been and what is not.
- I express love for myself by saying "no" when it feels right.
- I love myself enough to walk away from negative people.
- I seek relationships that empower me.
- I tell a new story about what is possible for me.
- I am willing to learn new ways of being in the world.
- I let go of what no longer supports me.
- I stay focused in the direction of my dreams.
- My siblings are perfect just as they are.
- I embrace my family with compassion and love.
- All my relationships are harmonious.
- I allow myself the time I need to work through my grief.

- I am free. I can choose again.
- I attract love wherever I go.
- I tell a new life story in which I am the hero and problem solver.
- I know better now, so I make better choices.
- I learn my lessons the first time so I don't get a harder lesson.
- My purpose in life is to learn to love unconditionally.
- I say "cancel" to every negative thought that comes into my mind.
- No person, place or thing has any power over me.
- Love is everywhere, and I experience love wherever I go.
- I know in each moment, I am free to decide.
- As I stand in my power, I send healing, love and compassion to all my relationships.
- No matter how much I protest, I am responsible for everything that happens to me.
- Comparisons are the thief of joy, so I let go of all comparisons.
- Looking within gives me the answers to all the questions I shall ever ask.
- I release the need to blame anyone, including myself.
- Whatever I need to know is revealed to me in the right time/ space sequence.
- All of my past except its beauty is gone; nothing is left but a blessing.
- By taking action, the Universe puts into motion ways to accomplish my goals.
- The point of power is always in the present moment.
- As I give this a light touch, this too shall pass.
- The Universe sends me the perfect people for the perfect

lessons.

- All people and all situations are delivering me toward my higher good.
- Life is simple. What I give out, I get back.
- My past is nothing more than the trail I have left behind. What drives my life today is the energy I generate in each of my present moments.
- My judgments keep me from seeing the good that lives behind appearances.
- I now release all known and unknown negative images.
- I let go of all destructive cellular memories.

Source Energy (God) Affirmations

- I am guided by Divine Intelligence.
- Spirit is always active in me.
- I know I am one with God.
- I know that God in me is perfect.
- I let go and let God run my life.
- I trust my Higher Self and listen with love to my own inner voice.
- I am one with the Power that created me.
- This Power has given me the ability to create my own life circumstances.
- I am willing to release old negative beliefs.
- I choose new thoughts that are positive and affirming.
- God is what I am.
- I know the Presence of the Living Spirit is in me and all around me.
- God is right where I am.

- I trust my Higher Self.
- The mind of God is flowing through me.
- The mind of God is right where I am.
- The mind of God is ever available and always operating.
- Spirit within me is alive, awake and aware.
- Truth lies at the center of my being.
- Divine Guidance is always available to me.
- Divine Guidance is at the center of my being.
- I rejoice in the Divine Presence within me.
- I live in the Kingdom of Heaven that is within me.
- I know I am not alone, so I trust Spirit's guidance.
- I trust the Divine Intelligence within me.
- Today I see God in everything and everyone.
- In this moment, I am one with God.
- I know Divine Spirit is operating in me right now.
- I know that the Truth is making me free.
- I am here for the delight of God.
- I am as God created me.
- I release every burden to Spirit.
- I am fully equipped for the Divine Plan for my life.
- I am nourished by the Spirit within.
- I see God in every person I meet.
- All is in Divine right order.
- We are all Divine, magnificent expressions of Life.
- There is a power for good in the Universe and I can use it.
- This Power is creative and unlimited and works through me now.
- My mind is centered on peace.
- I am surrounded by the white light of Spirit.

- My eyes are God's eyes, perfect and flawless.
- I know just what to do. I am always directed and guided by God.
- I know I can connect my mind with the Divine Mind and have peace in each moment.
- I will radiate my sacred self outward for the collective good of all.
- I am truly grateful for Spirit expressing as me.
- I trust Spirit to take care of everything that concerns me.
- Freed of worry and filled with faith, I have a heavenly experience today.
- I love everyone and everyone loves me.
- I now step aside and watch God work.
- With God, all things are easy and possible now.
- I have perfect confidence in God and He in me.
- God is always at the helm, guarding, guiding and directing my journey.
- My spiritual growth unfolds in wonderful ways.
- I know that I know and wait upon the Lord for my next steps.
- I feel joyful as I let Spirit be my guide.
- The mind of God is right where I am.
- My heart's desire is a perfect idea in God's mind.
- Today I listen intently to God's Voice.
- I KNOW Universal Intelligence is ever available to me.
- I now step aside and let God do the work.
- God is my unfailing and immediate source of my supply.
- With God, seemingly impossible doors open.
- There is no place where God is not.
- Today I allow God within to express freely.

- I am fully equipped to execute the Divine Plan of my life.
- I am completely open to Divine Love and gratitude.
- God is closer to me than I am to myself.
- Everything is in Divine and Perfect Order right now.
- I am a Divine, magnificent expression of life.
- The wisdom within reveals itself clearly through my writing and speaking.
- I open my mind and heart to the wisdom within.
- Enlightenment is my 24 hour a day job.
- There is within me a Power that knows what to do and how to do it.
- I accept Spirit's guidance flowing forth into action.
- God is the invisible partner in my life.
- I am willing to listen to Divine Guidance.
- The mind of God is my mind.
- I expect miracles to happen, for nothing can inhibit God's actions.
- I accept Spirit's guidance to support me as I take the next step.
- God is right where I am.
- In God's right action I place my full trust.
- This is a time of Divine Completion.
- Spirit, You are absolutely in control of this day.
- I listen as Spirit guides me to a greater experience of peace and joy.
- God's thoughts are my thoughts.
- I now recognize the role of Divine Timing.
- I now pay attention to each moment to receive God's love.
- God is the only source of my supply.
- I accept Divine Love and surrender my life to Spirit.

- I trust Spirit to guide me through each new day.
- I trust the Universe to find the perfect solution.
- God's perfect action is my life.
- I am guided by Divine Intelligence.
- I am the trust and peace of God.
- I honor my blessed journey with Spirit.
- Divine Love flows from me to each person I meet.
- I am a creative, talented expression of God.
- I do not have to worry about what to say or do because Spirit will direct me.
- I am deeply loved and cherished by the Universe.
- I do matter to myself and to God.
- I let God be the only presence acting now in my life.
- Spirit vitalizes, invigorates and renews me.
- Everything in my life is God expressing.
- There is one life, one presence, one Spirit, one God.
- I now invite Spirit to be in every idea and action.
- Peace and harmony is God expressing in my life.
- All my thoughts are formulated in Divine Mind.
- I now surrender to the one Power.
- Bless our marriage with Divine Love.
- Spirit will respond to the degree that I am conscious.
- I trust Spirit to resolve every situation.
- Universal wisdom inspires me.
- Life loves me and I love life.
- Today I enter more fully into my divine companionship.
- Out of the limitless creativity of Spirit I accept the flow of new ideas.
- I expect more good as a world of new ideas, new people and

new situations open to me.

- There is Divine Order in the Universe.
- I have utter abandonment in trusting Spirit.
- It is the Father within that does the work.
- I accept Spirit's guidance.
- I am the radiant light of the One.
- All is in Divine and perfect order right now.
- God's creativity flows through me.
- I am never alone; Spirit always guides and protects me.
- Divine peace surrounds me and dwells within me.
- God is my Source.
- I am deeply loved and cherished by the Universe right now.
- I flow with Life easily and effortlessly.
- I radiate my sacred self outward.
- I propose and God disposes.
- I trust Source Energy to resolve every situation.
- I am one with the Universal Mind.
- All relationship issues are found, opened and healed by filling me with light, life and the love of God.
- God is with me in the region of my heart.
- I am open and receptive to my highest good.
- Never again will I question my ability to make my demonstrations. God honors my thoughts and the law produces it.
- Today I become even more aware of Spirt acting in my life.
- I know that Spirit is operating in all my affairs.
- God is my unlimited Source of my supply.
- Thank you God for providing me with this great source of income.
- I am a rich child of a loving Father.

- I am one with the good of God. I accept unlimited love and riches.
- I am deeply grateful to the Universe for giving me this incredible life.
- My money grows and grows as I accept God's unlimited abundance.
- Spirit and I create the great life I live.
- Divine Intelligence guides me to joy, happiness, peace and a perfect life.
- Spirit within knows the answer and what my next steps should be.
- I am the face of God.
- There is a Power and Intelligence greater than me, and I can use it.
- Your Will be done.
- My work is a stepping stone to a far greater expression of Spirit.
- I trust the Universe to find the perfect solution.
- Divine right action is always taking place in my life.
- I let go and let God run my life.
- God is the only source of my abundance.
- I now know that I am one with God's abundance.
- I keep my mind focused on serving God.
- I am on a mission for God. God is my source.
- I am a wealthy child of God.
- God is my immediate, limitless, boundless source of money.
- Every cell in my body surrenders to Spirit's unlimited power.
- I do not need to dominate anyone in order to be spiritually awake.
- I am among the ministers of God.

Employment Affirmations

- My mind is open to new ideas.
- I know that my mind is being acted upon by pure Spirit.
- I am at peace with where I am in my life.
- There are no mistakes, just lessons to be learned.
- I learn from every experience and am guided to my success.
- I am working at a career I really enjoy.
- Spirit knows the perfect answer to my employment question.
- Every moment is a new beginning.
- My present job is a stepping stone to much greater things.
- The work I love to do unfolds before me in miraculous ways.
- All my experiences are stepping stones to my greater good.
- I choose to focus on my successes, achievements and accomplishments.
- My work is a stepping stone to a greater expression of God.
- I release and let go of the need to be perfect.
- Everything I need to know is revealed to me in the right time-space sequence.
- My creativity is always in demand.
- I feel great about the work I do.
- I am free to think wonderful thoughts.
- I am becoming all I was created to be.
- I flow with life easily and effortlessly.
- Let me never wander from my heart's desire.
- All obstacles in my pathway to achieving my dreams are removed.
- Today is filled with unexpected miracles.
- I rid myself of my doubts by remembering that there is a valid reason for everything that happens to me.

- I make right decisions quickly because I trust my inner guidance.
- I relax and appreciate the perfect unfolding of my Divine potential.
- My demonstrations come to me at the precise, perfect timing.
- My work is fun and easy and deeply fulfilling.
- My inner spirit blesses me with fulfilling work.
- In the checkerboard of life, someone is looking for exactly what I have to offer, and we are being brought together in the perfect time/space sequence.
- My career is providing financial rewards.
- I do work that I love and I am well paid for it.
- I embrace new opportunities.
- I use my imagination to see good things happening to me.
- I can use what I know to solve new problems because I already know so much.
- I am powerful and my gifts are needed.
- I accept all opportunities when they come. I feel confident about my future.
- I am as successful as I make up my mind to be.
- I open myself to new ideas and new horizons.
- I now open the door to more good in my life.
- My uniqueness is a gift to the world.
- I have everything I need to be successful.
- I let go of all fear as I handle my work challenges.
- I lovingly support myself as I learn new skills.
- I am so close to that which I desire.
- I trust the Universe to find the perfect employment solution.
- Out of this situation only good can come.

- I now experience a good beyond my wildest dreams.
- Whatever I need is available to me right now.
- I am now more successful than I could ever imagine.
- I let every thought of discord float away.
- I will work this day at my purest intentions for the highest good of all.
- Everything that needs to be done will be done on time and with ease.

ACKNOWLEDGMENTS

I would like to thank my parents for giving me life.

I want to thank my siblings, my husband and my daughters for understanding that I had to write this memoir, and that it is their story too.

Thanks to everyone who purchased my first book, read my story and encouraged me to keep on writing, especially the Stanley Lake Library Book Club.

Thanks to my editors, Debby Bernau and Kerry Parry. Without their invaluable assistance, my memoir would never have been possible. Both of them met with me many times to edit this book and make my story come alive. I am deeply grateful to them for reading and re-reading and pushing me forward.

Thank you to Sis Jarling St. John for typing the notes from our hitch-hiking trip so many years ago. She must have had a premonition that someday they would come in handy—and they did.

Finally, thank you to the Centers for Spiritual Living community for giving me hope and guidance through the years, especially to Rev. Karen Paschal, my long-time friend and spiritual coach, and to Rev. Kathleen Lenover for her coaching and her courage to go to John of God and sharing that journey with me.

ABOUT THE AUTHOR

Janice McDermott grew up in a small town in Eastern Iowa. She worked as an early childhood Montessori educator in urban schools for twenty-nine years in Illinois, Wisconsin, and Colorado. All her life, she's been interested in the ways her early experiences have impacted her life-view.

Janice currently works as a life, leadership and spiritual coach. She lives in Colorado with her husband.

To have Janice speak at your event, please contact her through her website: www.janicemcdermott.com.

Made in the USA
Lexington, KY
31 October 2019

56344000R00219